The Life of a

House

A house goes through everything with you. It hosts friends, throws parties, keeps you safe and warm during hard times, welcomes new humans and watches them grow, and so much more every day.

Capture the big things and the little things that make life so wonderful. These are the special events and everyday moments you'll look back on and remember fondly, forever.

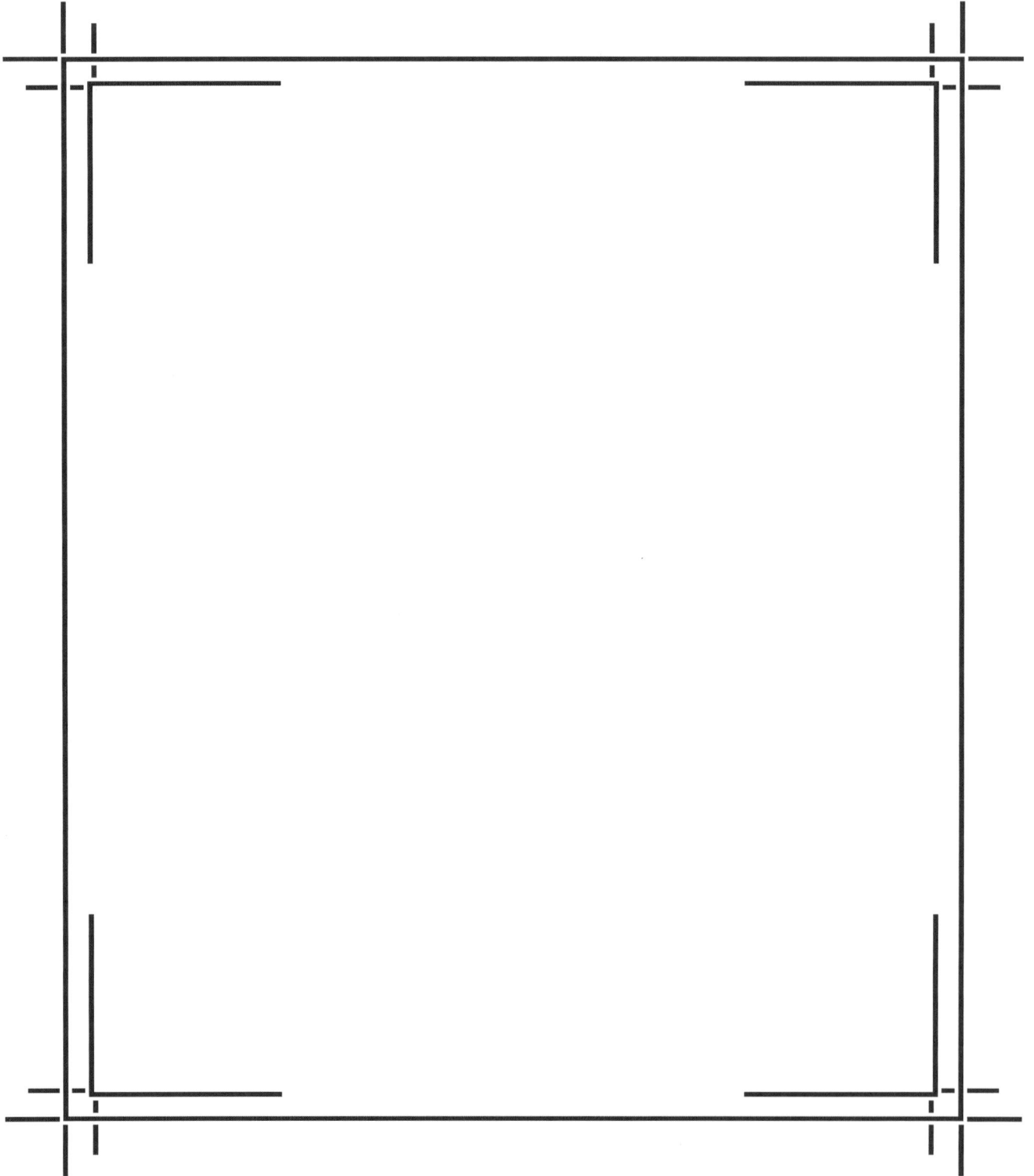

Your canvas...

It is _____ ___, ____

Month   Day   Year

Today, we...

_____

_____

_____

_____

_____

We will always remember...

_____

_____

_____

_____

_____

_____

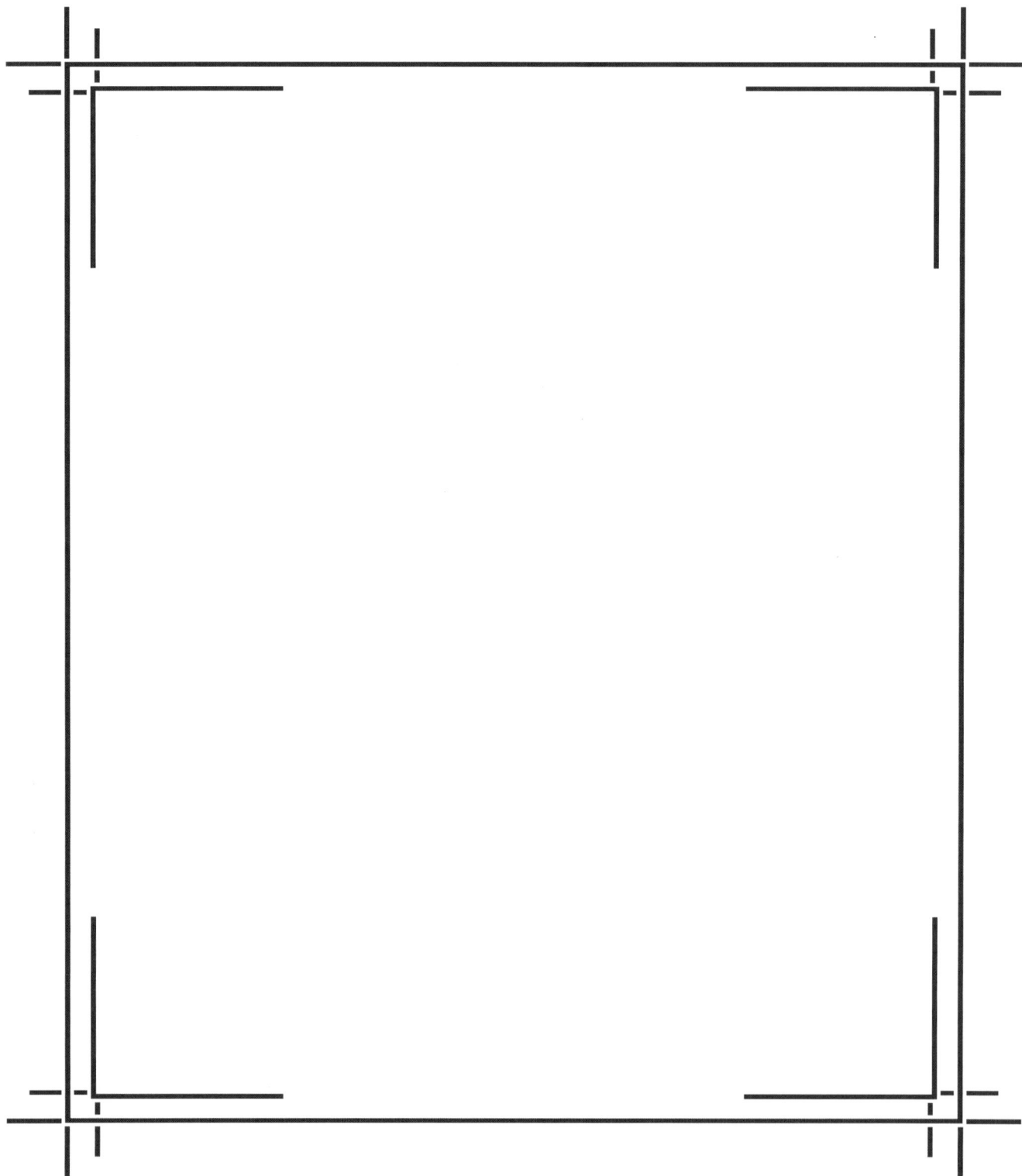

Your canvas...

It is _____ ___, ____

Today, we...

_____
_____
_____
_____
_____

We will always remember...

_____
_____
_____
_____
_____

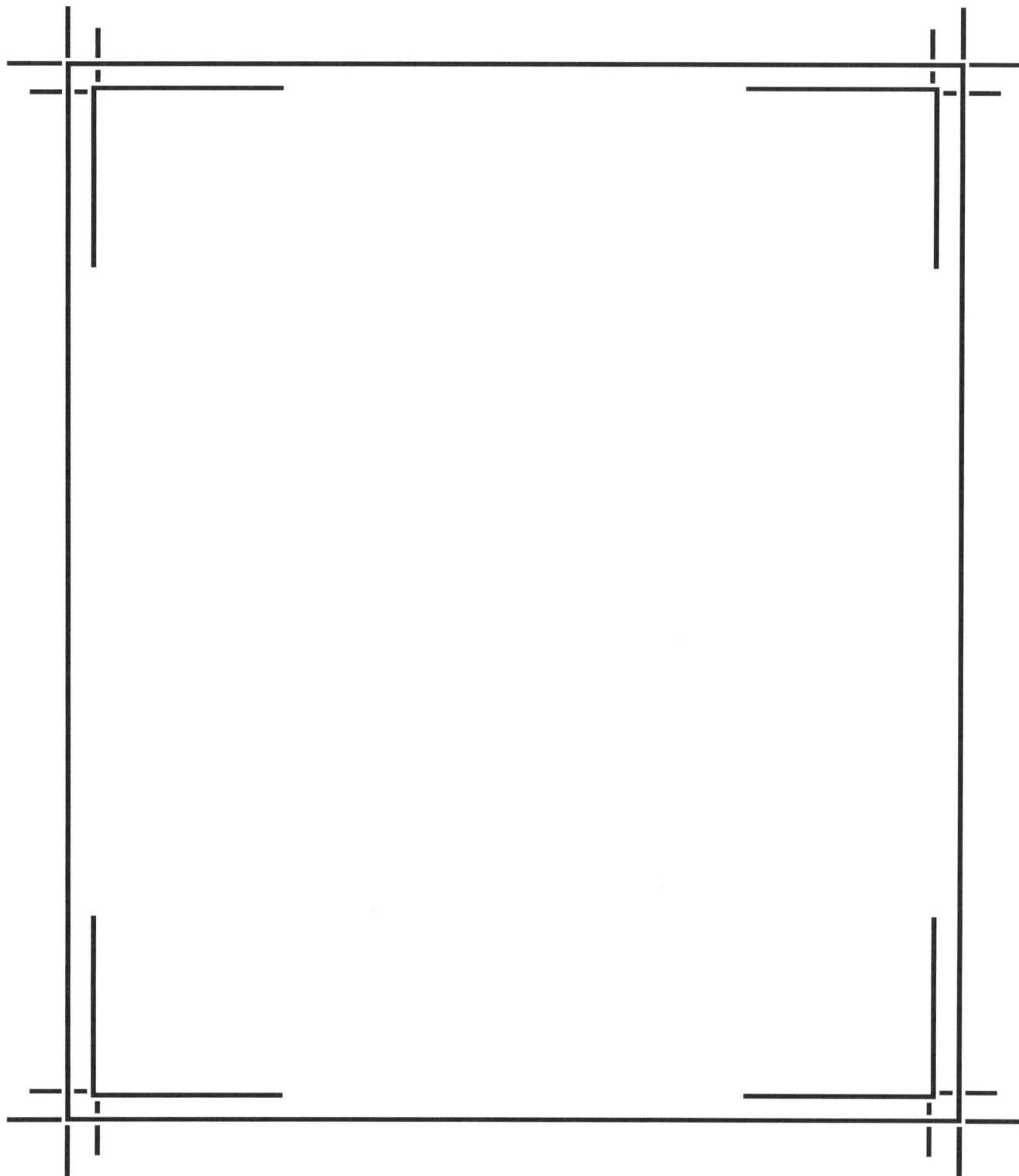

Your canvas...

It is _____ ___, _____
Month   Day   Year

Today, we...

_____
_____
_____
_____
_____
_____

We will always remember...

_____
_____
_____
_____
_____
_____

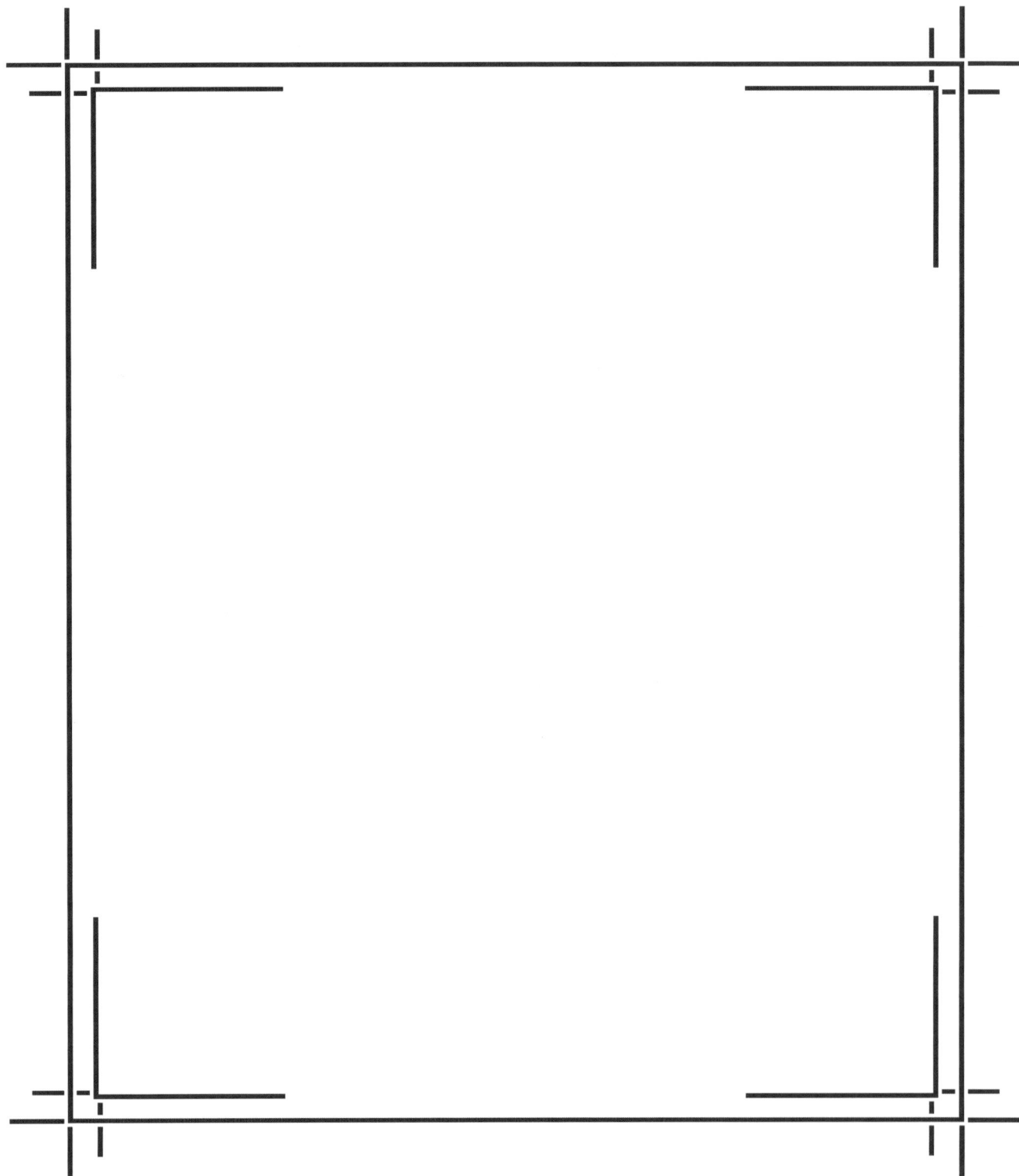

Your canvas...

It is _____ ___, ____
Month Day   Year

Today, we...

_____

_____

_____

_____

_____

We will always remember...

_____

_____

_____

_____

_____

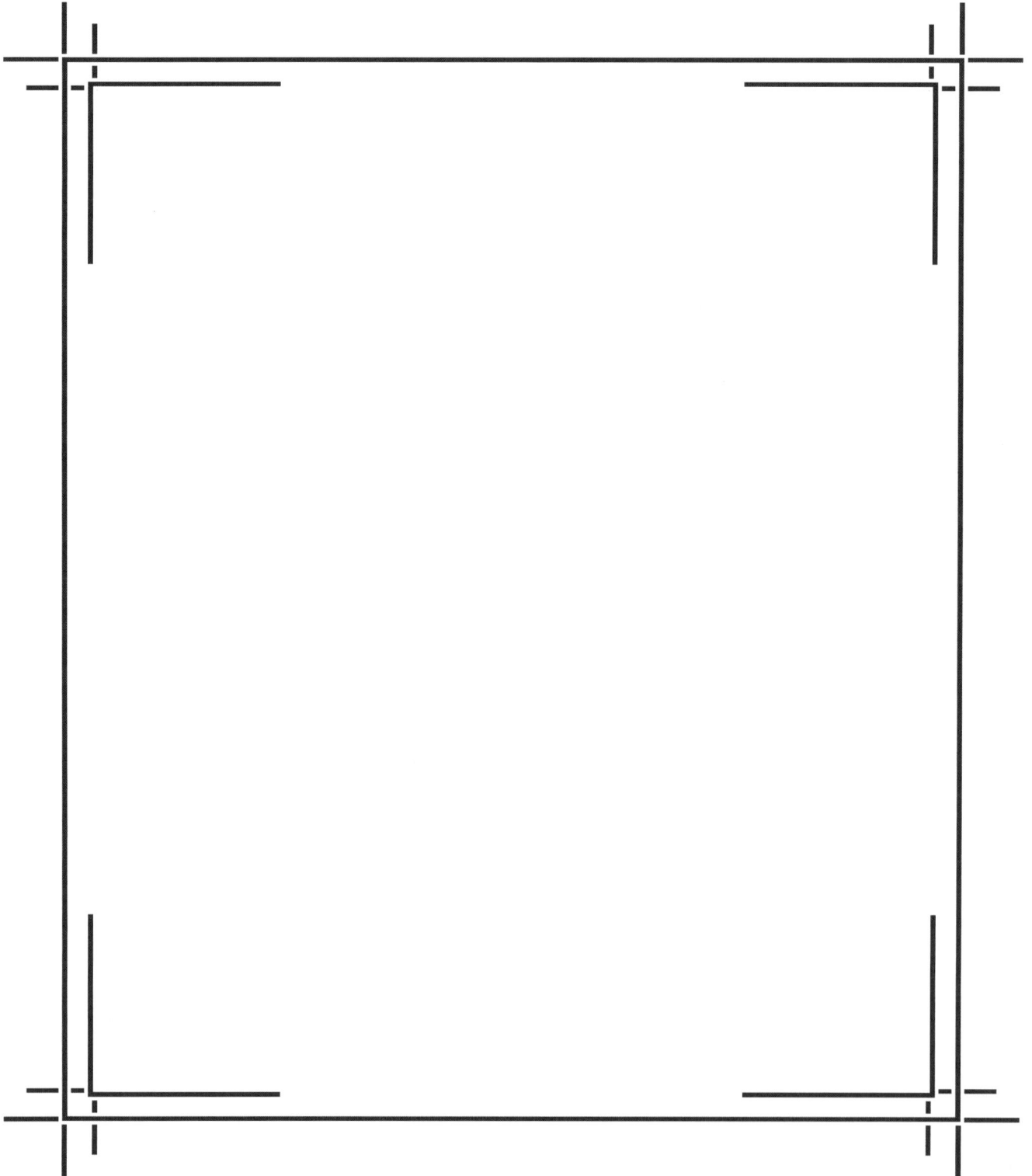

Your canvas...

It is _____ ___, ____
Month   Day   Year

Today, we...

_____

_____

_____

_____

_____

We will always remember...

_____

_____

_____

_____

_____

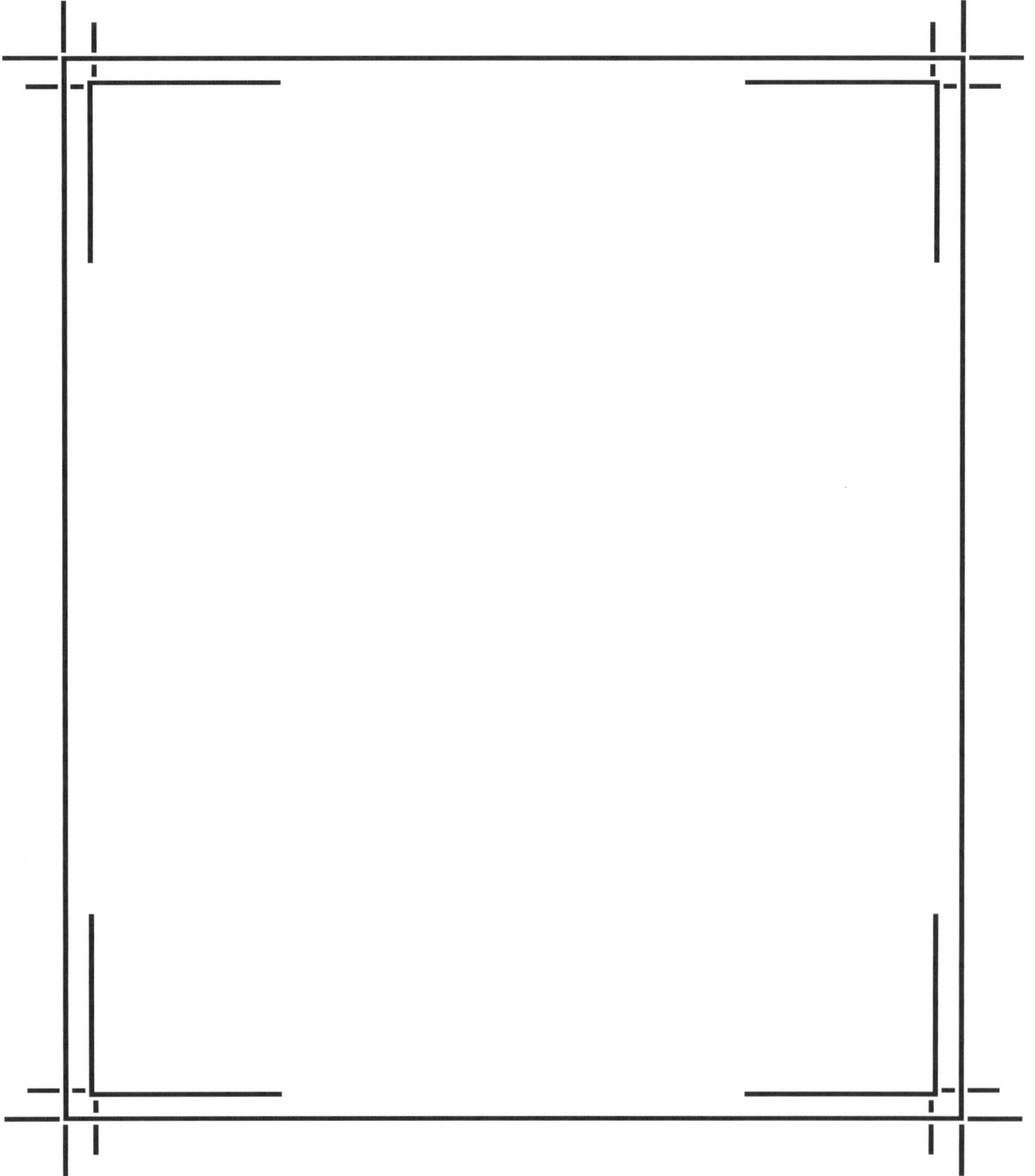

Your canvas...

It is _____ ___, ___
Month   Day   Year

Today, we...

_____

_____

_____

_____

_____

We will always remember...

_____

_____

_____

_____

_____

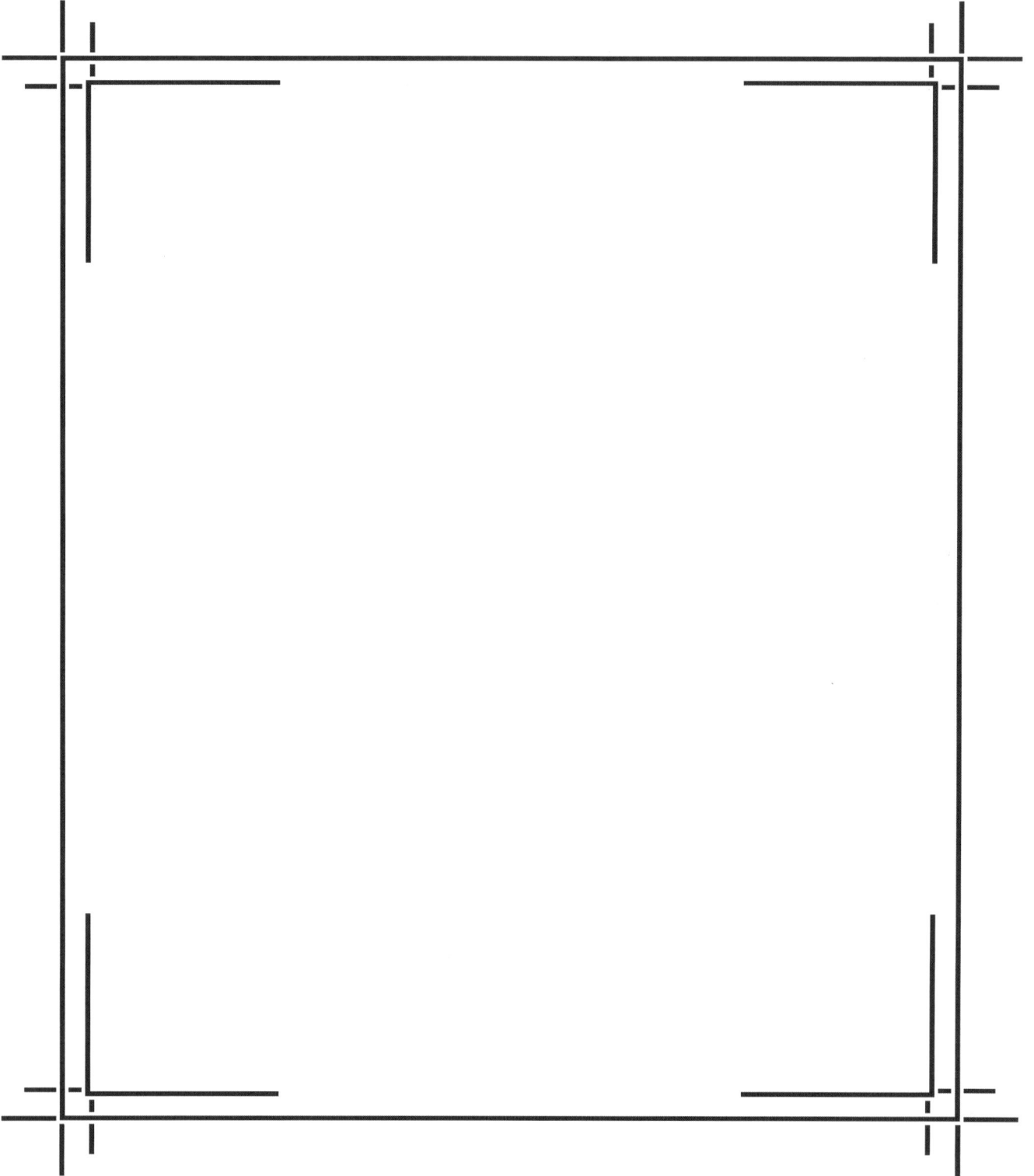

Your canvas...

It is _____ ___, _____
Month   Day   Year

Today, we...

_____

_____

_____

_____

_____

_____

We will always remember...

_____

_____

_____

_____

_____

_____

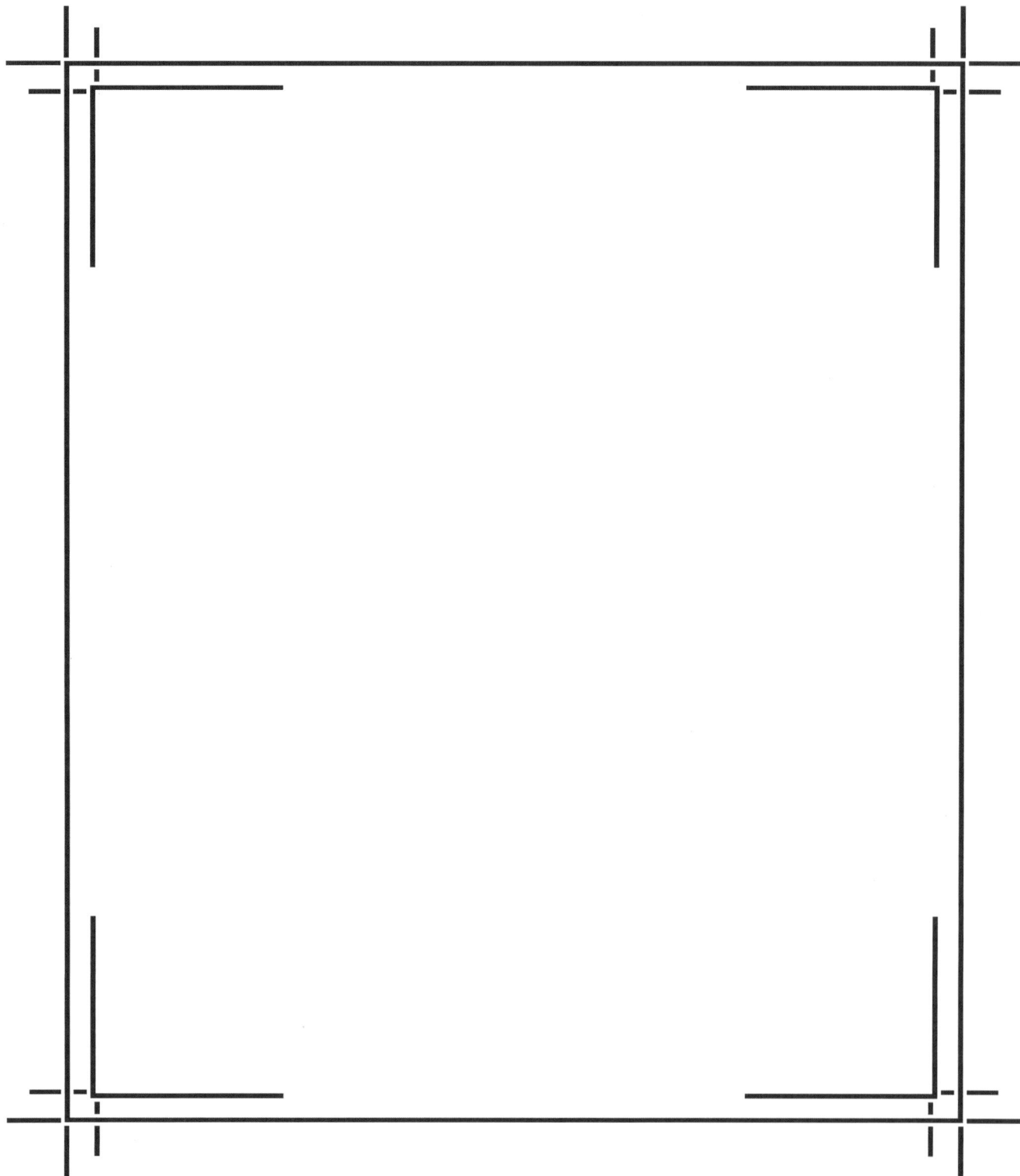

Your canvas...

It is _____ ___, _____
Month   Day   Year

Today, we...

_____

_____

_____

_____

_____

_____

We will always remember...

_____

_____

_____

_____

_____

_____

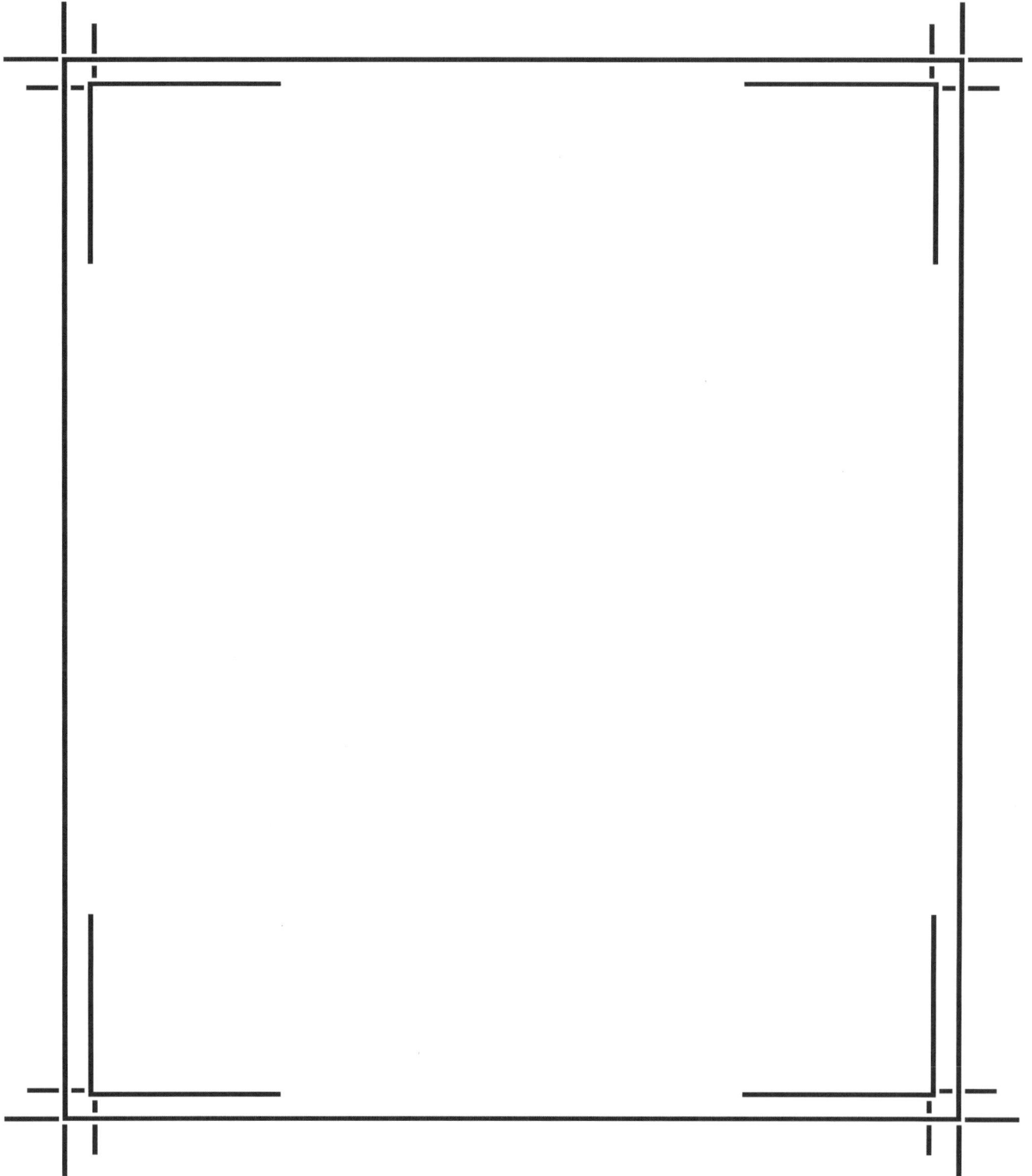

Your canvas...

It is _____ ___ , ____

Today, we...

_____

_____

_____

_____

_____

We will always remember...

_____

_____

_____

_____

_____

_____

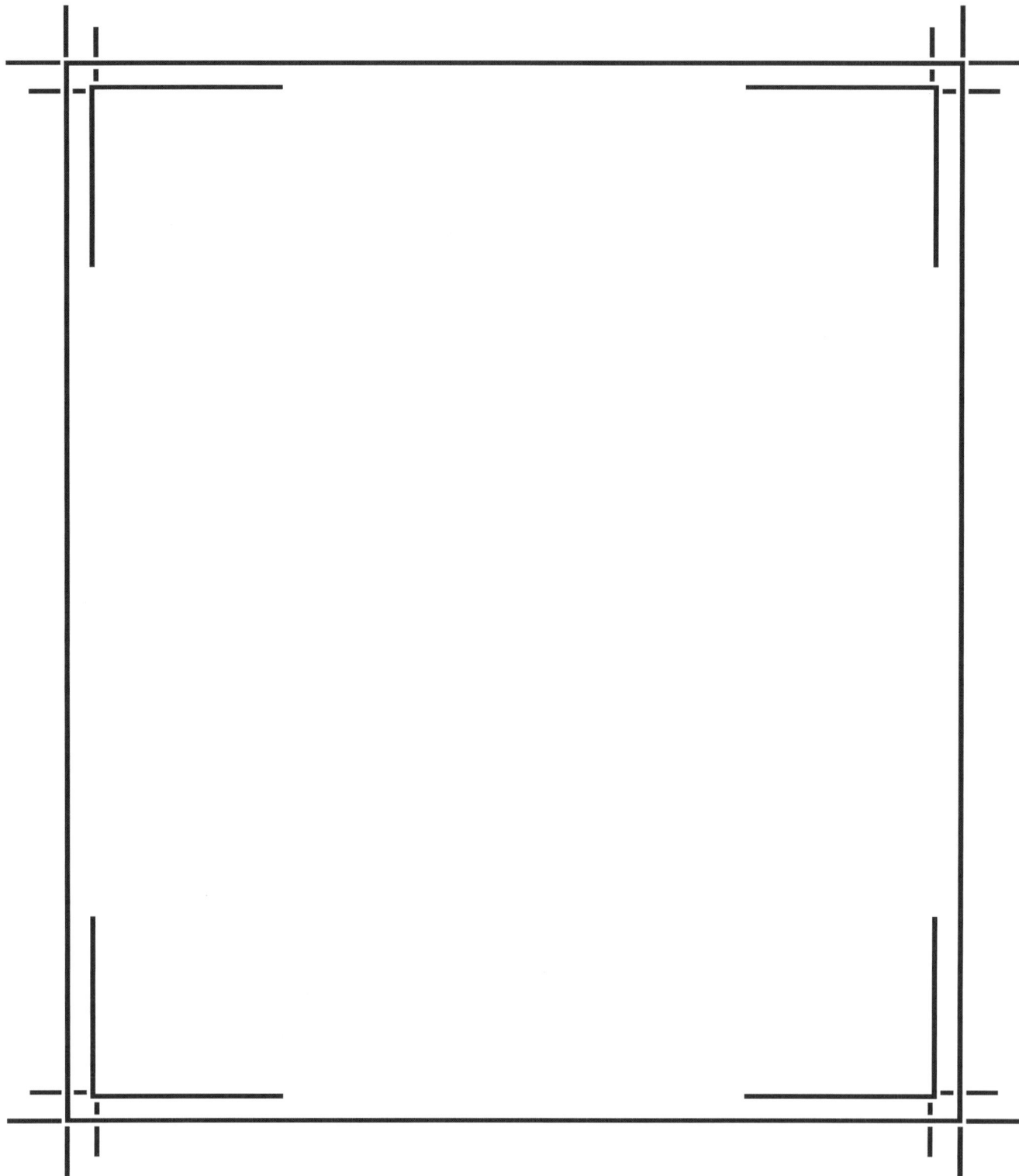

Your canvas...

It is _____ ____ , _____
Month   Day   Year

Today, we...

_____

_____

_____

_____

_____

We will always remember...

_____

_____

_____

_____

_____

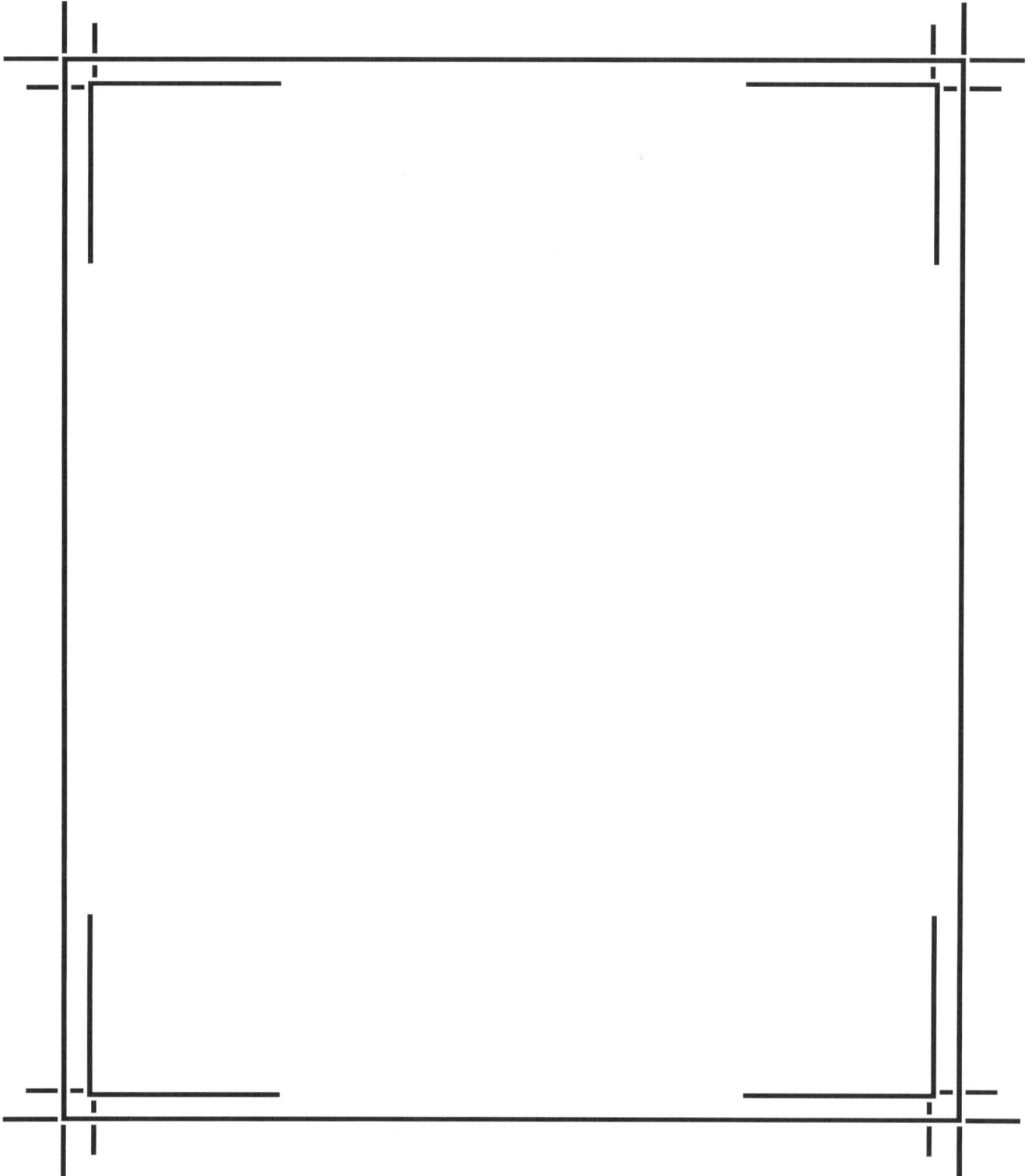

Your canvas...

It is _____ ___, ____
Month   Day,   Year

Today, we...

_____

_____

_____

_____

_____

We will always remember...

_____

_____

_____

_____

_____

_____

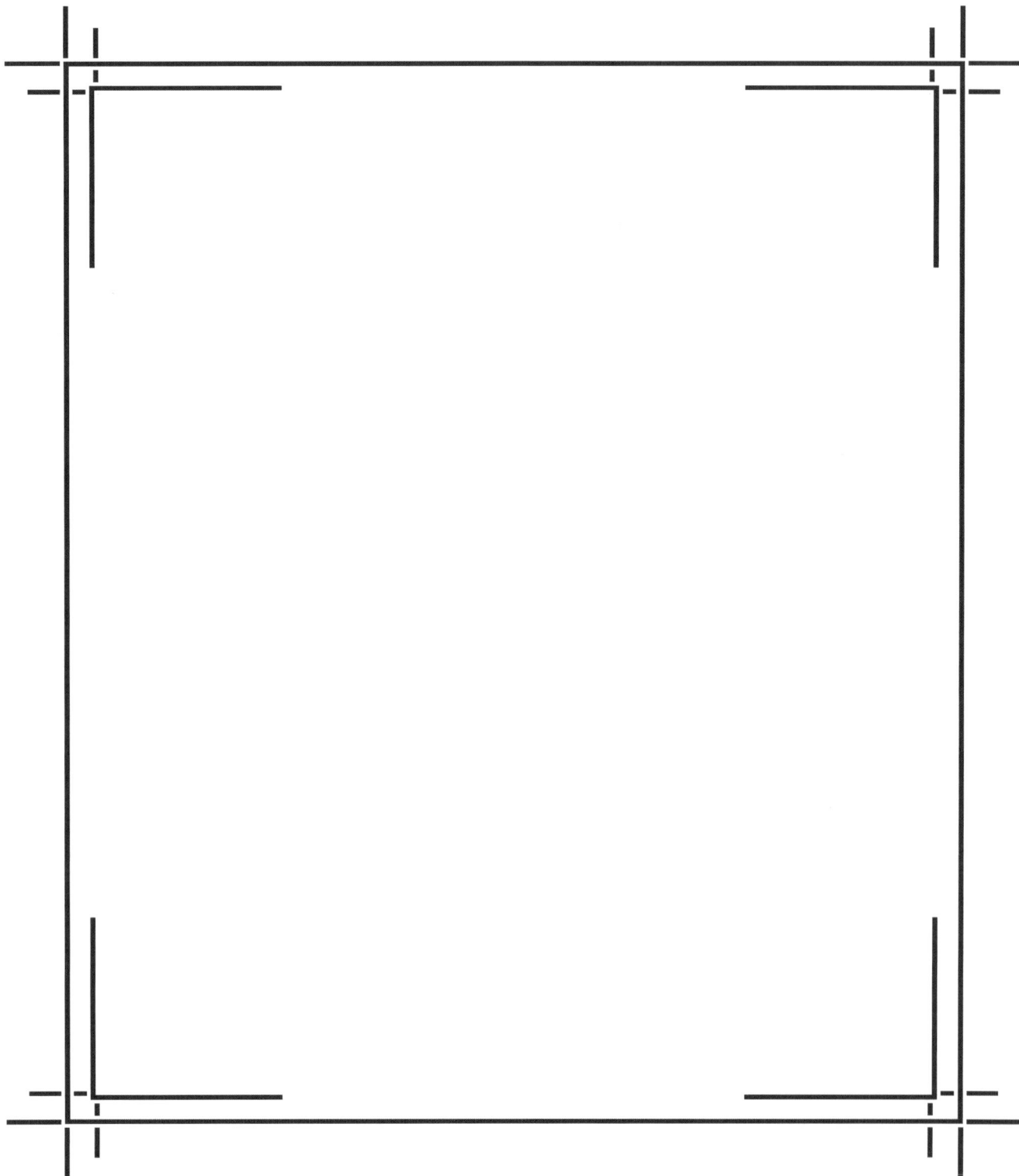

Your canvas...

It is _____ ____, ____
Month   Day   Year

Today, we...

_____

_____

_____

_____

_____

_____

We will always remember...

_____

_____

_____

_____

_____

_____

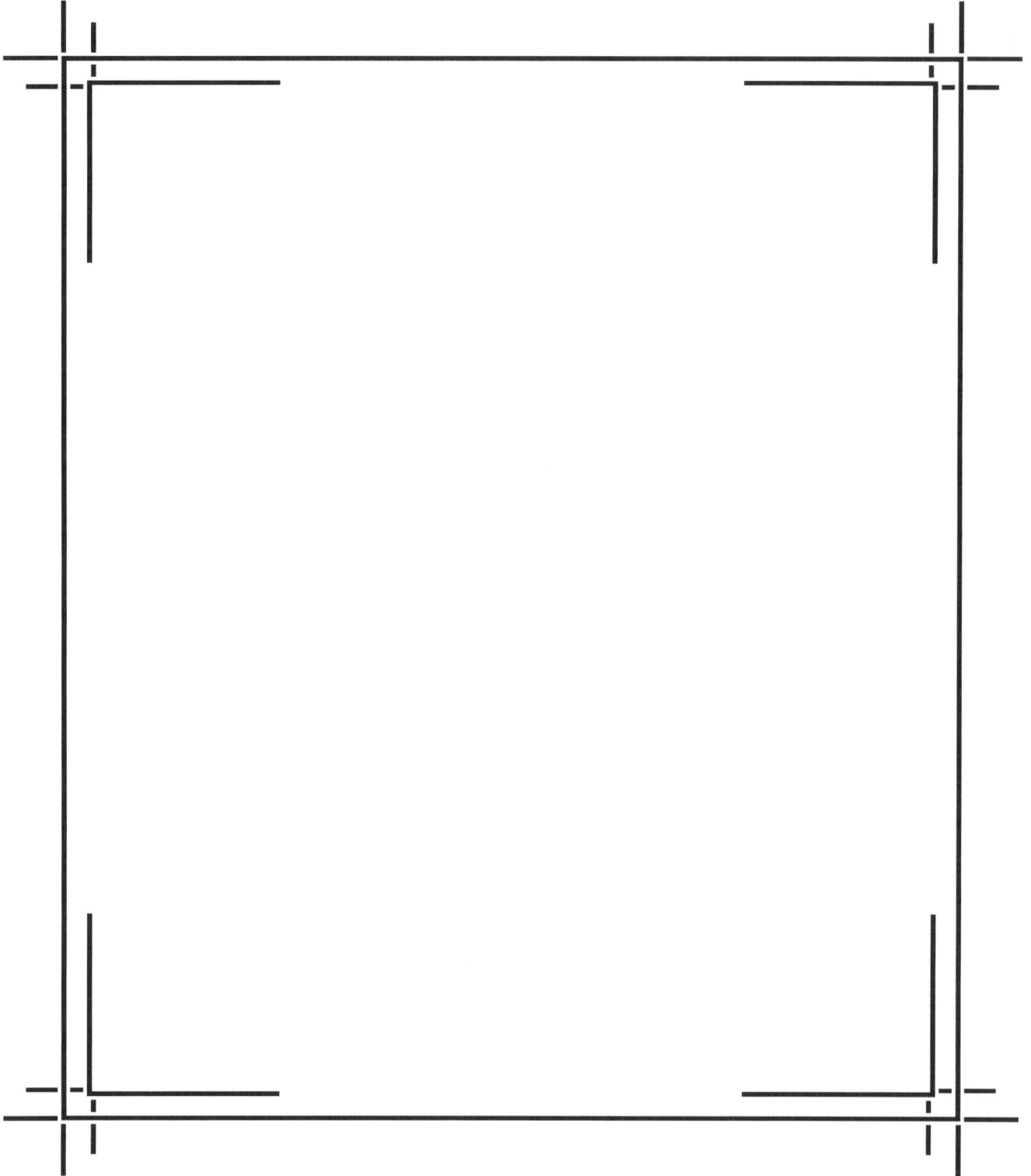

Your canvas...

It is _____ ___, _____
Month   Day   Year

Today, we...

_____

_____

_____

_____

_____

We will always remember...

_____

_____

_____

_____

_____

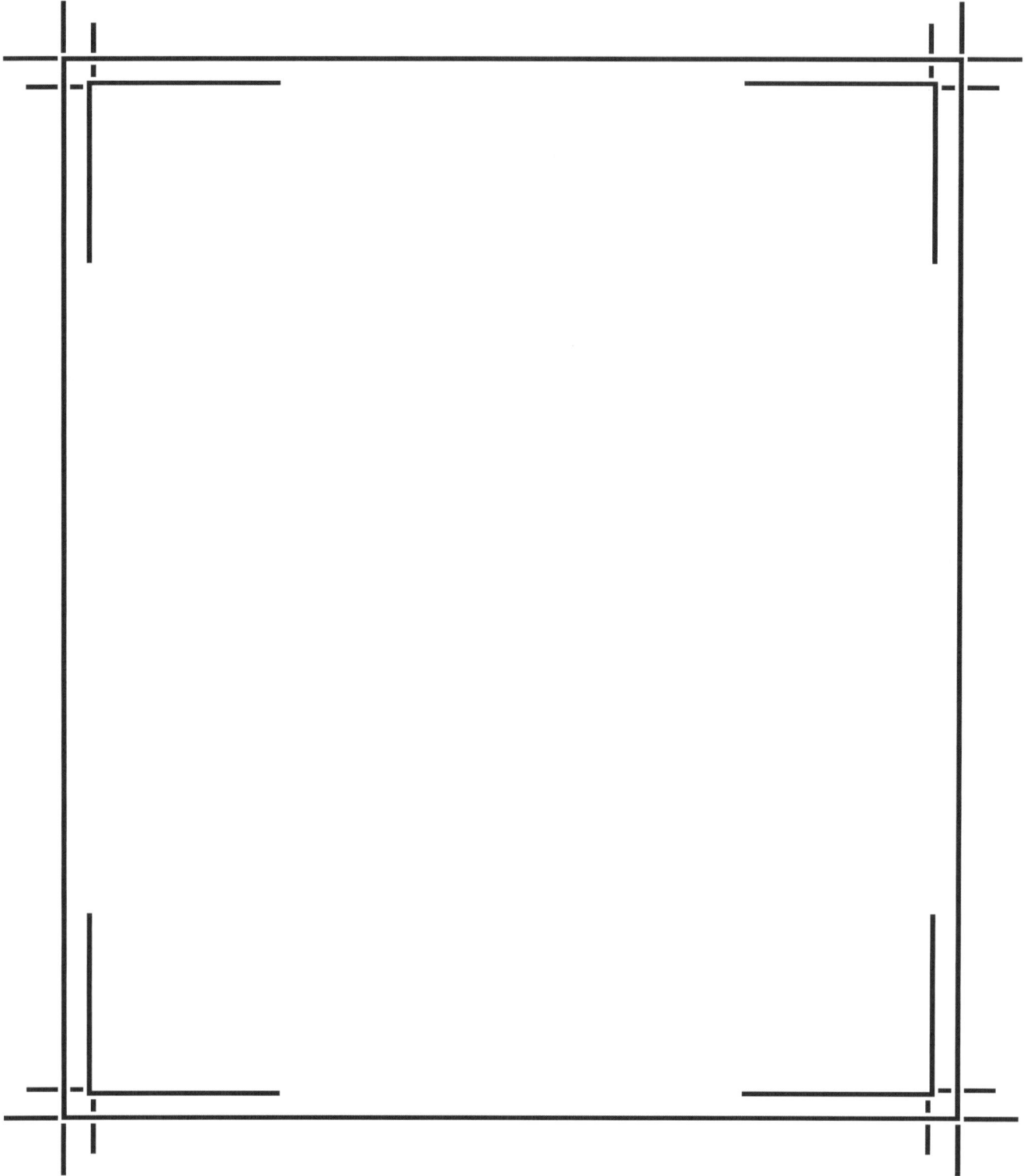

Your canvas...

It is _____ ___, _____
Month　　Day　,　Year

Today, we...

_____

_____

_____

_____

_____

_____

We will always remember...

_____

_____

_____

_____

_____

_____

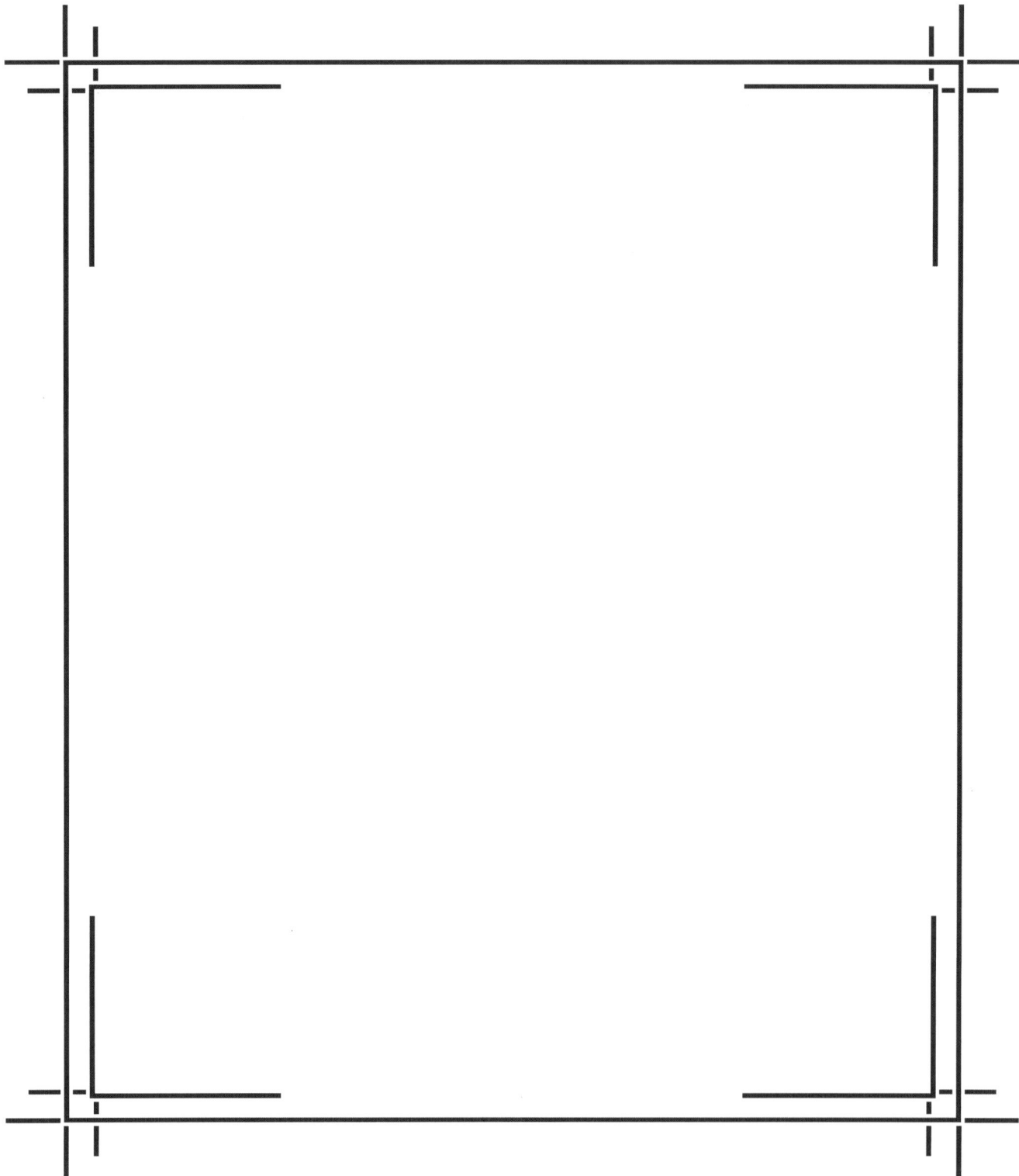

Your canvas...

It is _____ ___, ____
Month   Day,   Year

Today, we...

_____
_____
_____
_____
_____
_____

We will always remember...

_____
_____
_____
_____
_____
_____

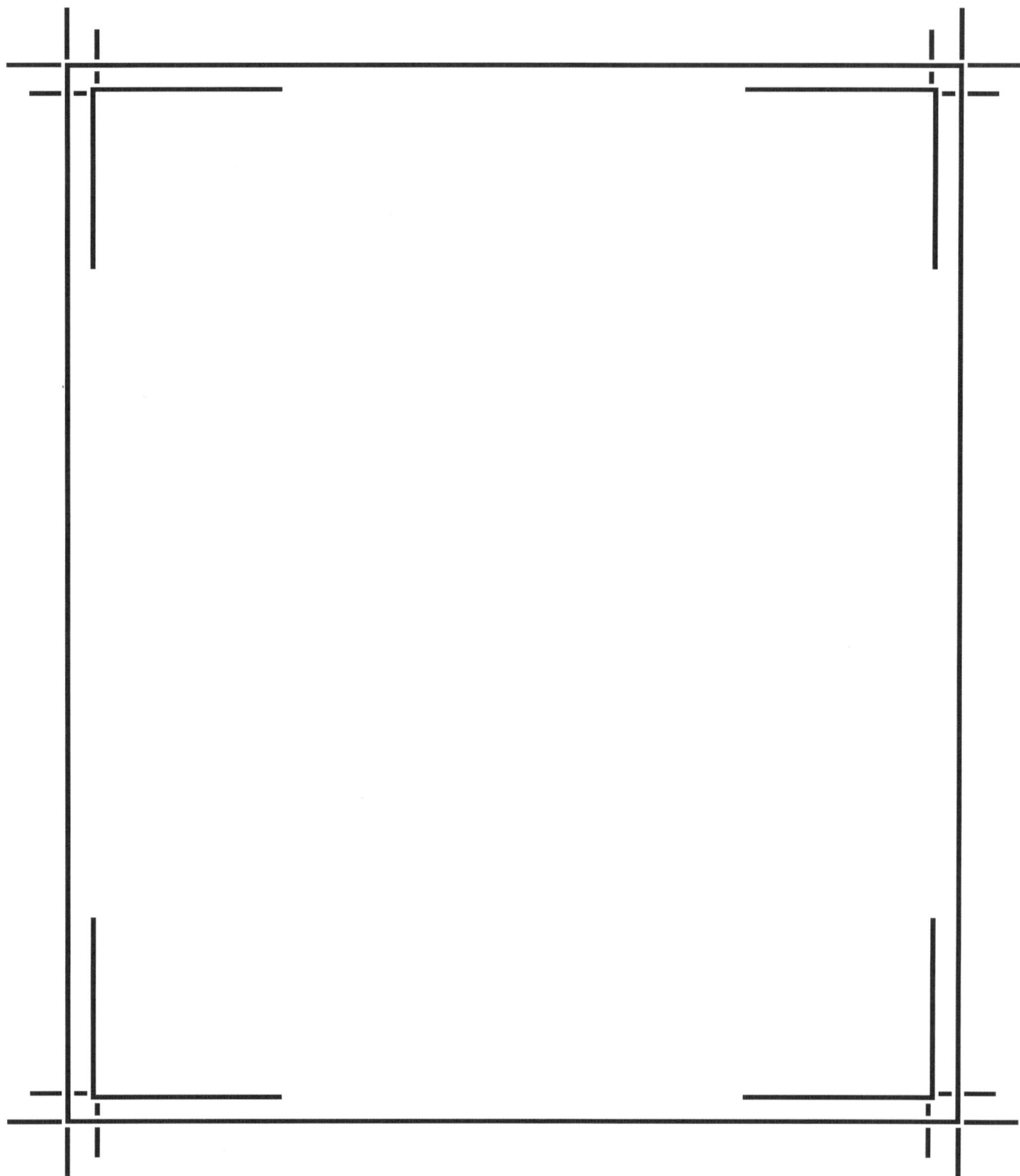

Your canvas...

It is _____ ___, ____

Today, we...

_____

_____

_____

_____

_____

_____

We will always remember...

_____

_____

_____

_____

_____

_____

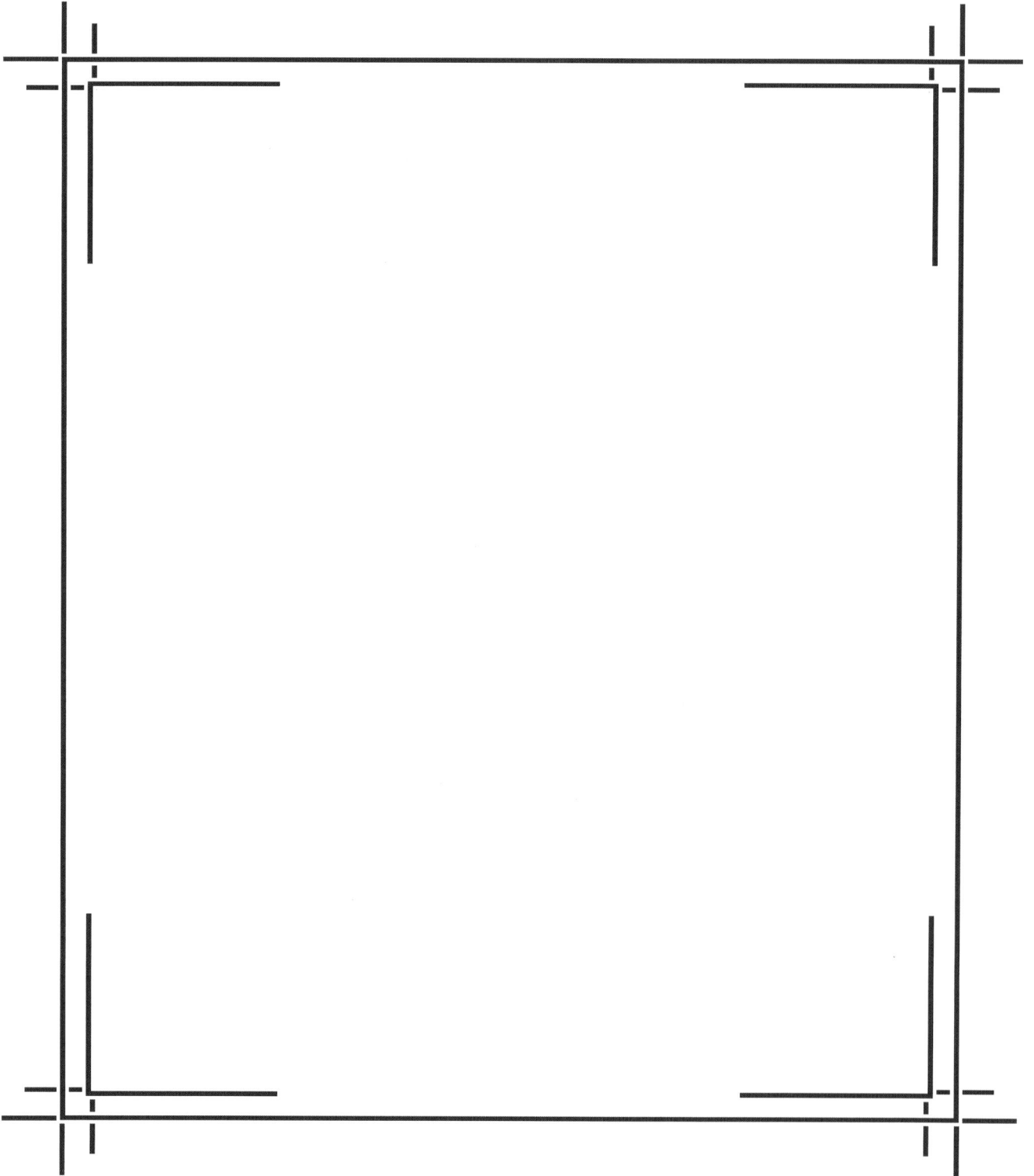

Your canvas...

It is _____ _____, _____

Today, we...

_____

_____

_____

_____

_____

We will always remember...

_____

_____

_____

_____

_____

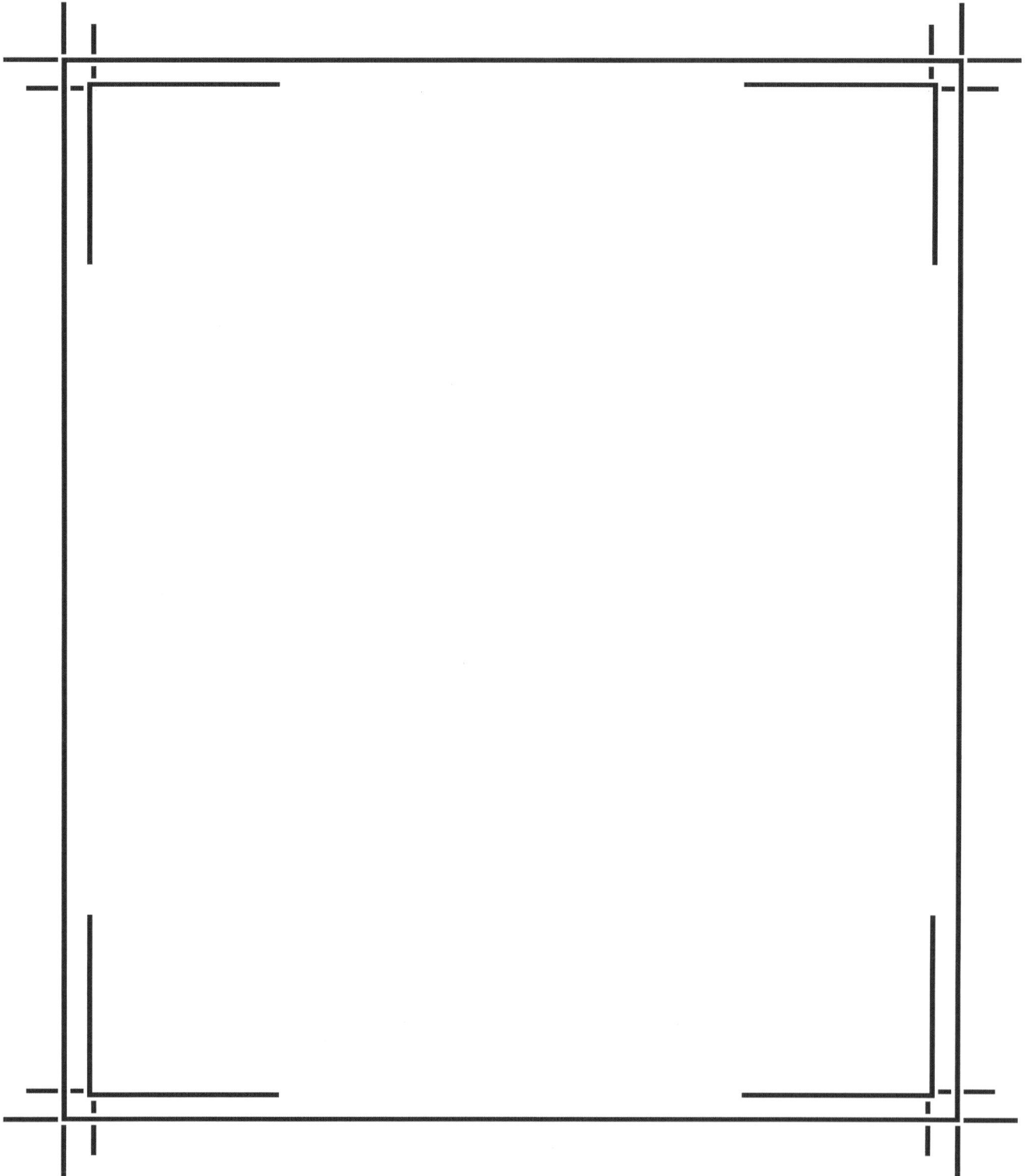

Your canvas...

It is _____ ___, ____
Month   Day   Year

Today, we...
_____
_____
_____
_____
_____
_____

We will always remember...
_____
_____
_____
_____
_____
_____

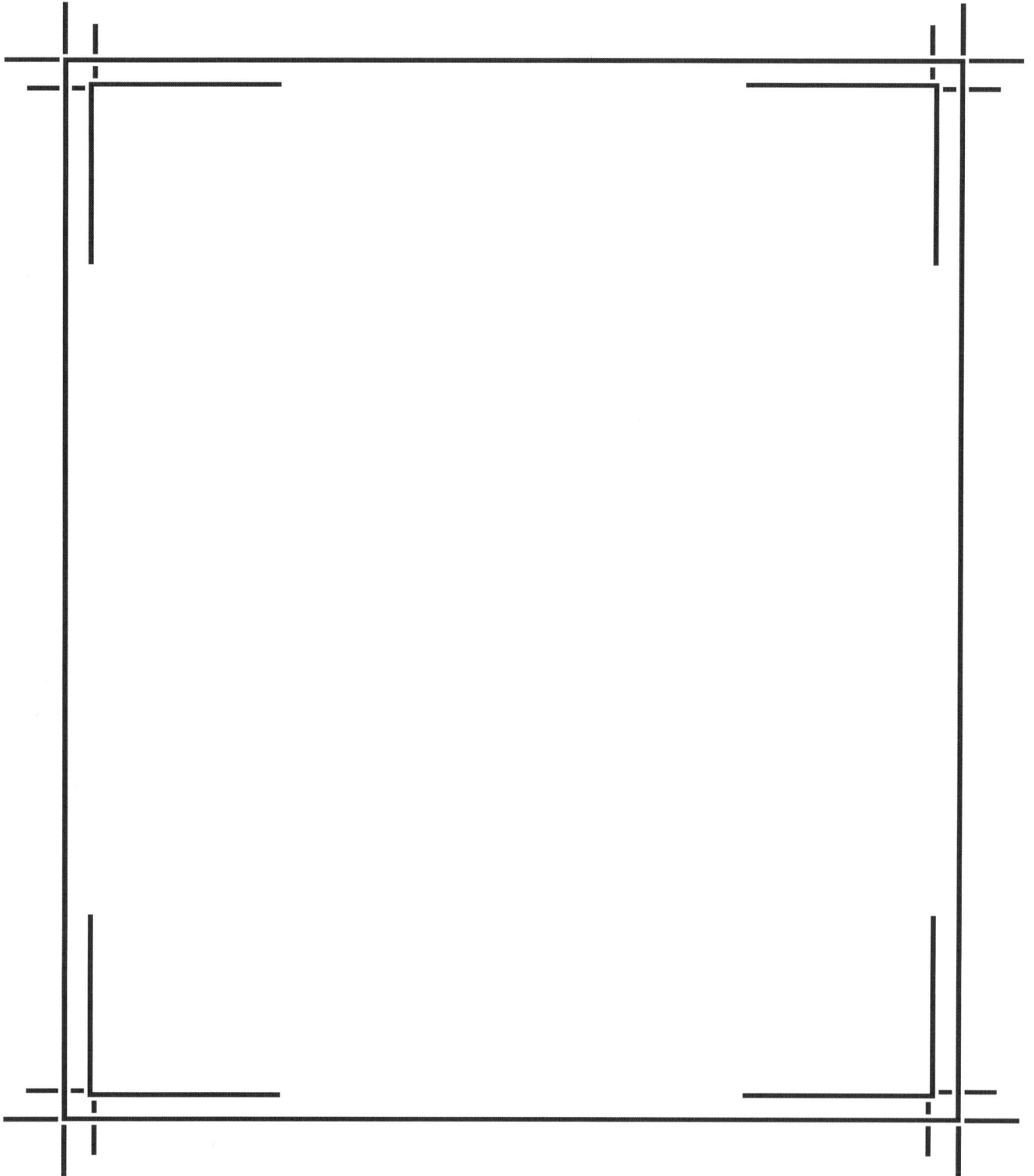

Your canvas...

It is _____ ___, ____
Month   Day   Year

Today, we...

_____

_____

_____

_____

_____

We will always remember...

_____

_____

_____

_____

_____

_____

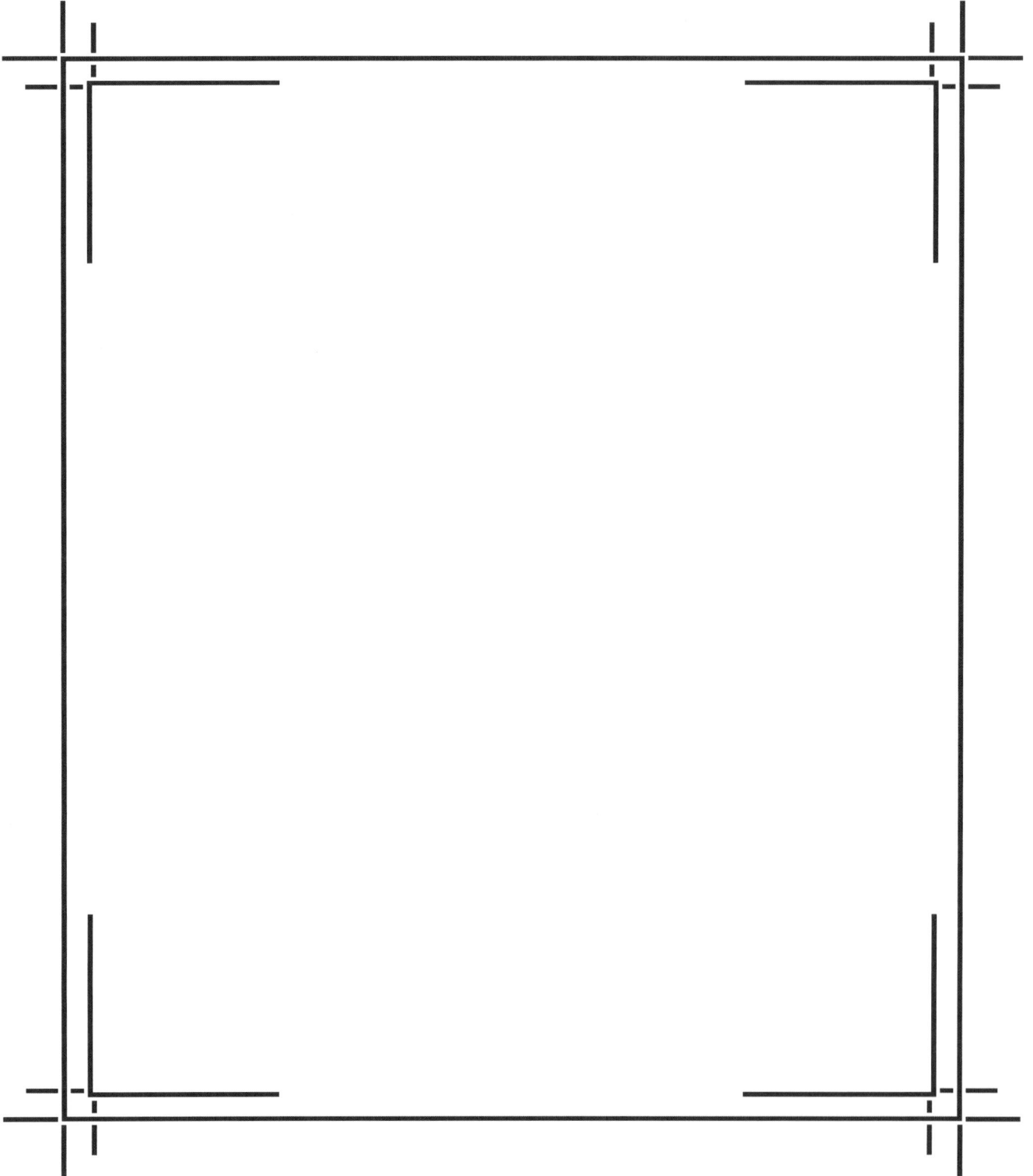

Your canvas...

It is _____ ___, ____
Month   Day   Year

Today, we...

_____

_____

_____

_____

_____

We will always remember...

_____

_____

_____

_____

_____

_____

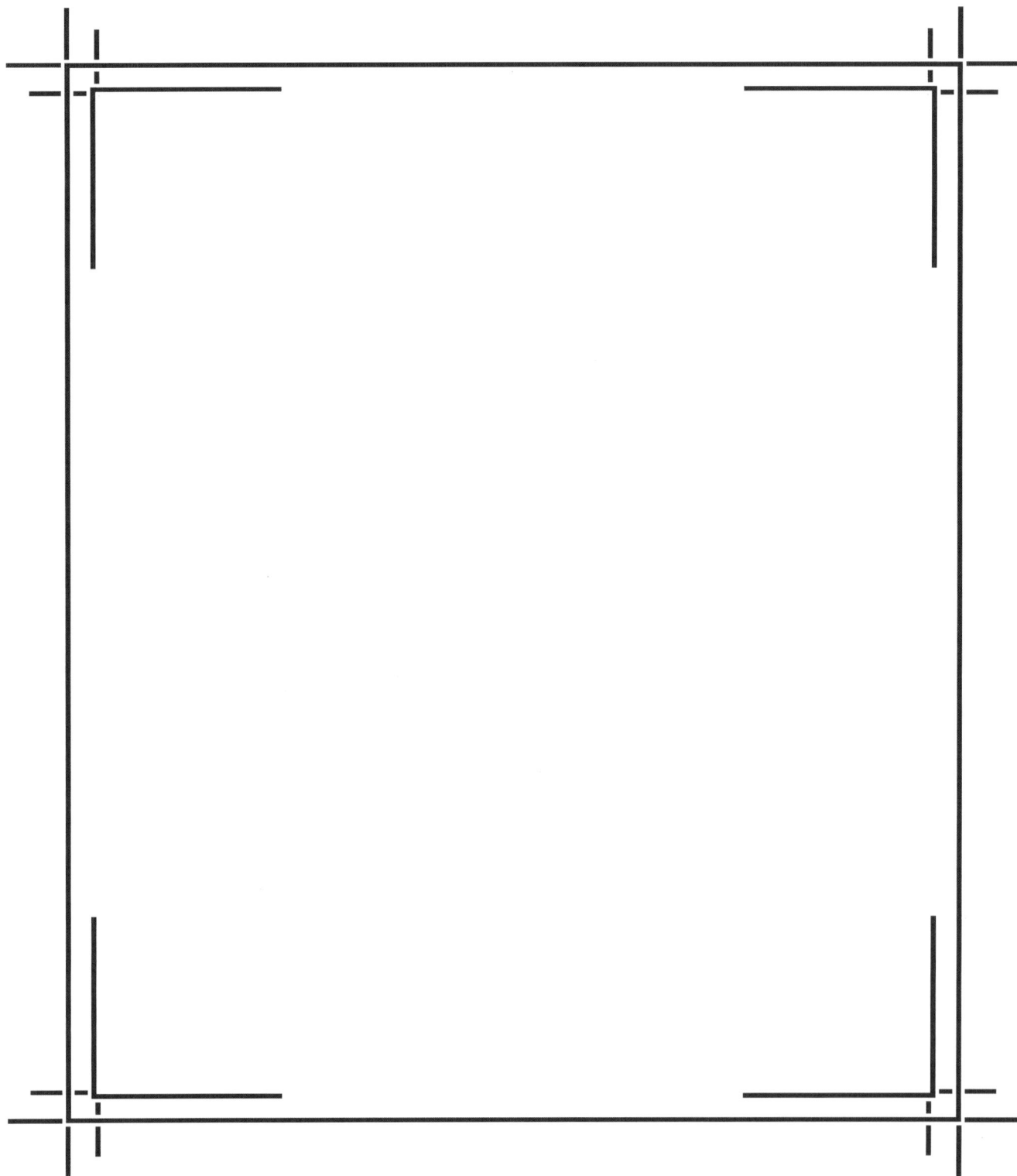

Your canvas...

It is _____ ___, ____
Month   Day   Year

Today, we...

_____

_____

_____

_____

_____

We will always remember...

_____

_____

_____

_____

_____

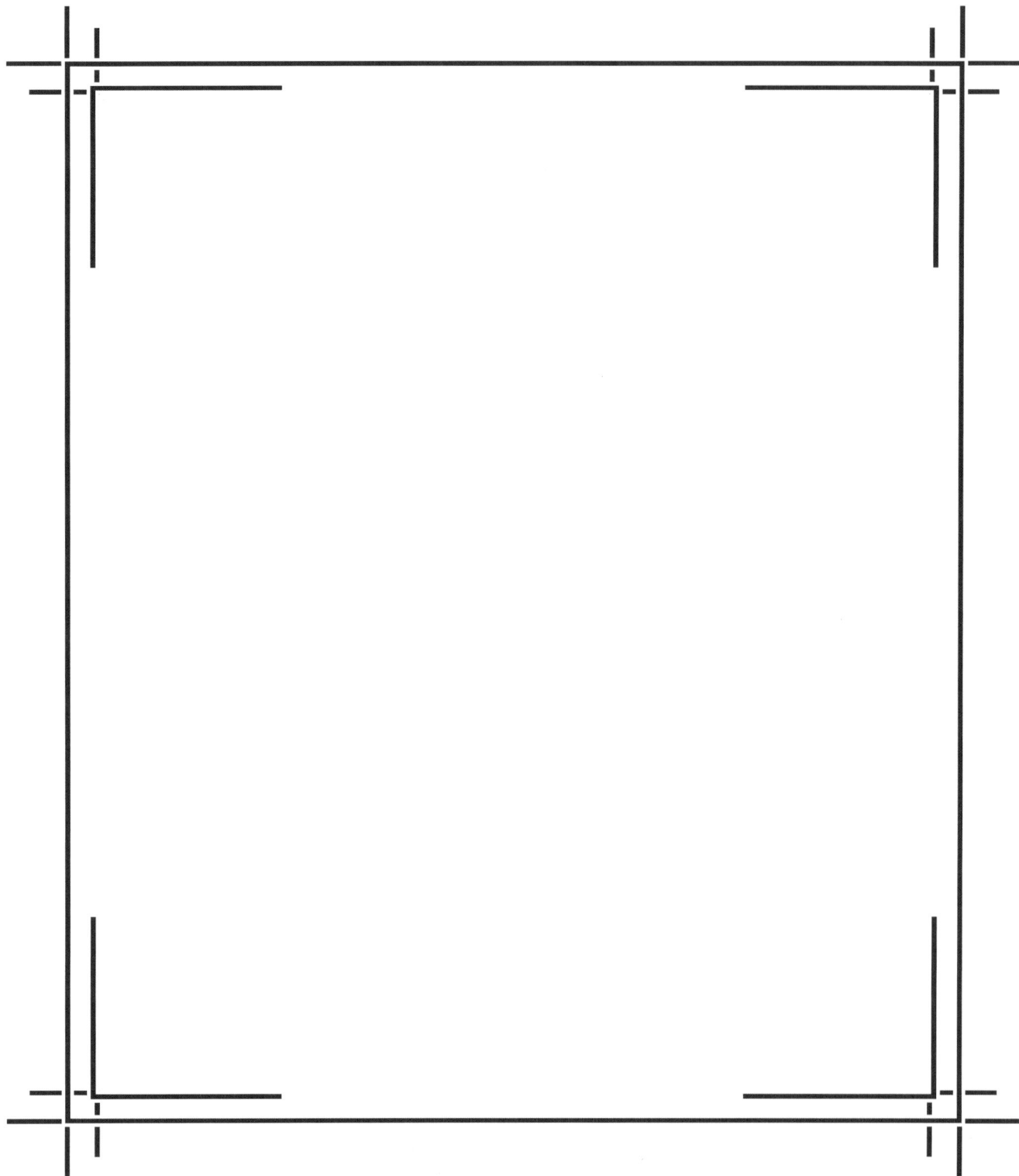

Your canvas...

It is _____ ___, ___
Month   Day   Year

Today, we...

_____

_____

_____

_____

_____

_____

We will always remember...

_____

_____

_____

_____

_____

_____

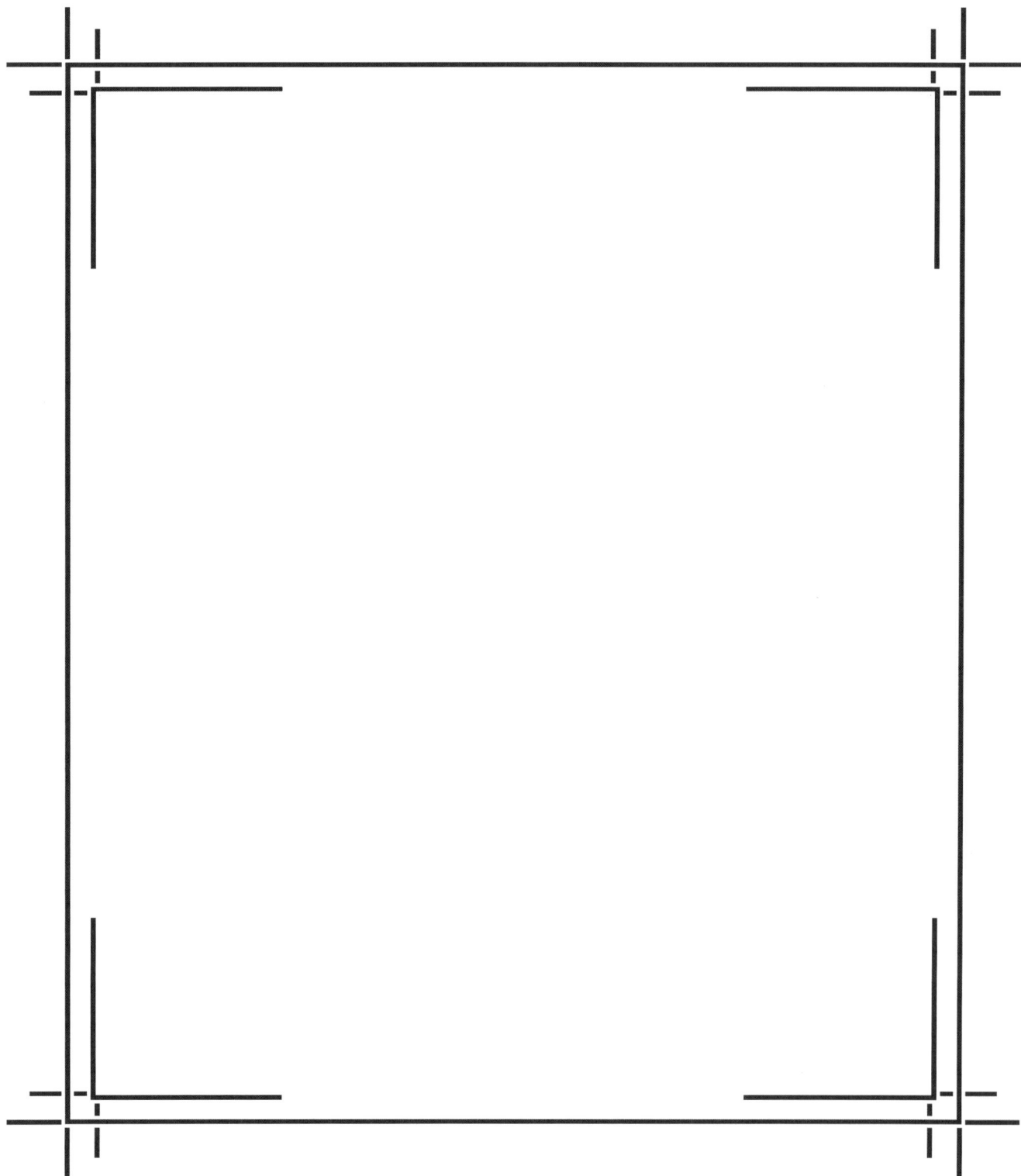

Your canvas...

It is _____ ___, ____

Today, we...

_____

_____

_____

_____

_____

We will always remember...

_____

_____

_____

_____

_____

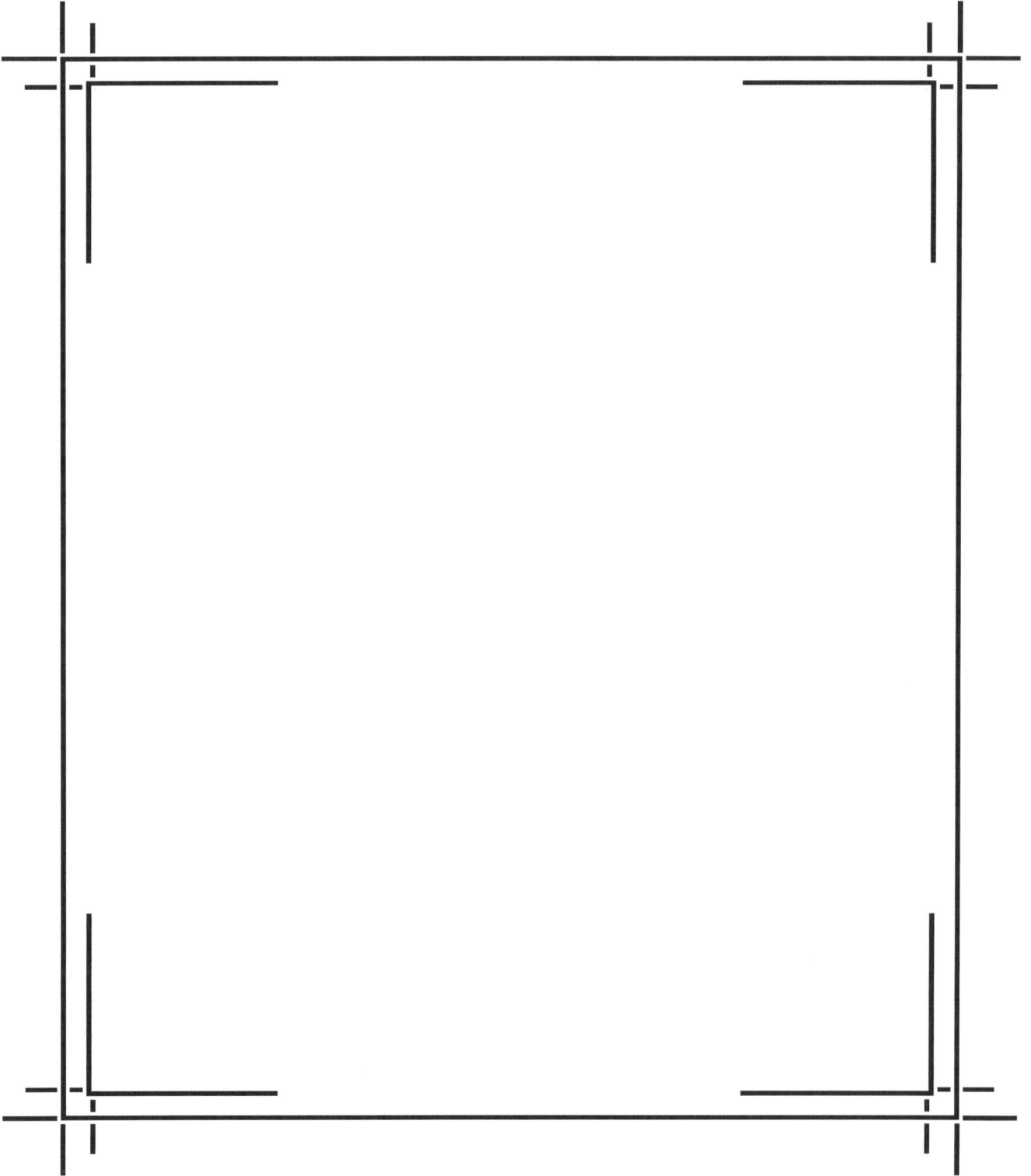

Your canvas...

It is _____ ___, _____
Month Day Year

Today, we...

_____

_____

_____

_____

_____

_____

We will always remember...

_____

_____

_____

_____

_____

_____

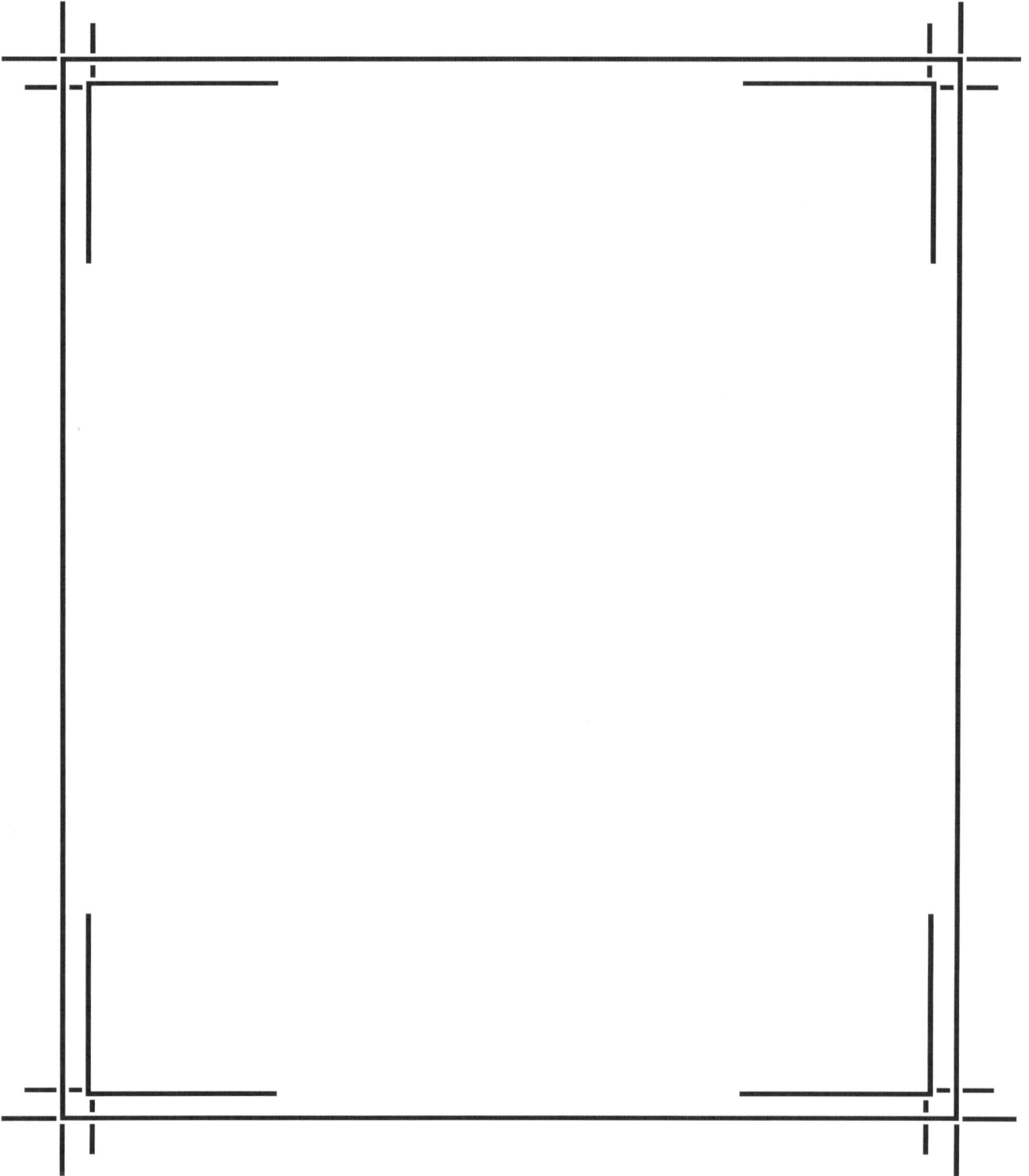

Your canvas...

It is _____ ___, ____
Month   Day   Year

Today, we...

_____

_____

_____

_____

_____

We will always remember...

_____

_____

_____

_____

_____

_____

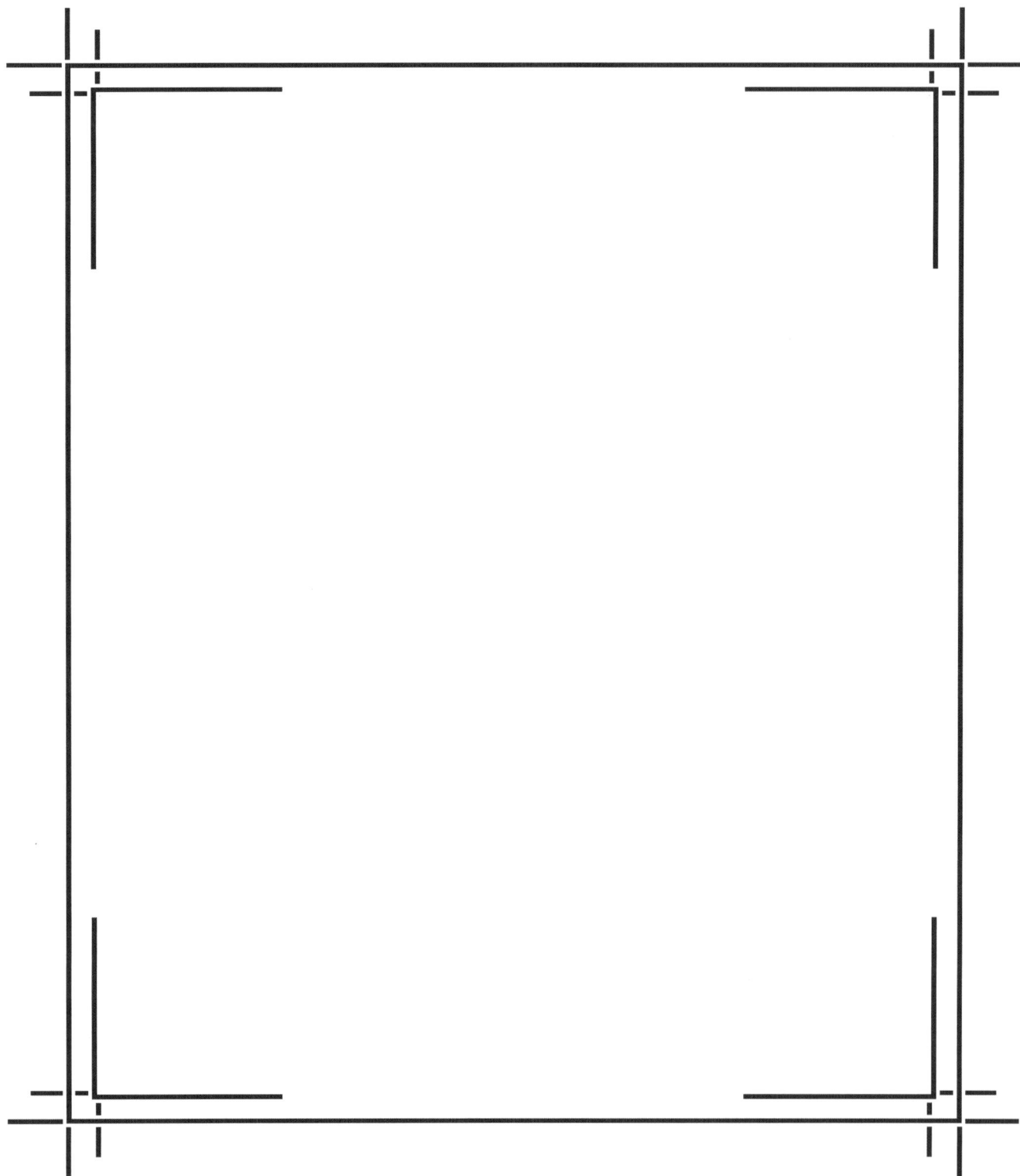

Your canvas...

It is _____ ___, ____
Month   Day   Year

Today, we...

_____

_____

_____

_____

_____

We will always remember...

_____

_____

_____

_____

_____

_____

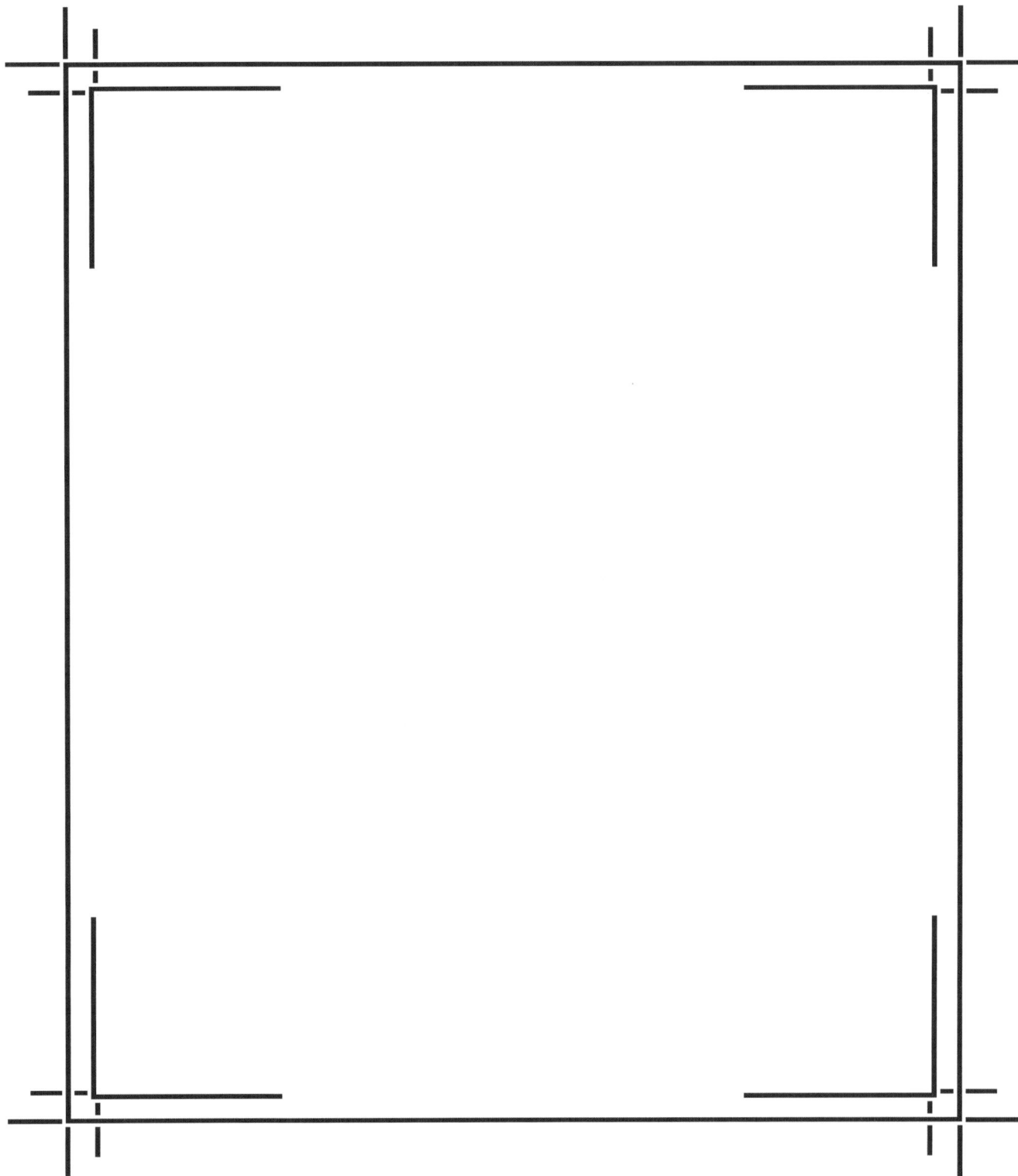

Your canvas...

It is _____ ___, _____
Month   Day,   Year

Today, we...

_____

_____

_____

_____

_____

_____

We will always remember...

_____

_____

_____

_____

_____

_____

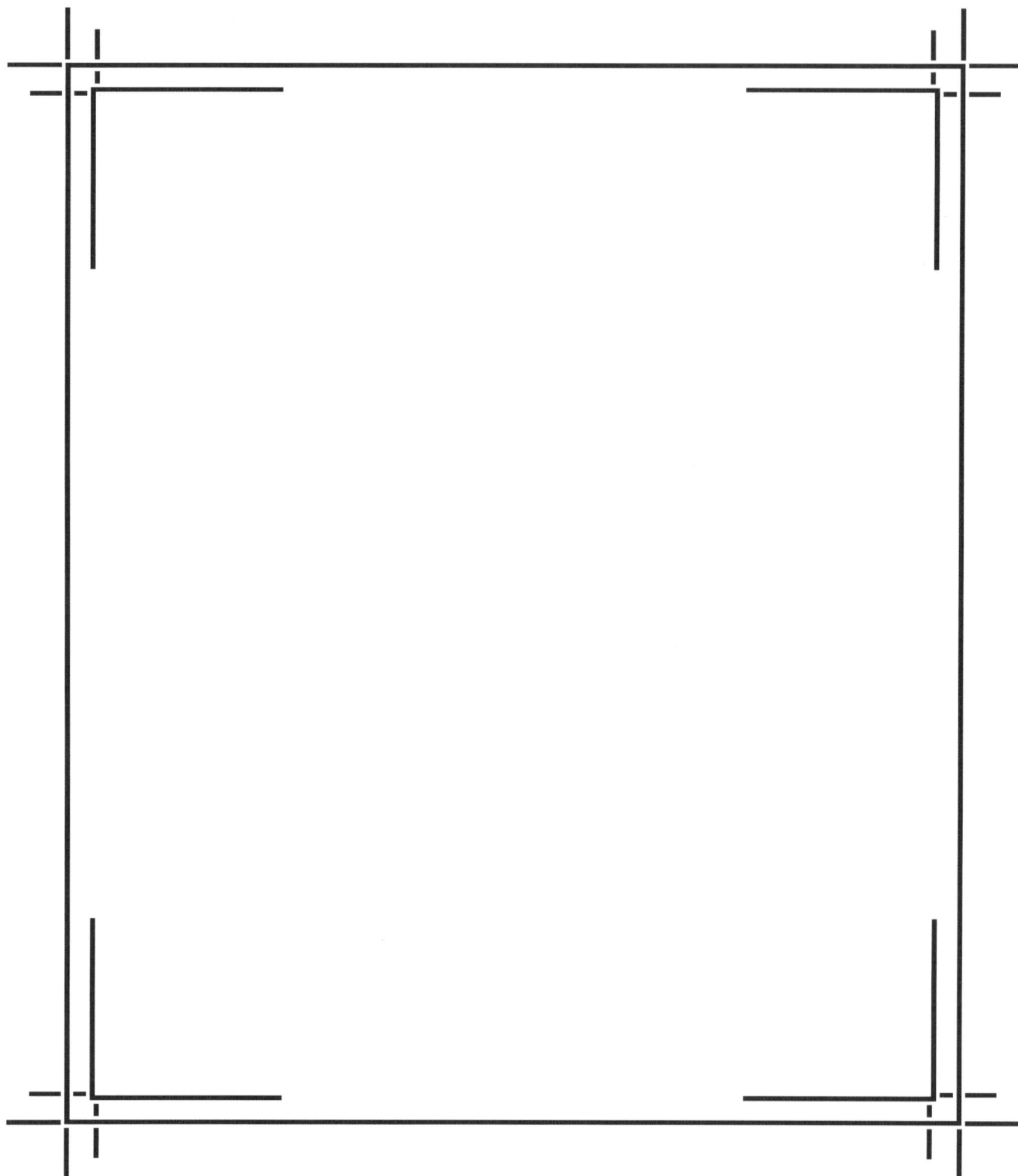

Your canvas...

It is _____ ___, ____
Month   Day   Year

Today, we...

_____

_____

_____

_____

_____

We will always remember...

_____

_____

_____

_____

_____

_____

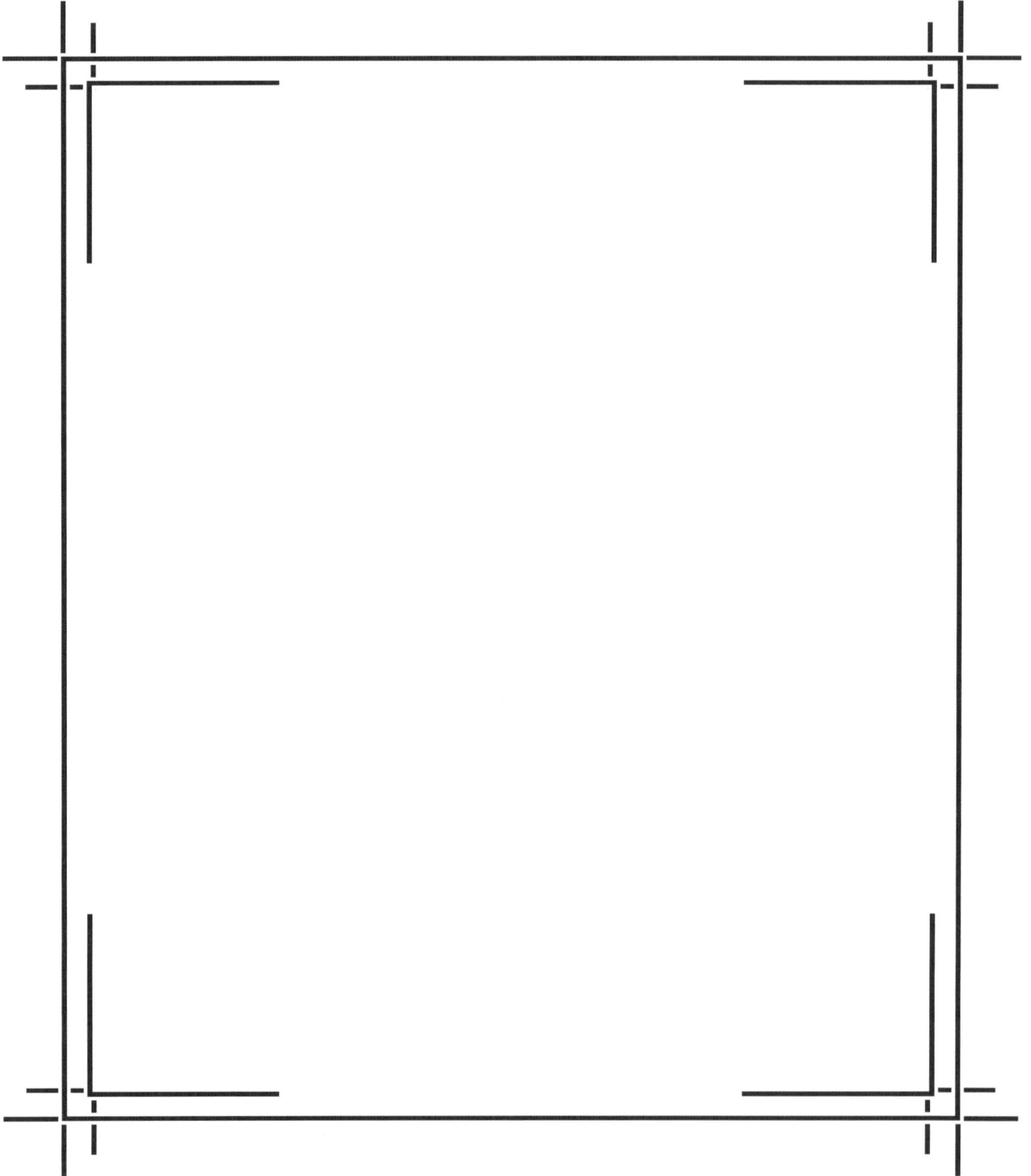

Your canvas...

It is _____ ___, ____
Month   Day   Year

Today, we...

_____

_____

_____

_____

_____

We will always remember...

_____

_____

_____

_____

_____

_____

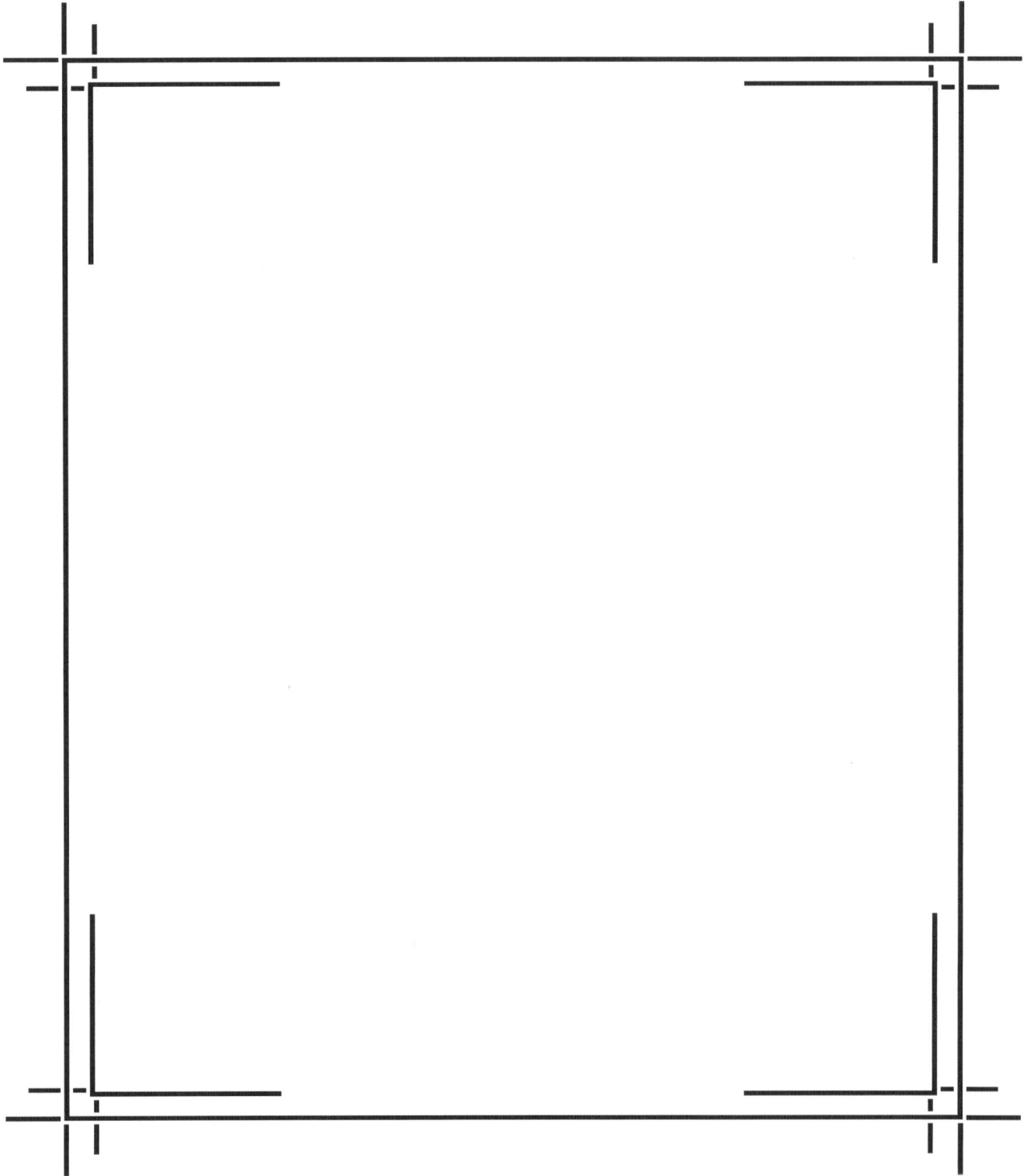

Your canvas...

It is _____ ___, ____

Today, we...

_____

_____

_____

_____

_____

We will always remember...

_____

_____

_____

_____

_____

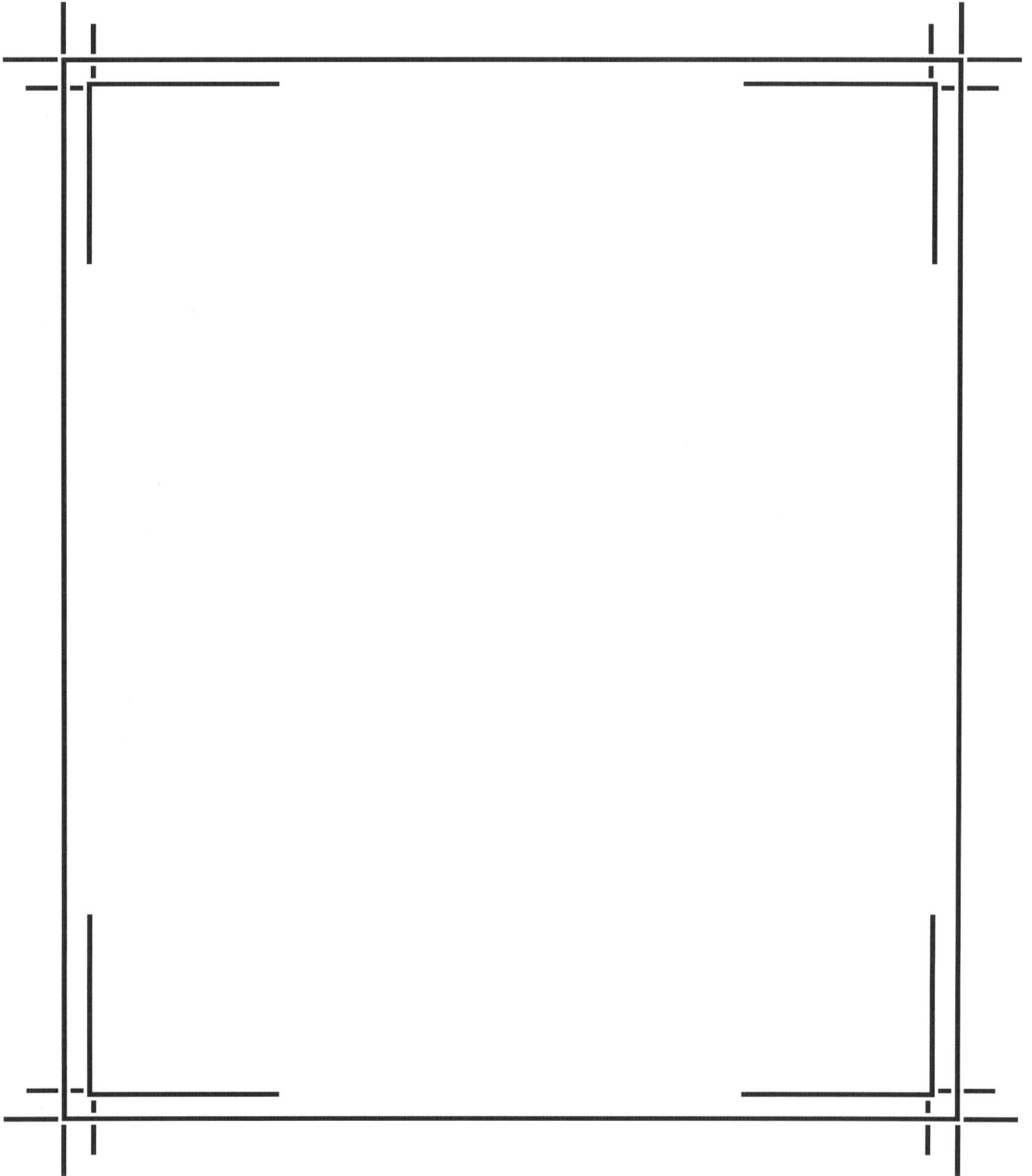

Your canvas...

It is ____ __, ____
Month   Day   Year

Today, we...

_____

_____

_____

_____

_____

We will always remember...

_____

_____

_____

_____

_____

_____

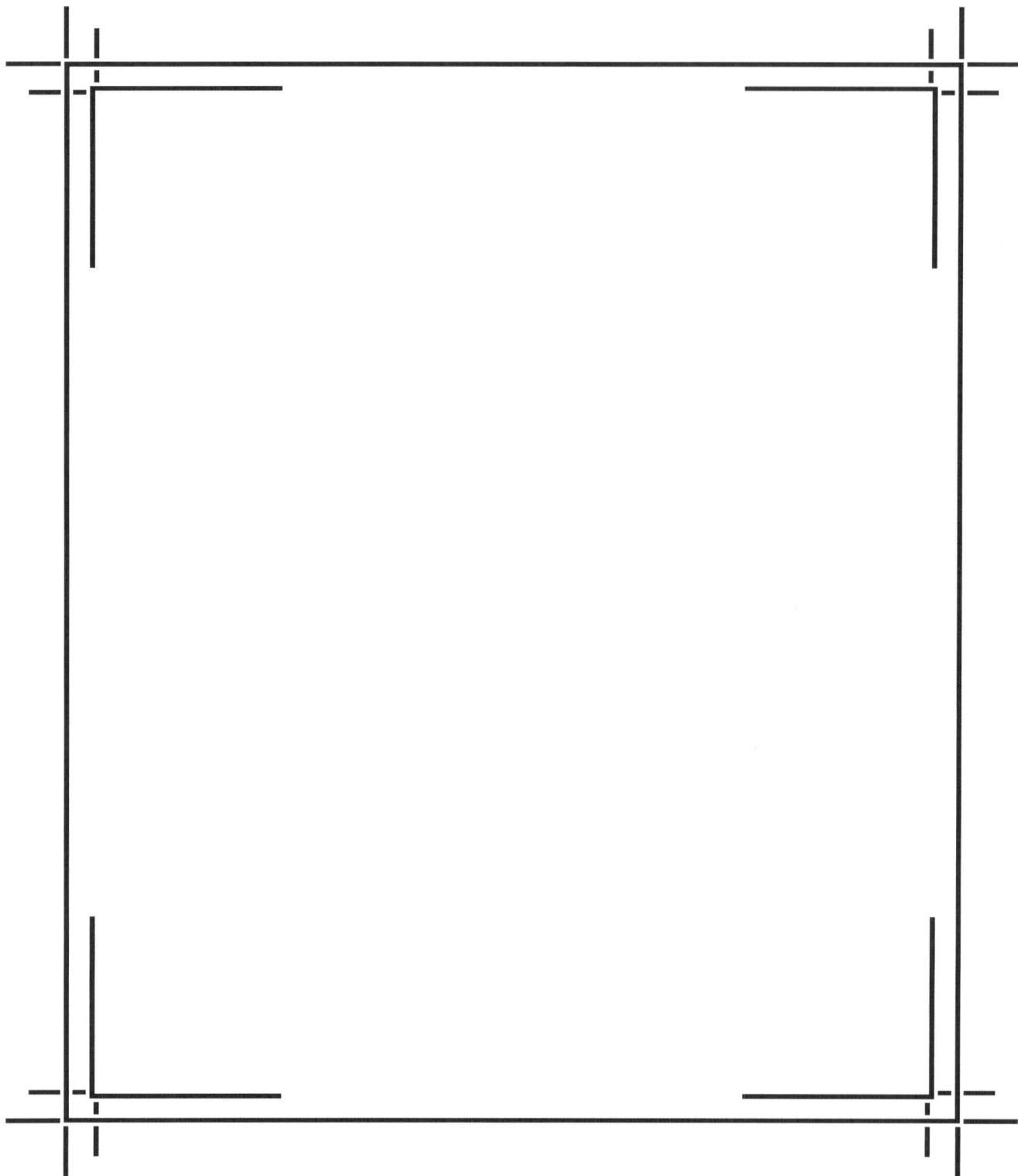

Your canvas...

It is _____ _____, _____
Month   Day   Year

Today, we...

_____

_____

_____

_____

_____

_____

We will always remember...

_____

_____

_____

_____

_____

_____

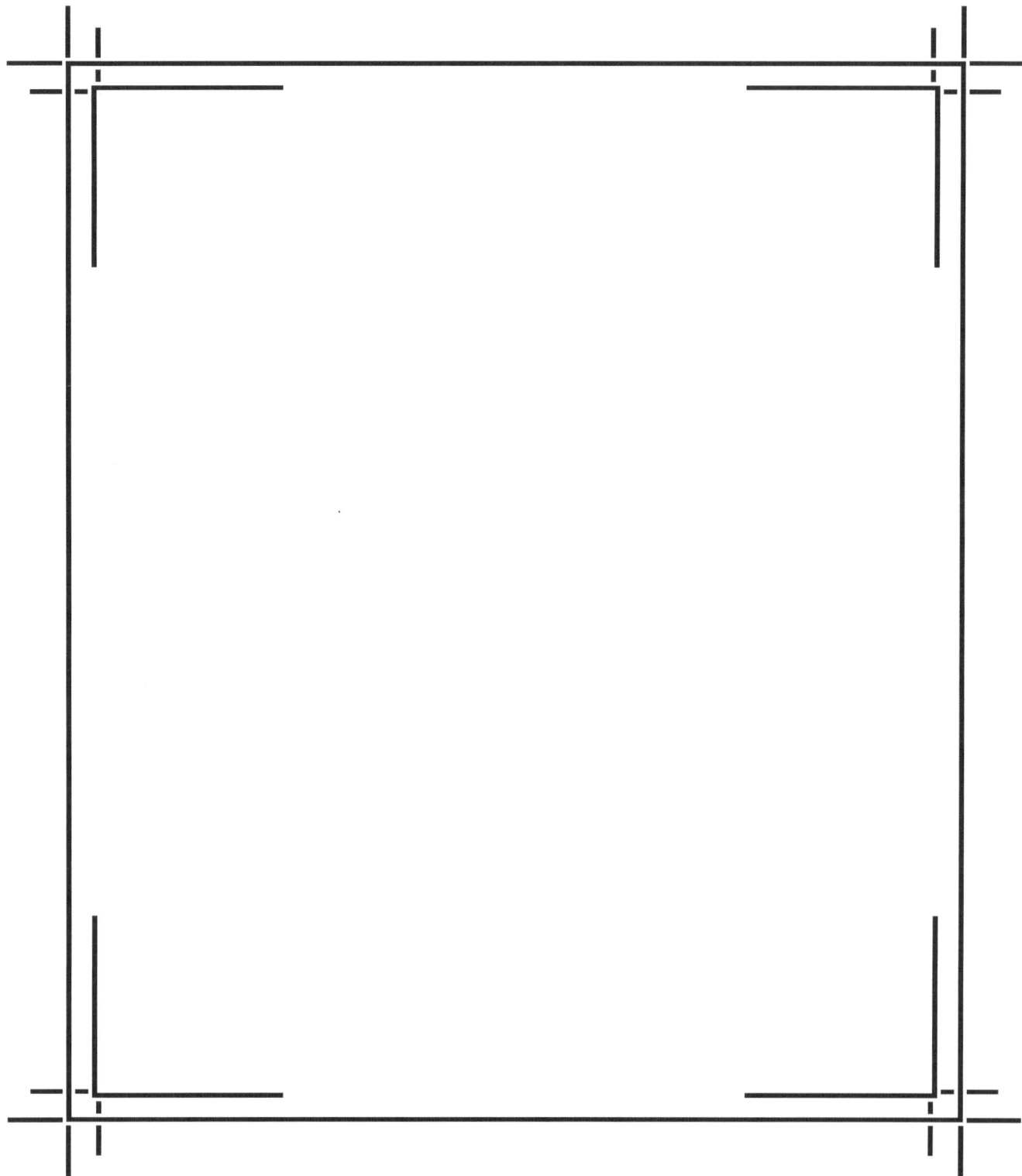

Your canvas...

It is _____ ___, ____
Month   Day   Year

Today, we...

_____

_____

_____

_____

_____

We will always remember...

_____

_____

_____

_____

_____

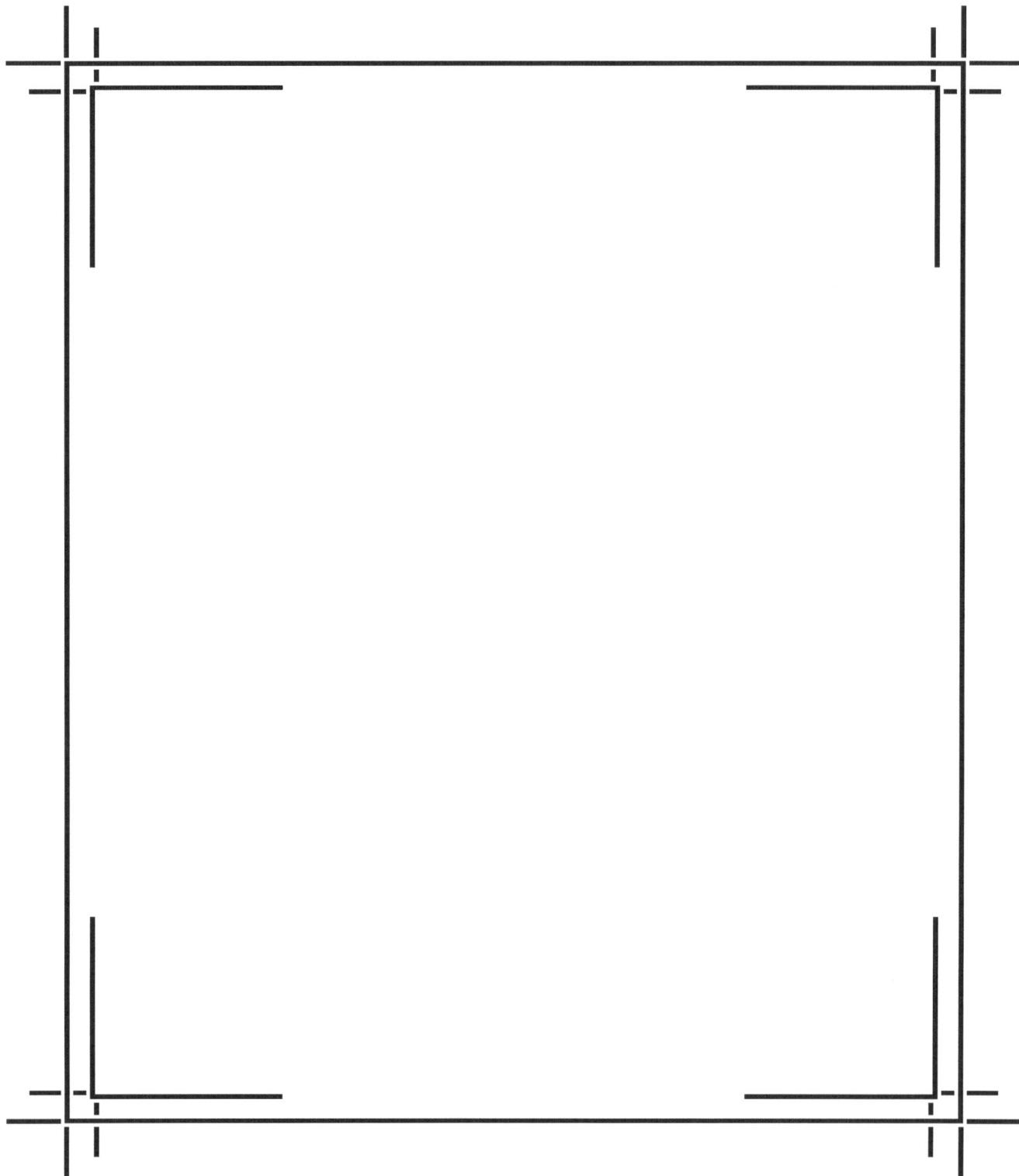

Your canvas...

It is ____ ___, ____
Month   Day ,   Year

Today, we...

_____

_____

_____

_____

_____

We will always remember...

_____

_____

_____

_____

_____

_____

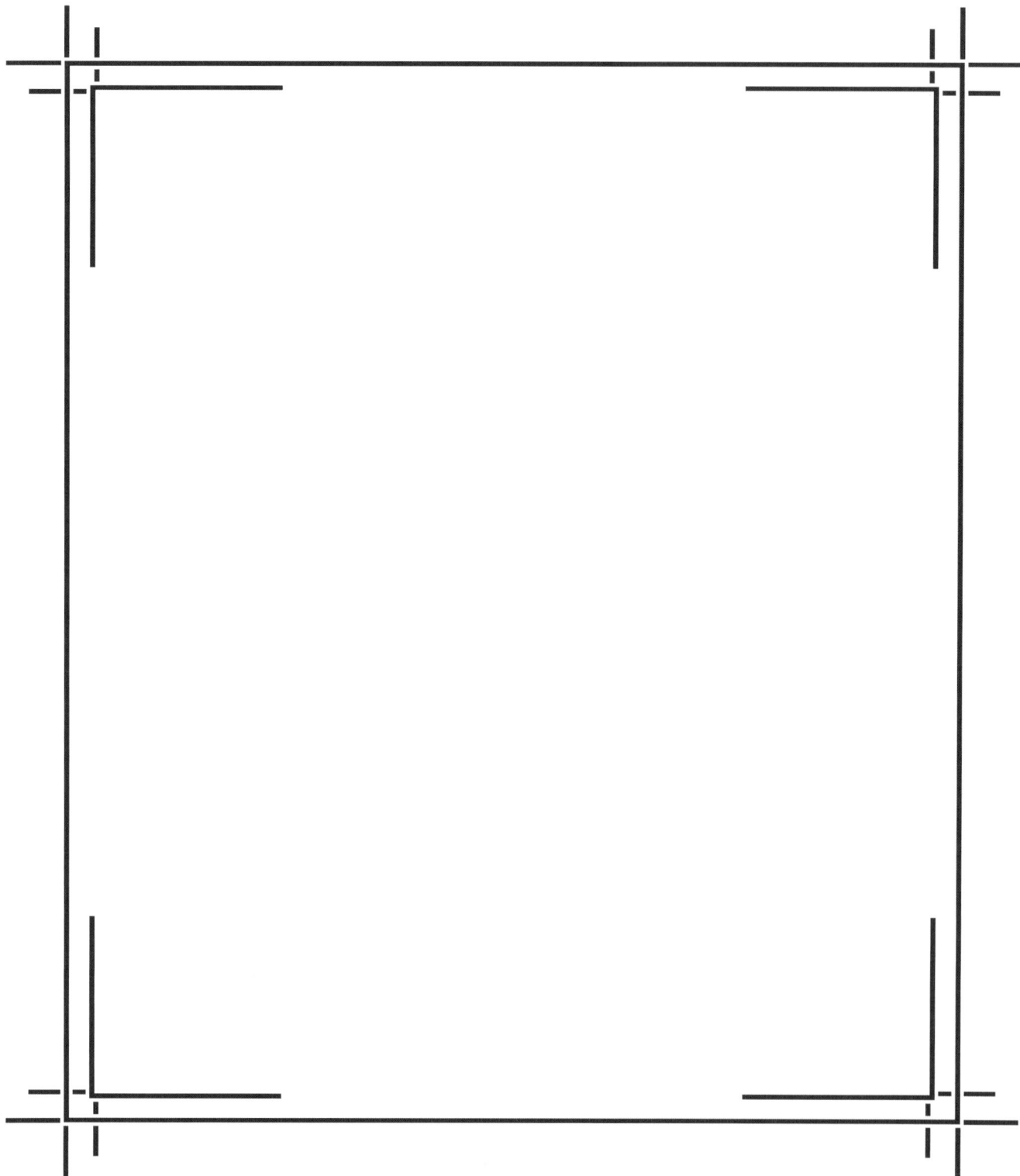

Your canvas...

It is _____ ___, ____

Today, we...

_____

_____

_____

_____

_____

We will always remember...

_____

_____

_____

_____

_____

_____

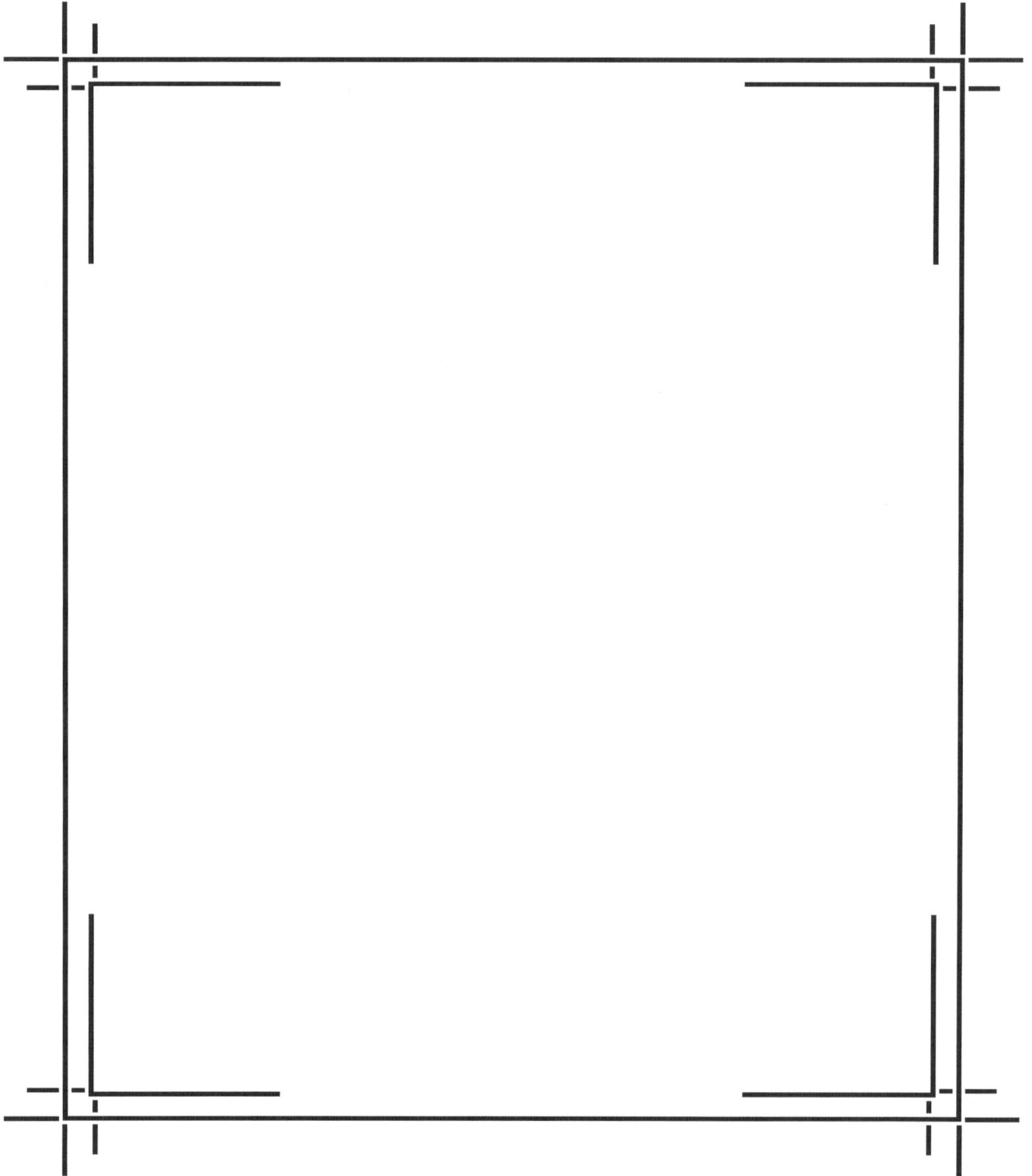

Your canvas...

It is _____ ___, ____
Month   Day , Year

Today, we...

_____

_____

_____

_____

_____

We will always remember...

_____

_____

_____

_____

_____

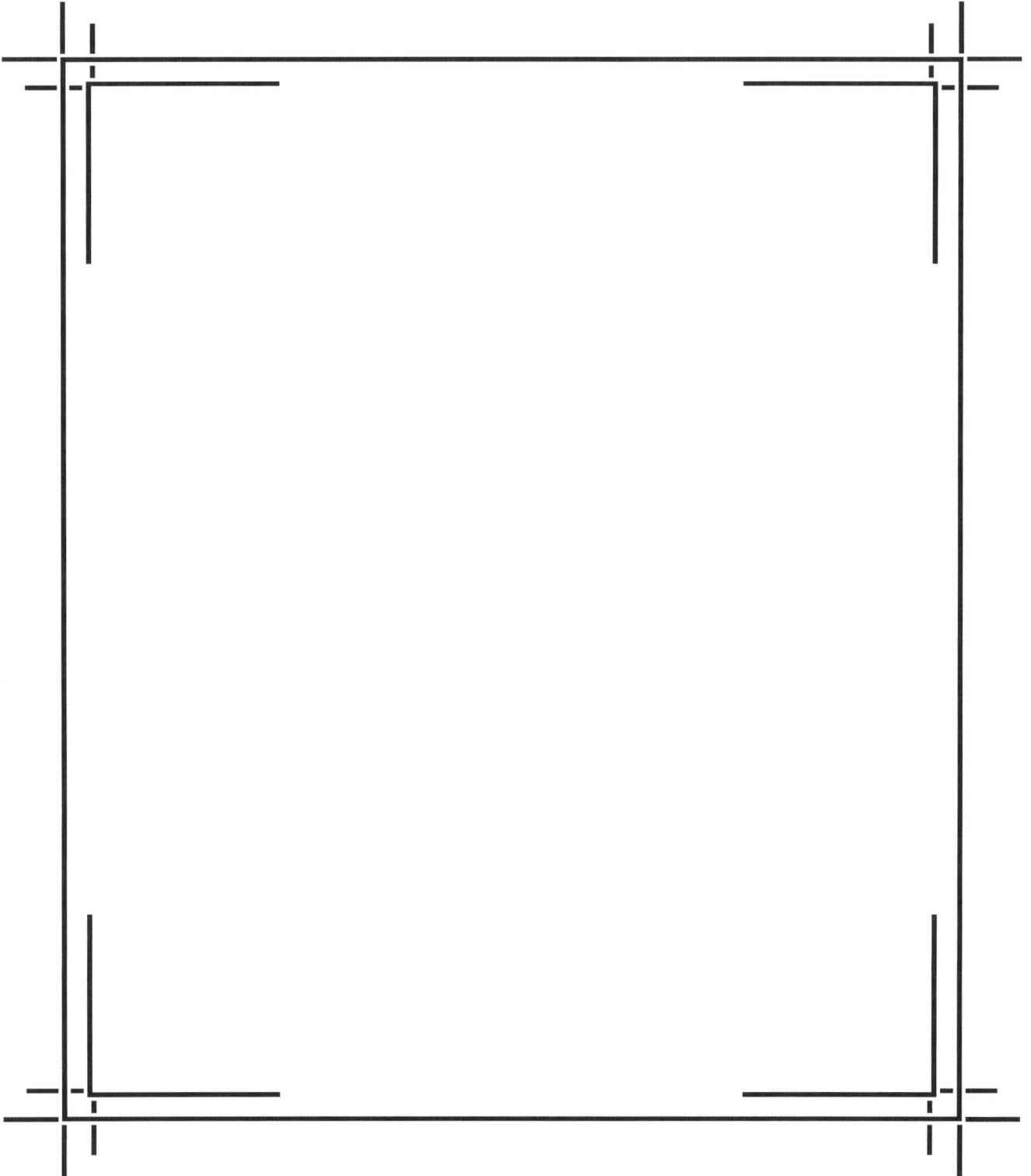

Your canvas...

It is ____ ____, ____
Month   Day   Year

Today, we...

_____

_____

_____

_____

_____

We will always remember...

_____

_____

_____

_____

_____

_____

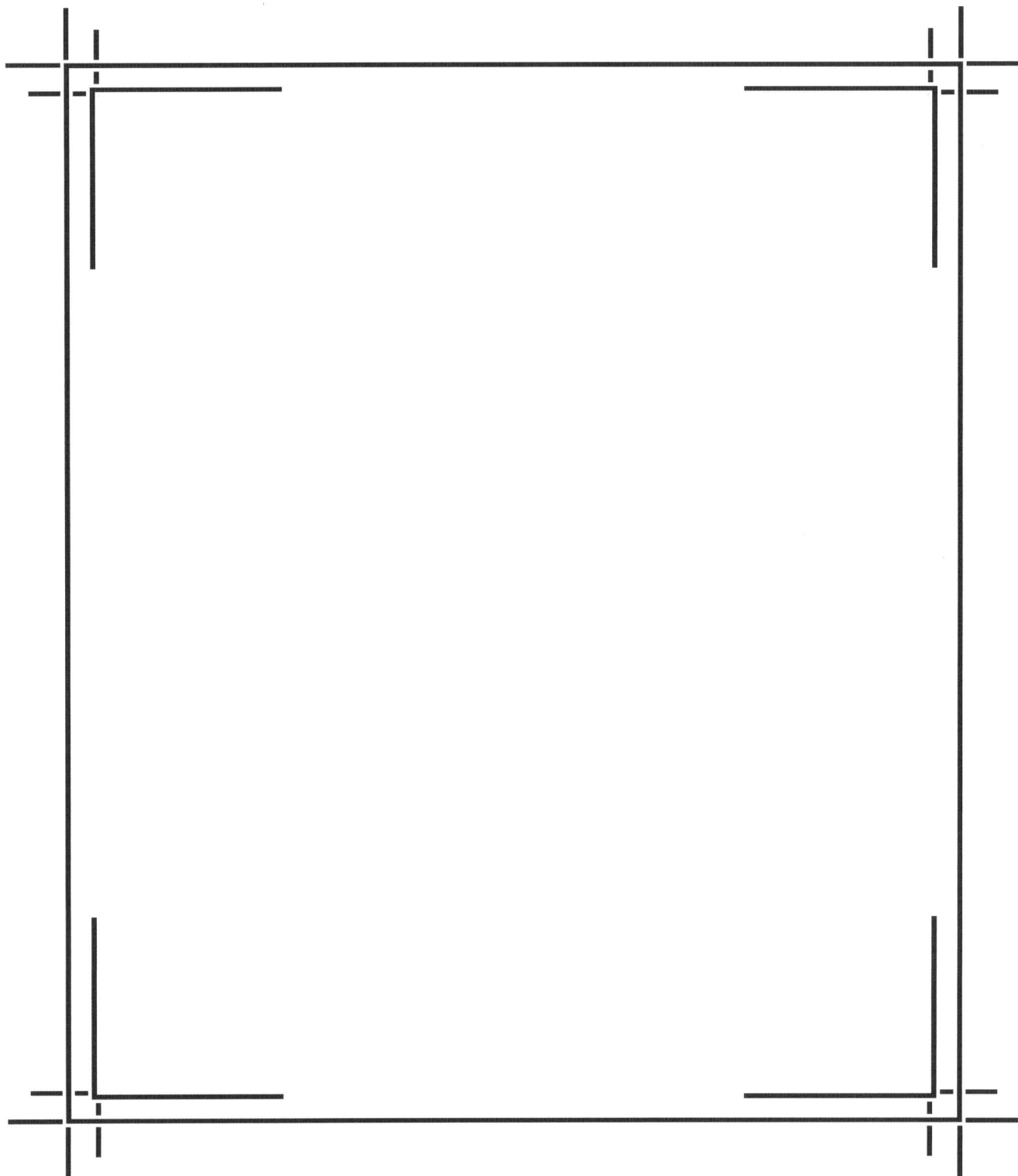

Your canvas...

It is _____ ___, _____

Today, we...

_____

_____

_____

_____

_____

_____

We will always remember...

_____

_____

_____

_____

_____

_____

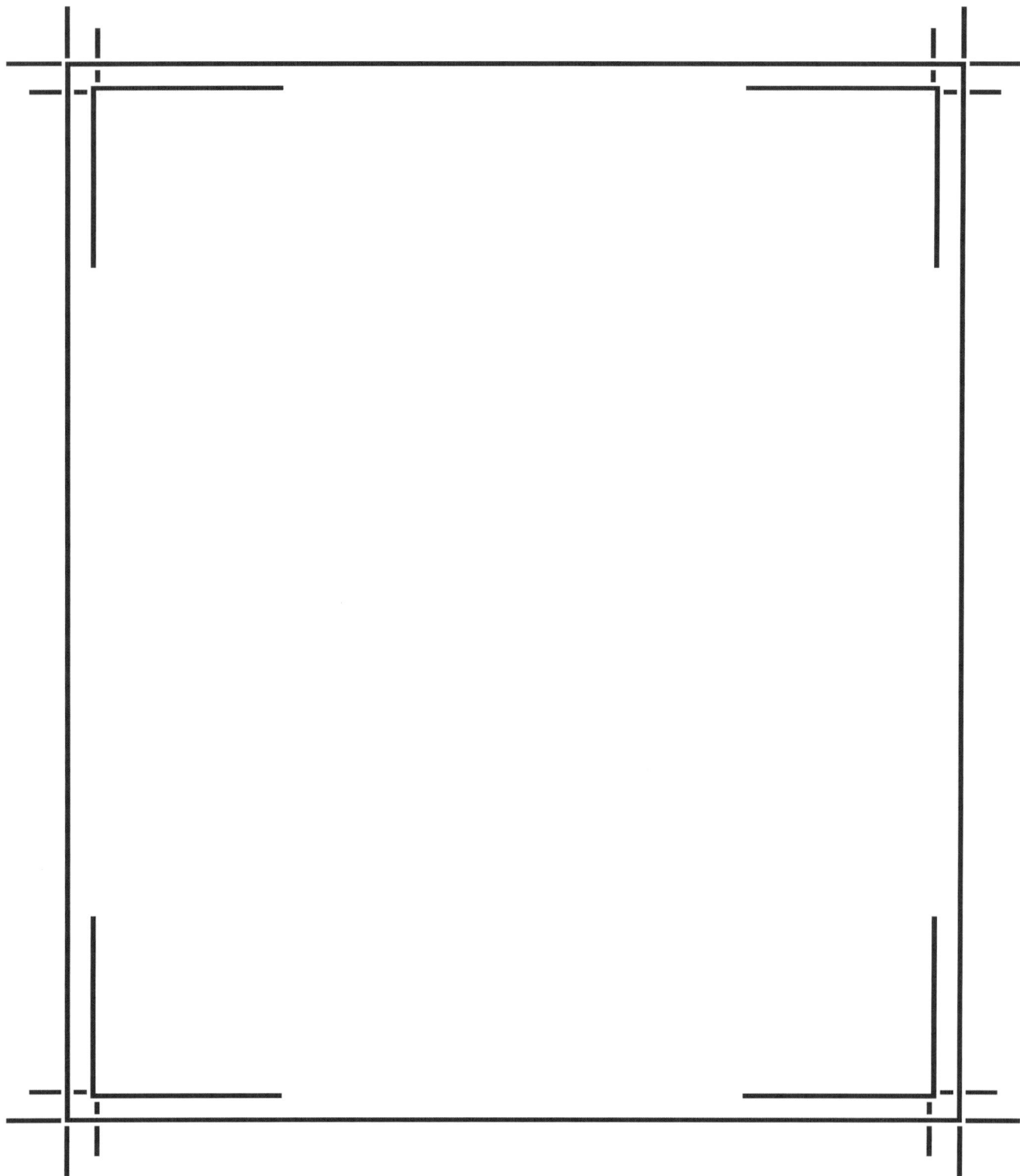

Your canvas...

It is _____ ___, _____
Month   Day   Year

Today, we...

_____

_____

_____

_____

_____

We will always remember...

_____

_____

_____

_____

_____

_____

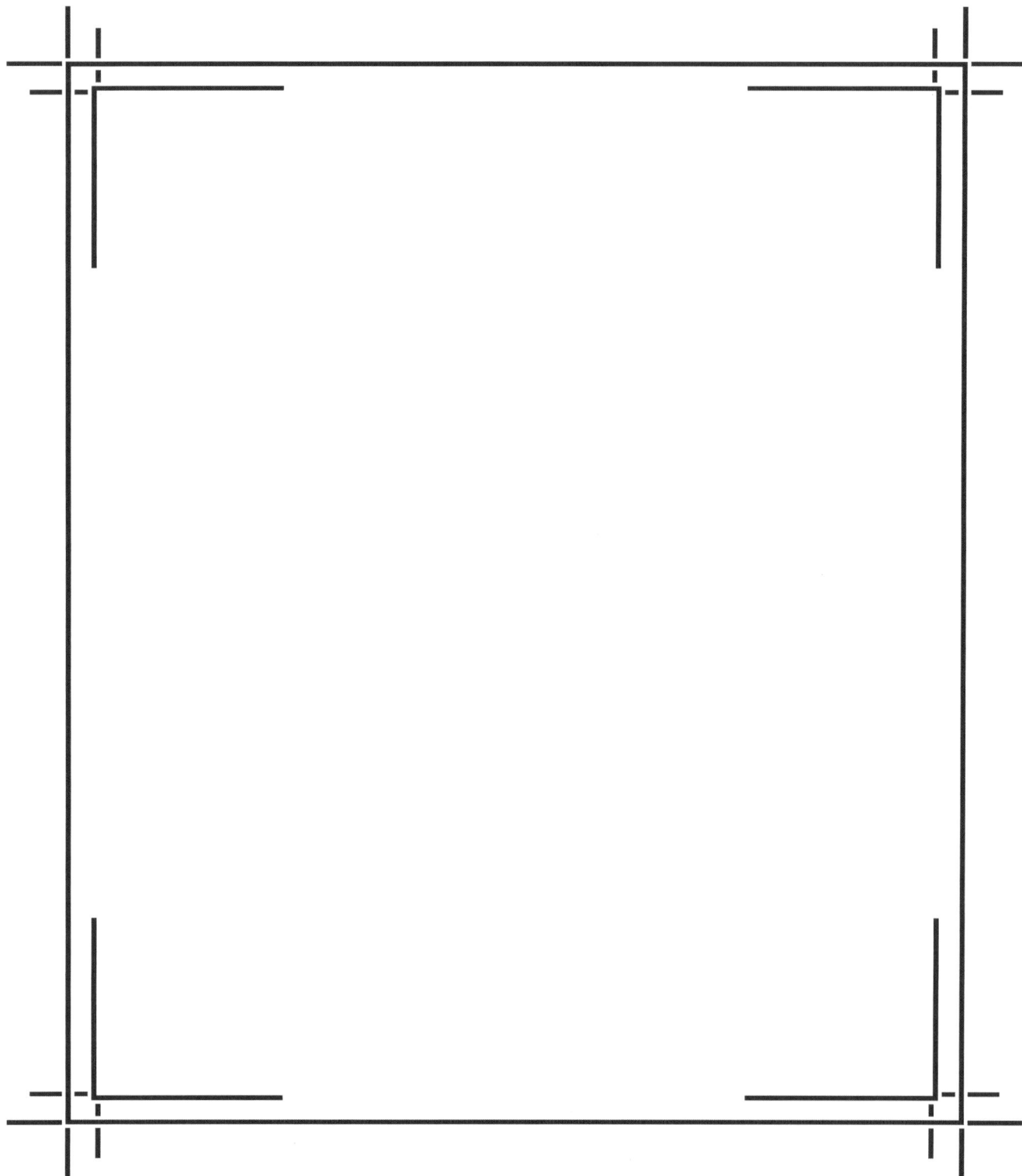

Your canvas...

It is _____ ___, ____
Month   Day   Year

Today, we...

_____

_____

_____

_____

_____

We will always remember...

_____

_____

_____

_____

_____

_____

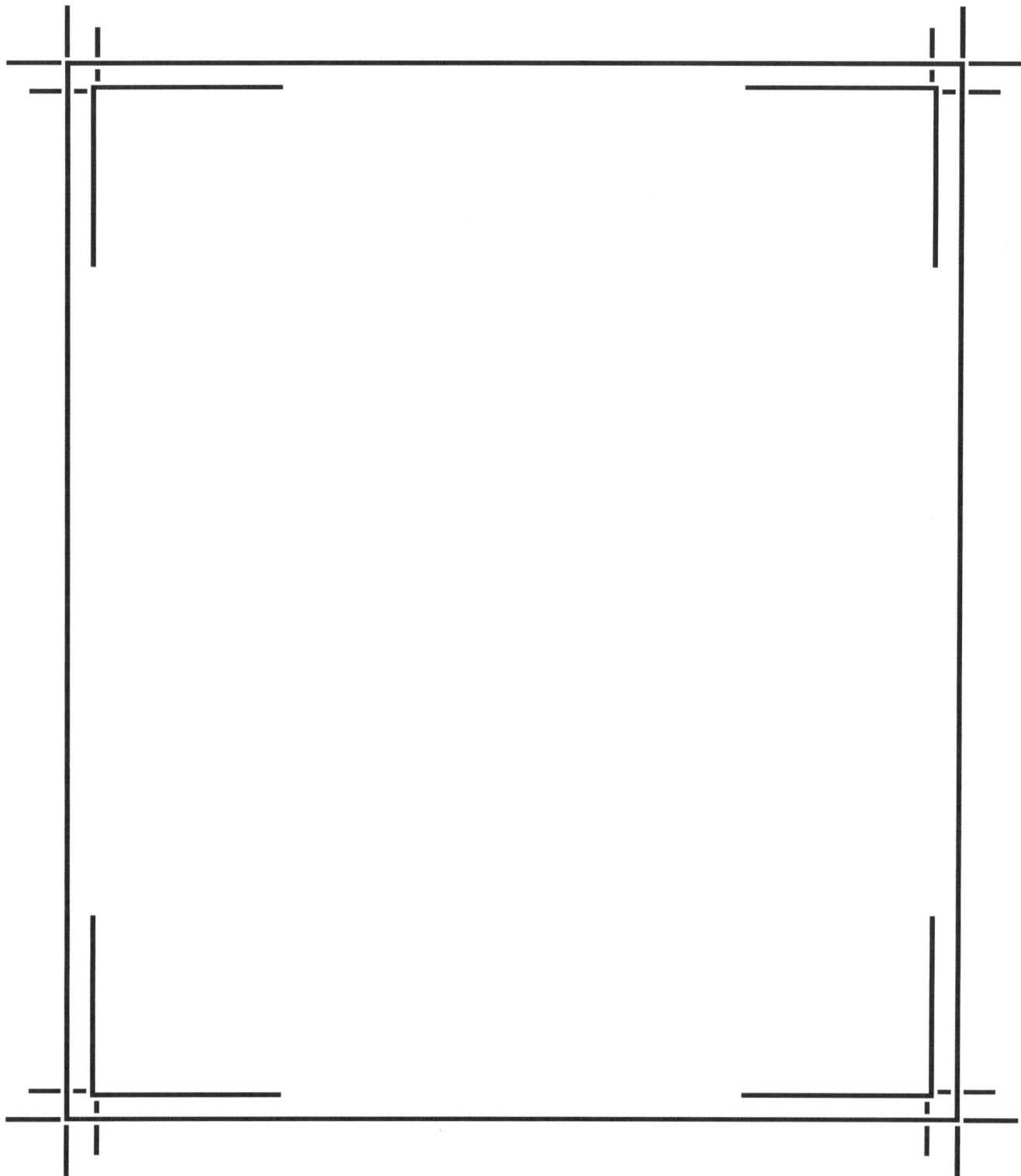

Your canvas...

It is _____ ____, ____
Month   Day   Year

Today, we...

_____

_____

_____

_____

_____

_____

We will always remember...

_____

_____

_____

_____

_____

_____

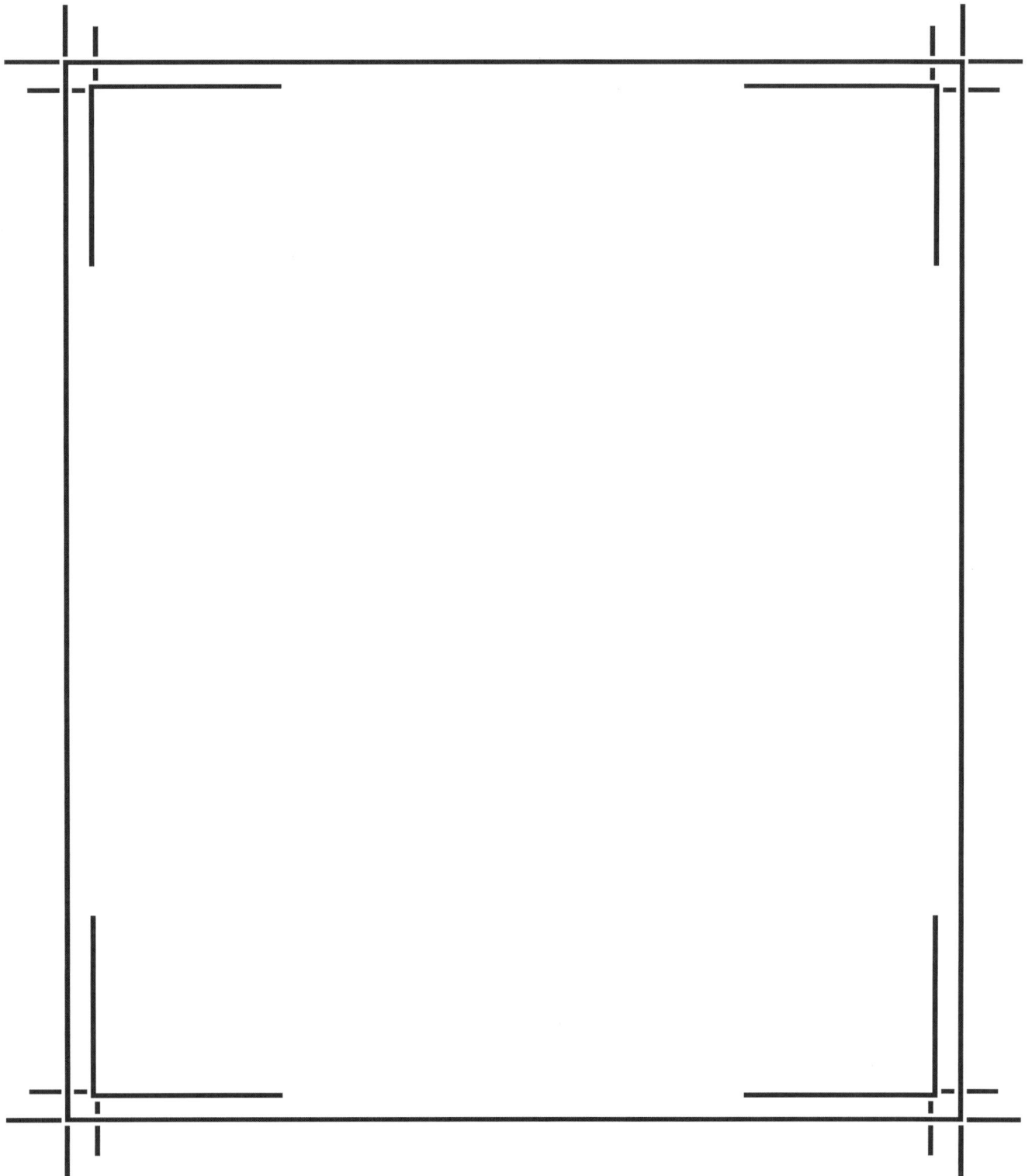

Your canvas...

It is _____ ___, _____
Month   Day,   Year

Today, we...

_____

_____

_____

_____

_____

We will always remember...

_____

_____

_____

_____

_____

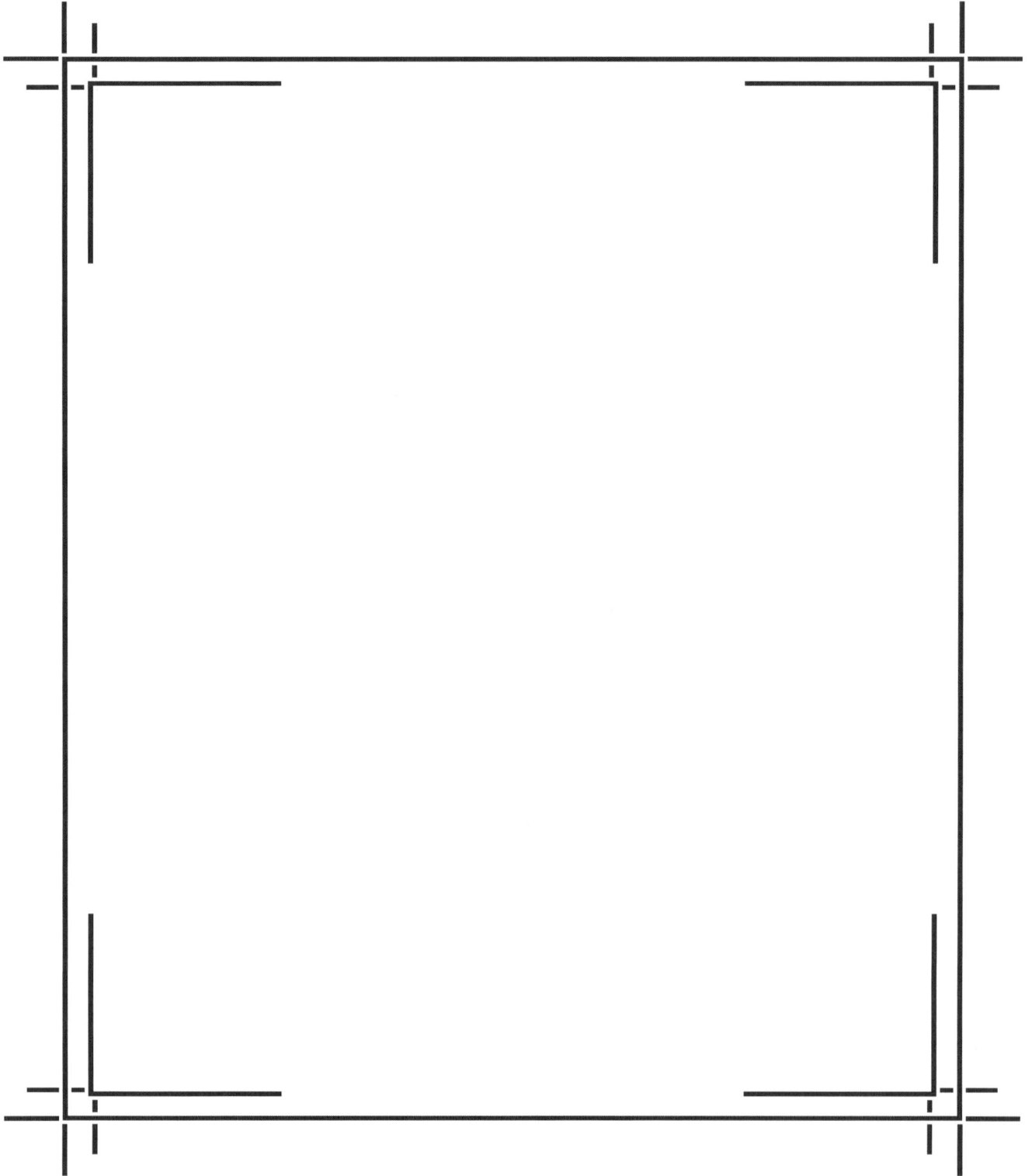

Your canvas...

It is _____ ___, _____
Month   Day ,   Year

Today, we...

_____

_____

_____

_____

_____

We will always remember...

_____

_____

_____

_____

_____

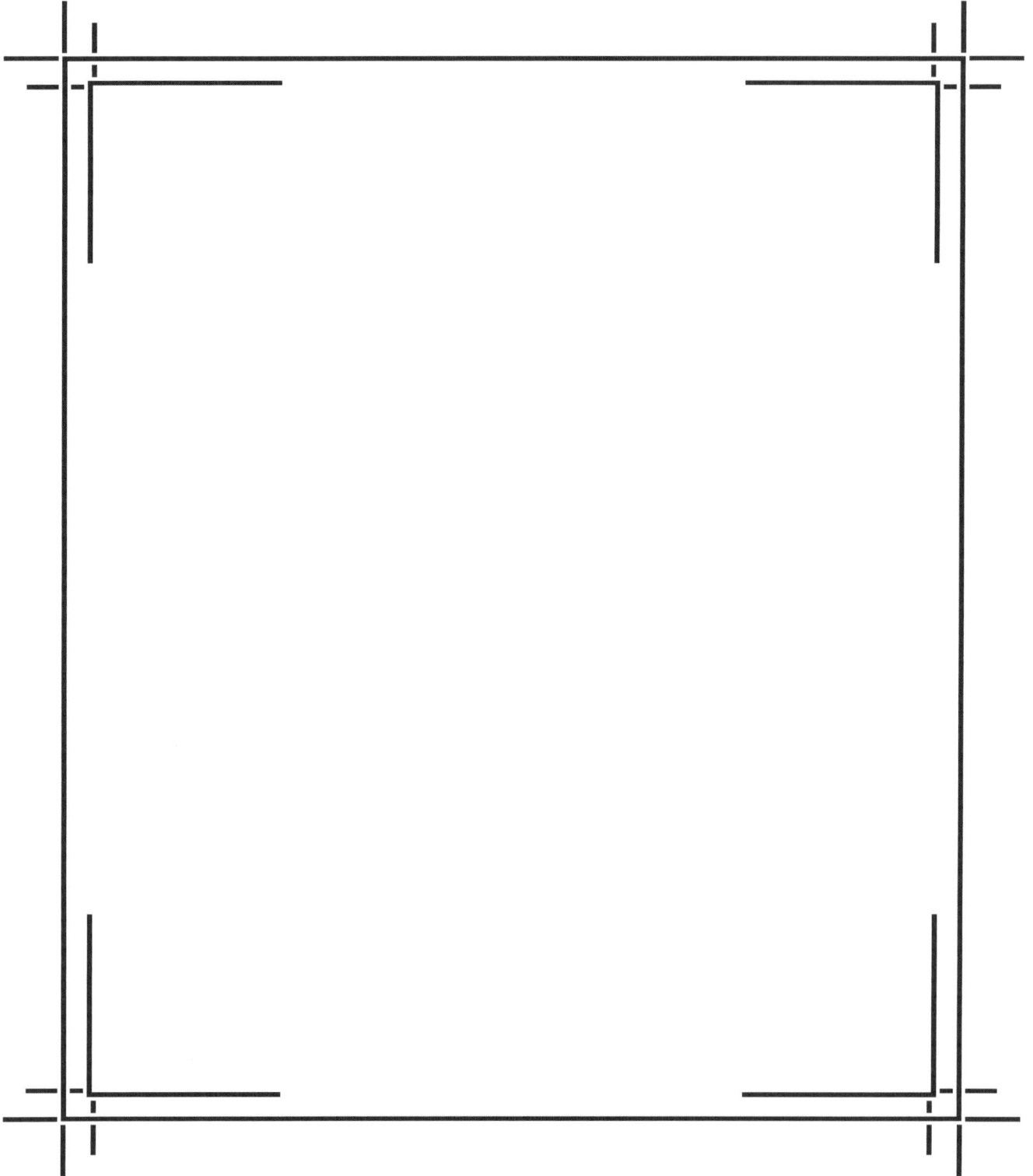

Your canvas...

It is _____ _____, _____
Month   Day   Year

Today, we...

_____

_____

_____

_____

_____

We will always remember...

_____

_____

_____

_____

_____

_____

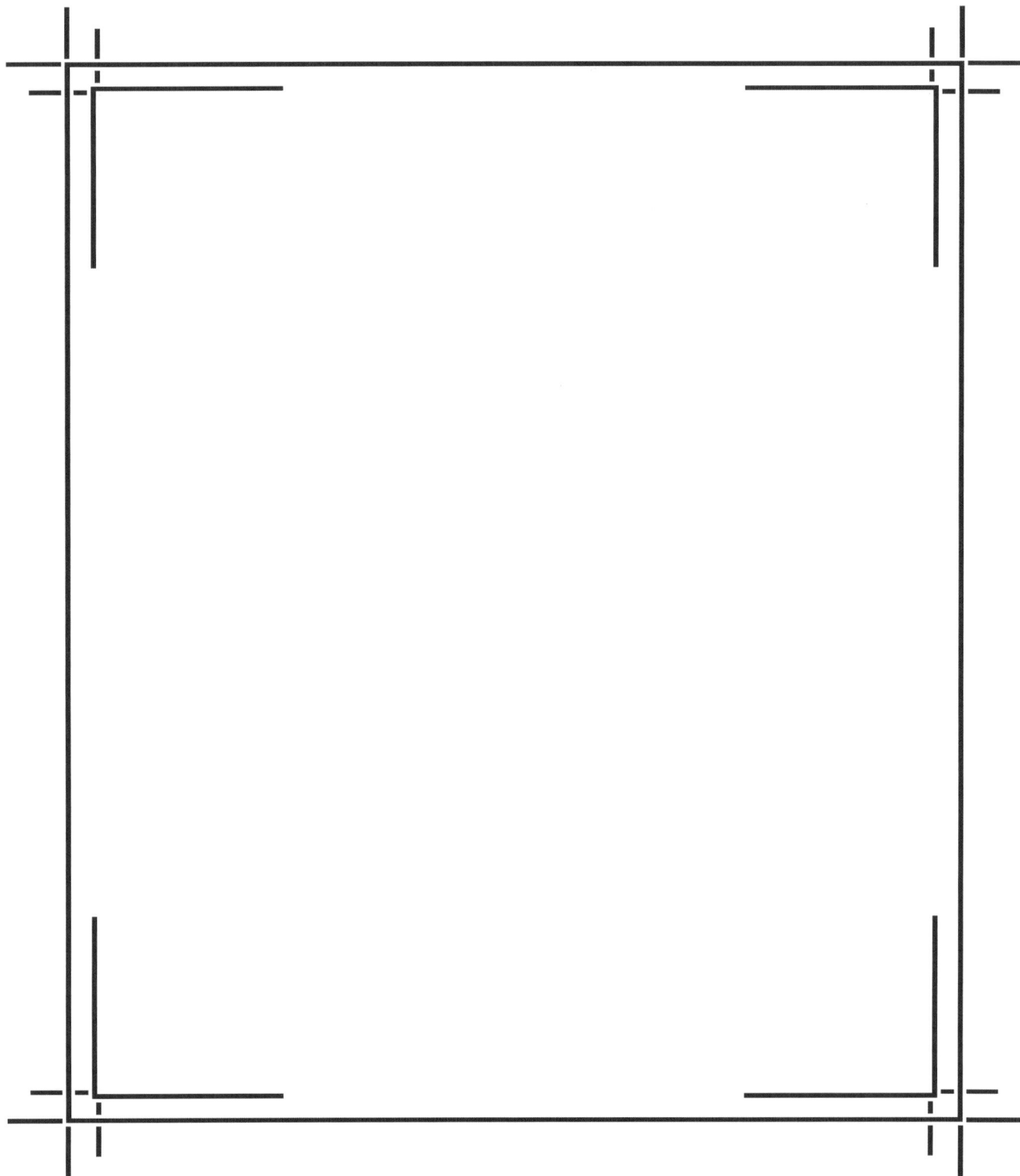

Your canvas...

It is _____ ___, ____
Month   Day   Year

Today, we...

_____

_____

_____

_____

_____

We will always remember...

_____

_____

_____

_____

_____

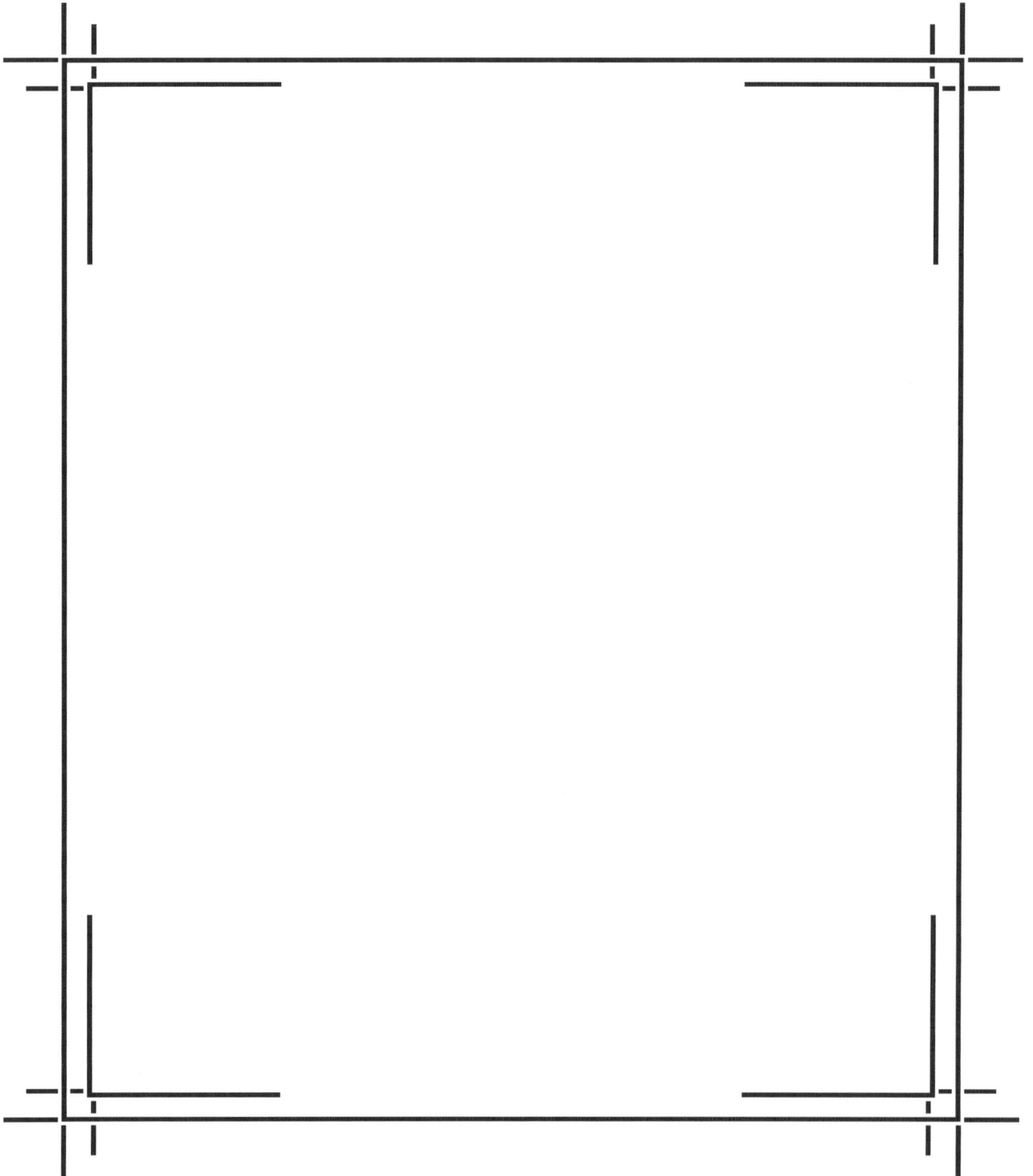

Your canvas...

It is _____ ___, _____
Month   Day   Year

Today, we...

_____

_____

_____

_____

_____

_____

We will always remember...

_____

_____

_____

_____

_____

_____

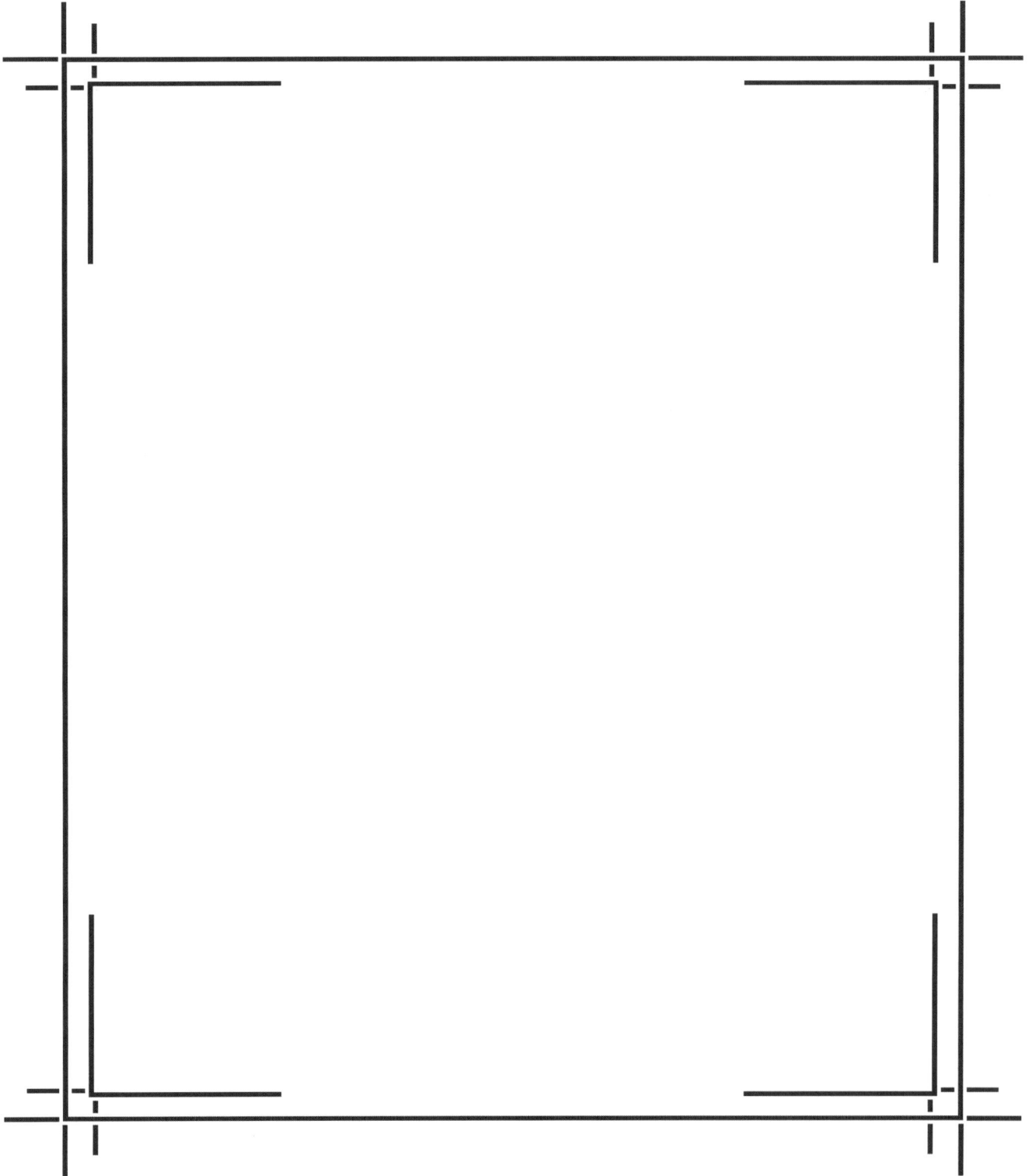

Your canvas...

It is

_____ ___, _____
Month   Day   Year

Today, we...

_____

_____

_____

_____

_____

We will always remember...

_____

_____

_____

_____

_____

_____

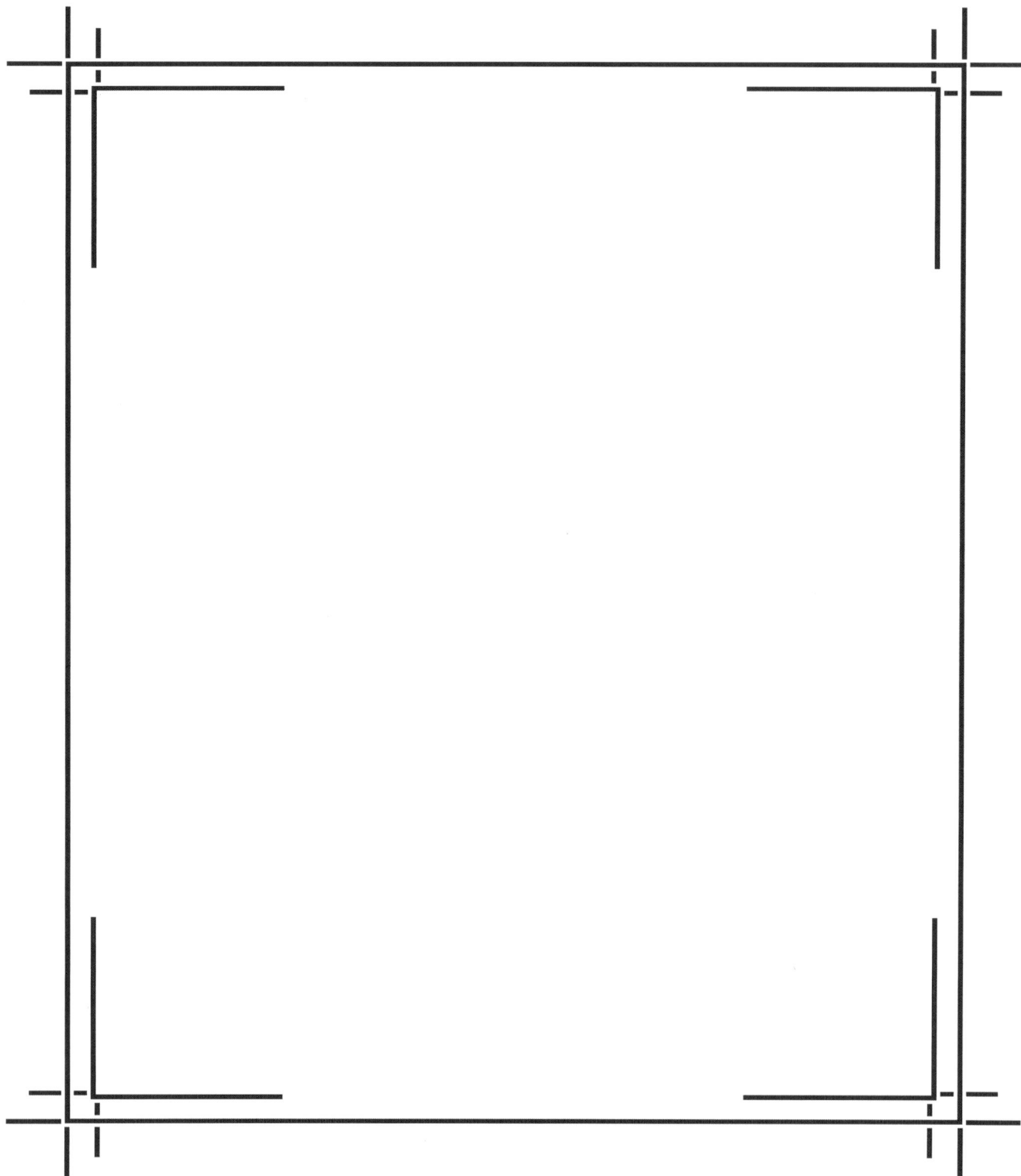

Your canvas...

It is _____ ___, _____
Month   Day   Year

Today, we...

_____

_____

_____

_____

_____

We will always remember...

_____

_____

_____

_____

_____

_____

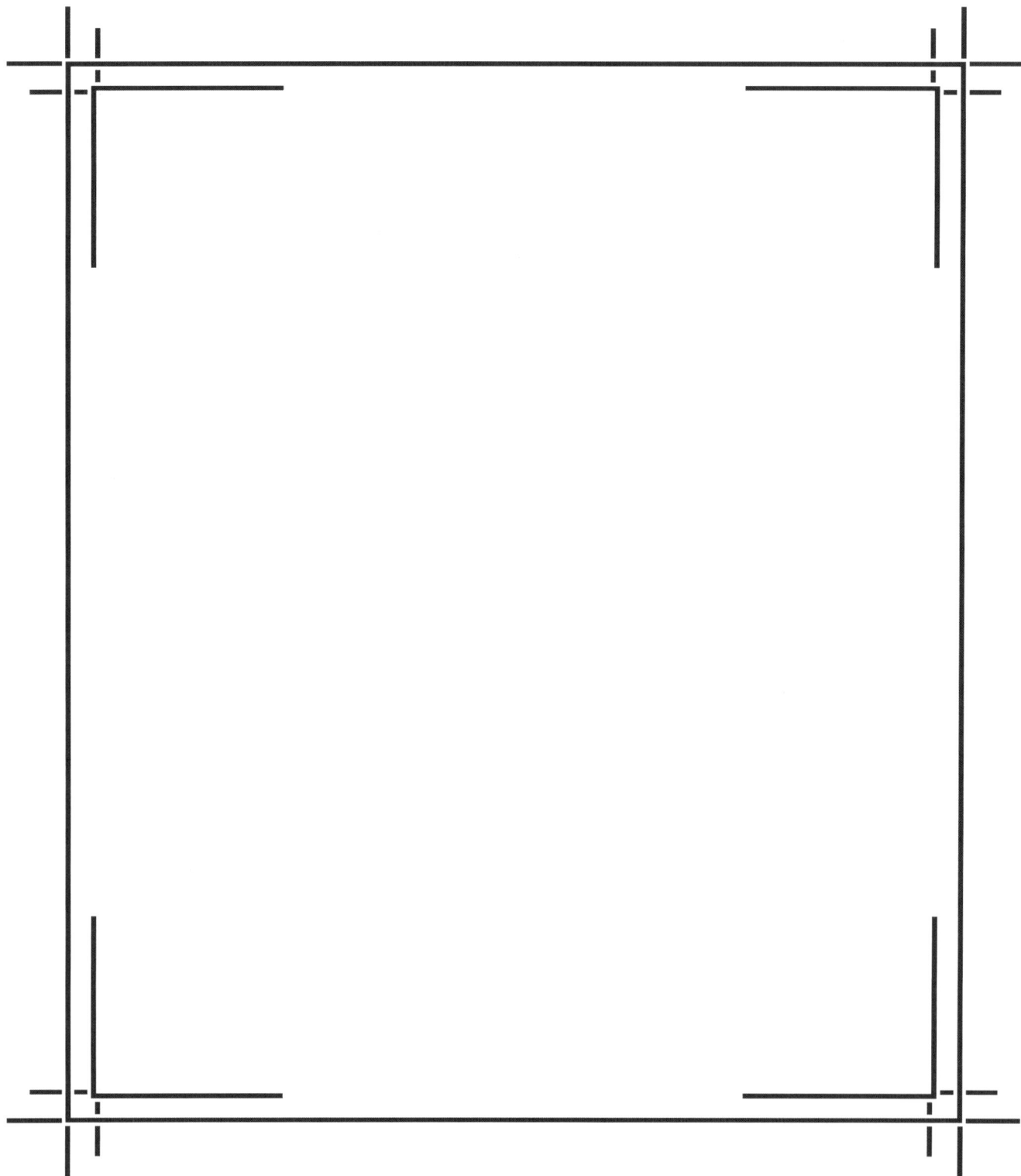

Your canvas...

It is _____ ___, ____
Month   Day   Year

Today, we...

_____
_____
_____
_____
_____

We will always remember...

_____
_____
_____
_____
_____
_____

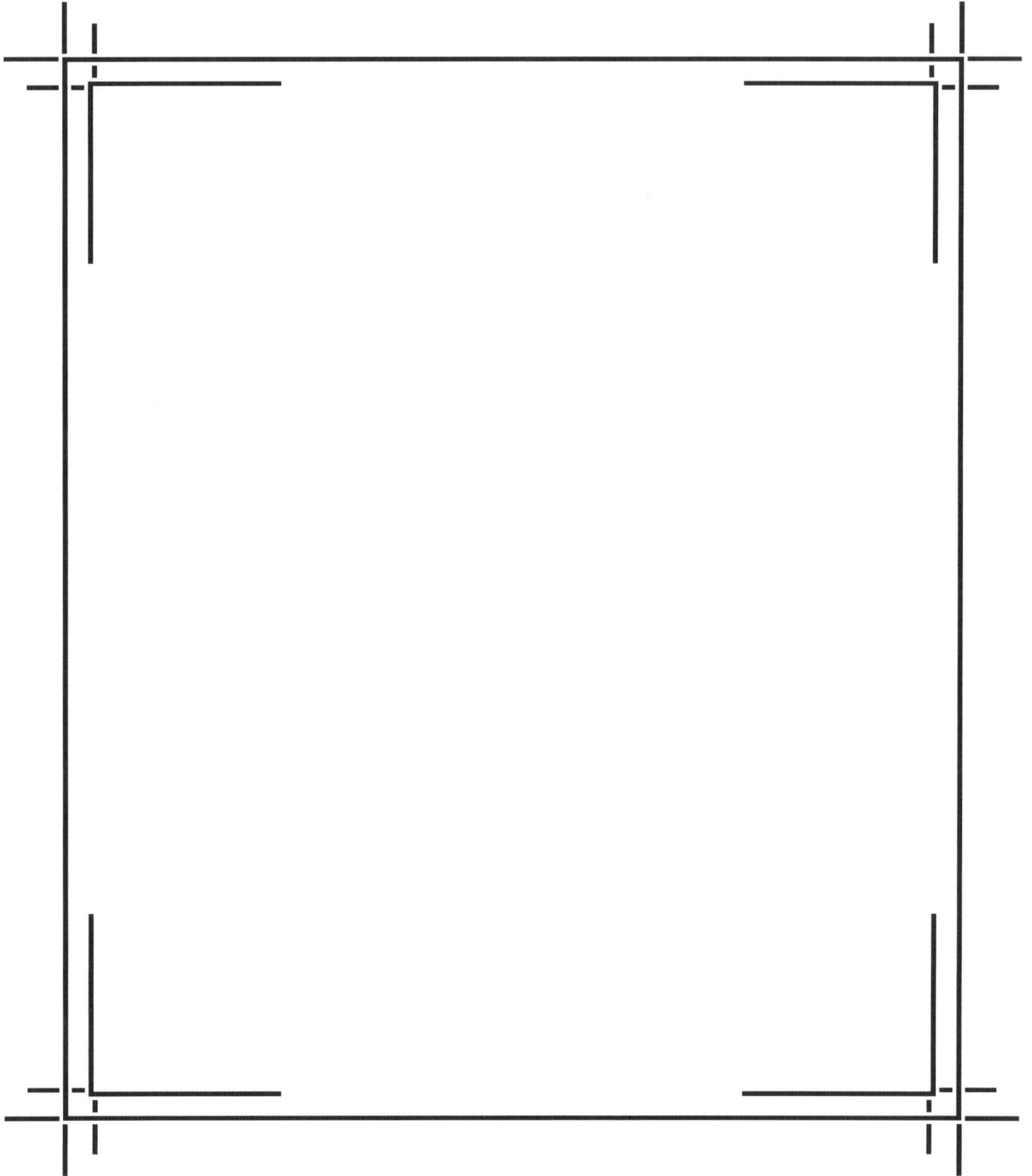

Your canvas...

It is _____ ___, ____
Month   Day   Year

Today, we...

_____

_____

_____

_____

_____

We will always remember...

_____

_____

_____

_____

_____

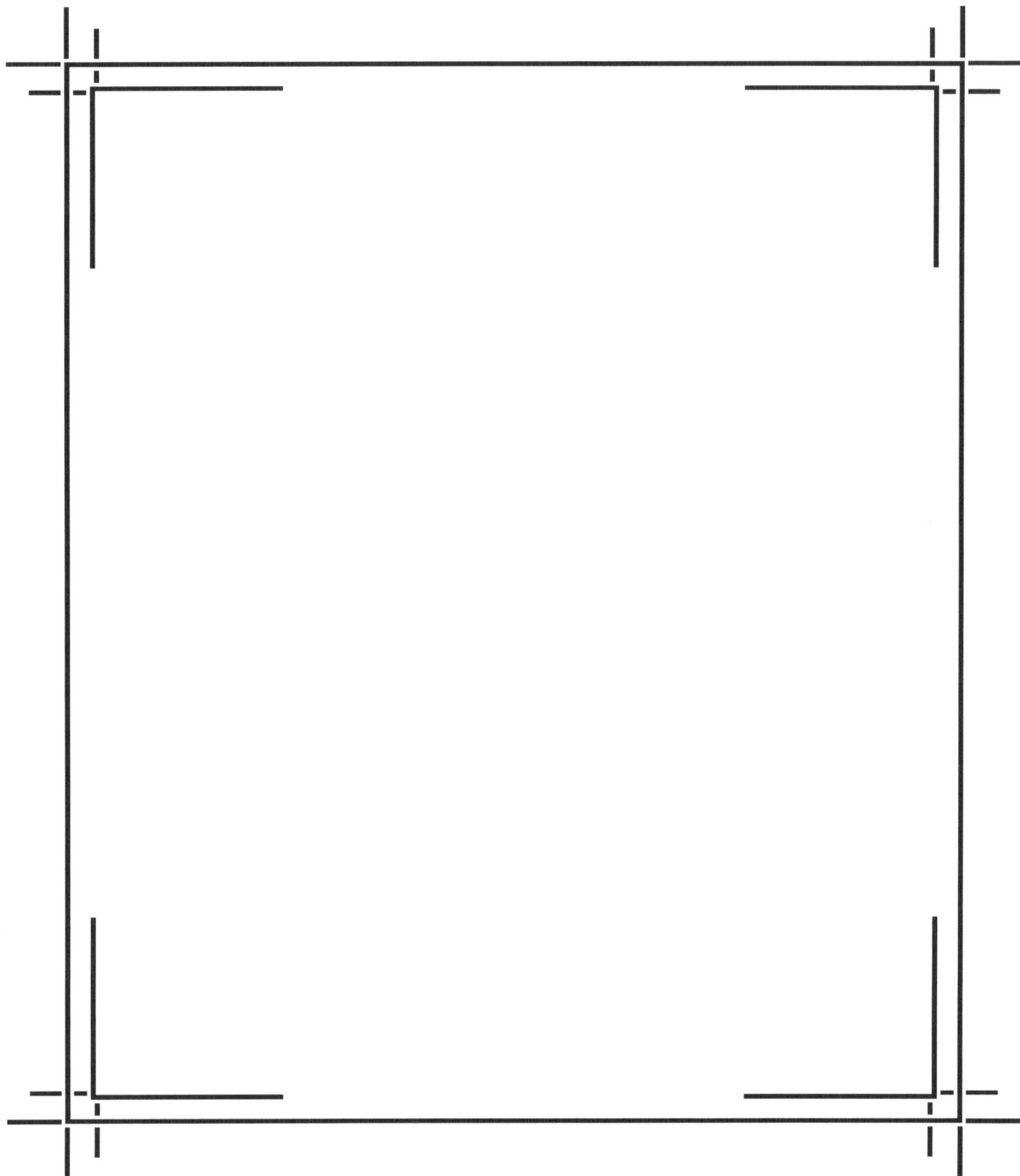

Your canvas...

It is _____ _____, _____
Month   Day   Year

Today, we...

_____

_____

_____

_____

_____

We will always remember...

_____

_____

_____

_____

_____

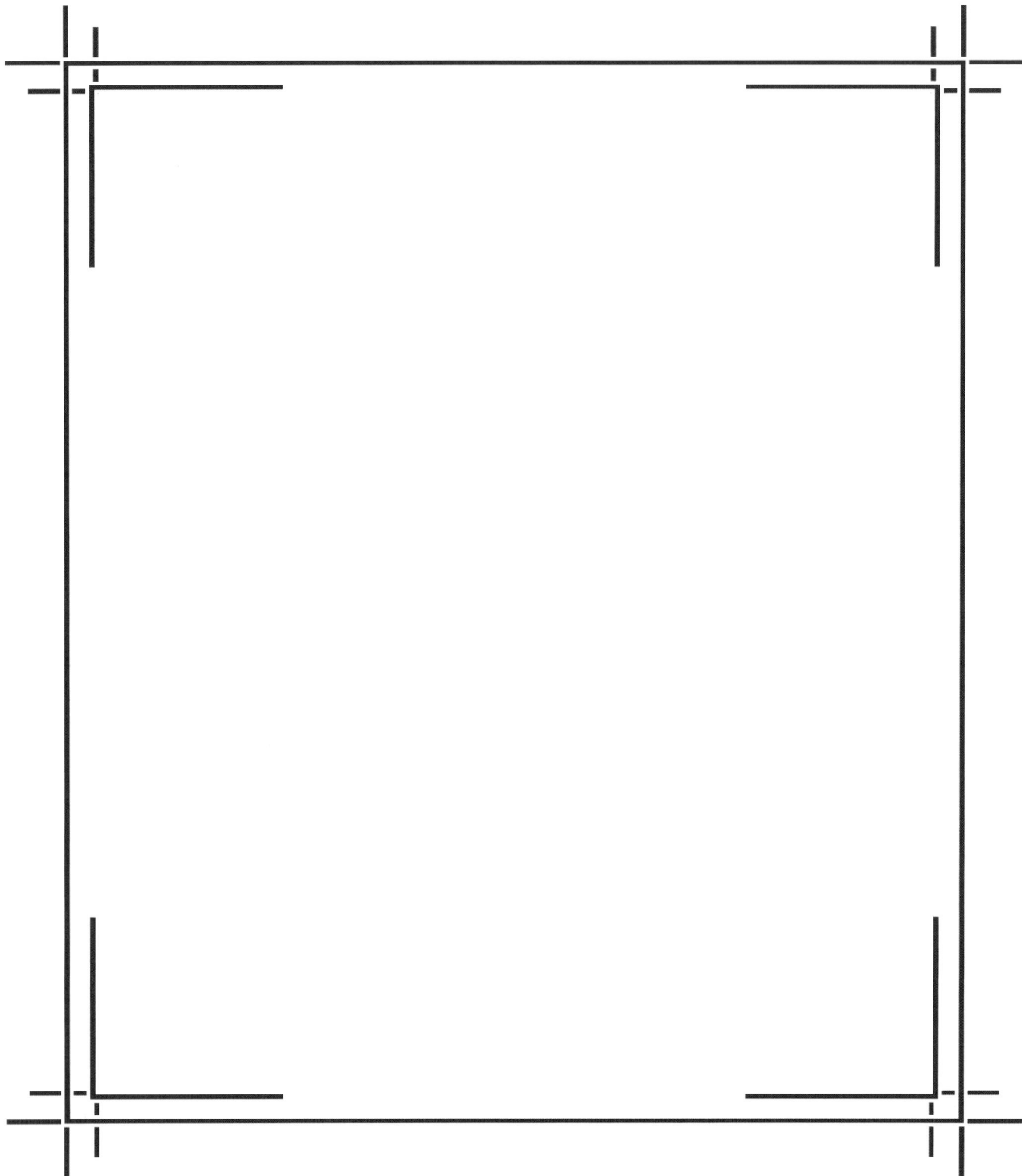

Your canvas...

It is _____ ___, ____
Month   Day   Year

Today, we...

_____

_____

_____

_____

_____

_____

We will always remember...

_____

_____

_____

_____

_____

_____

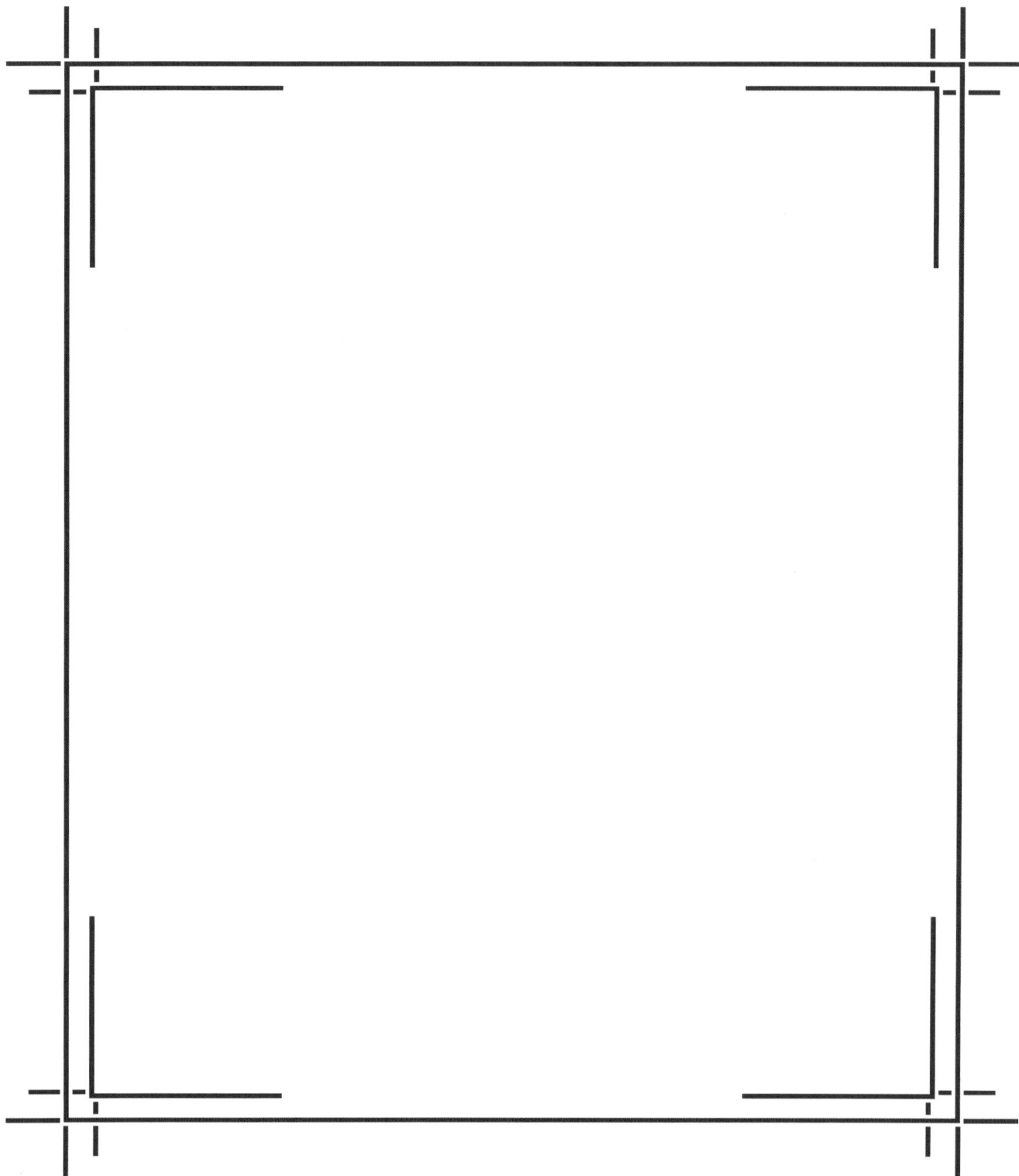

Your canvas...

It is _____ ___, _____
Month   Day   Year

Today, we...

_____

_____

_____

_____

_____

We will always remember...

_____

_____

_____

_____

_____

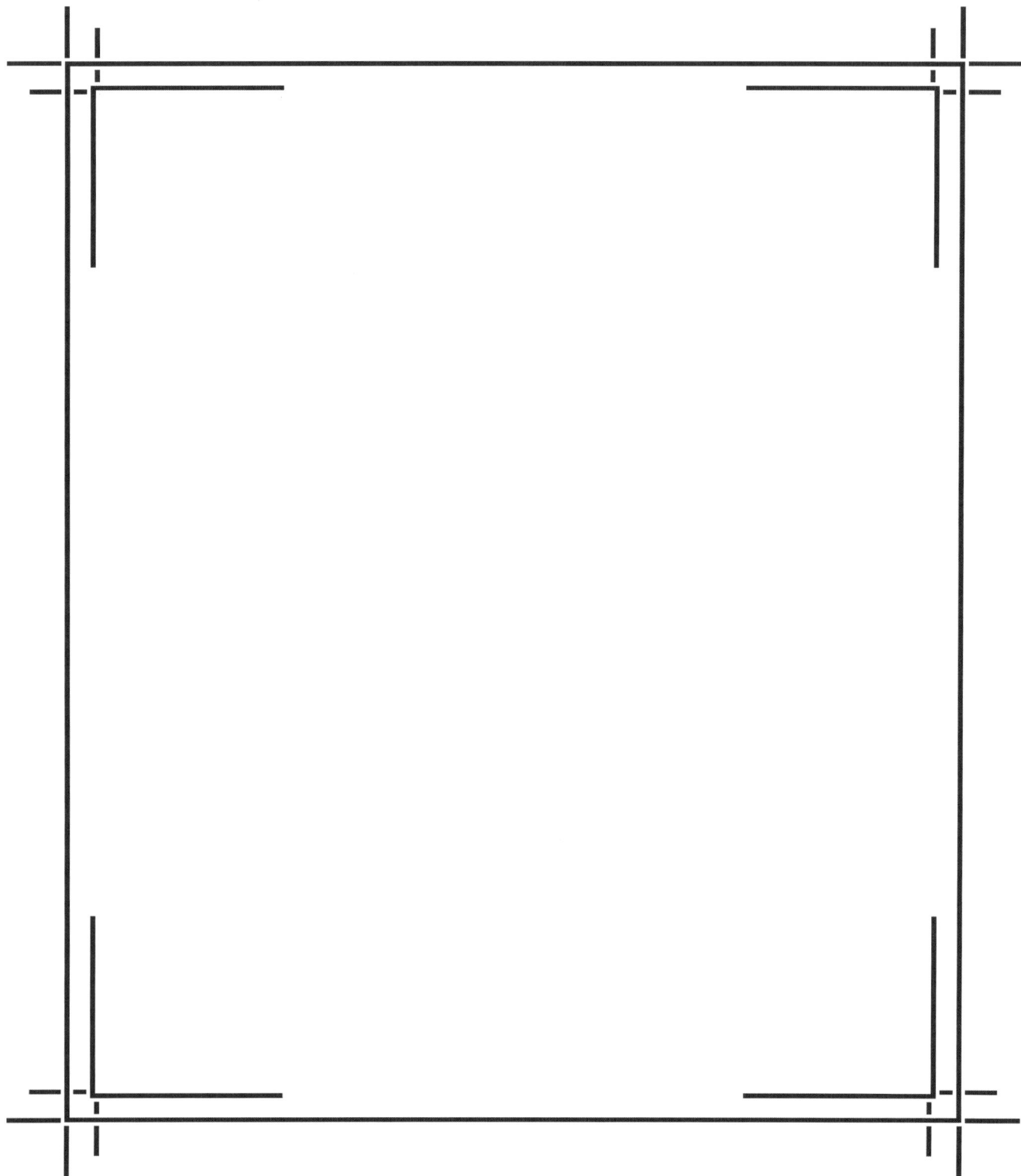

Your canvas...

It is _____ ___, _____

Today, we...

_____

_____

_____

_____

_____

_____

We will always remember...

_____

_____

_____

_____

_____

_____

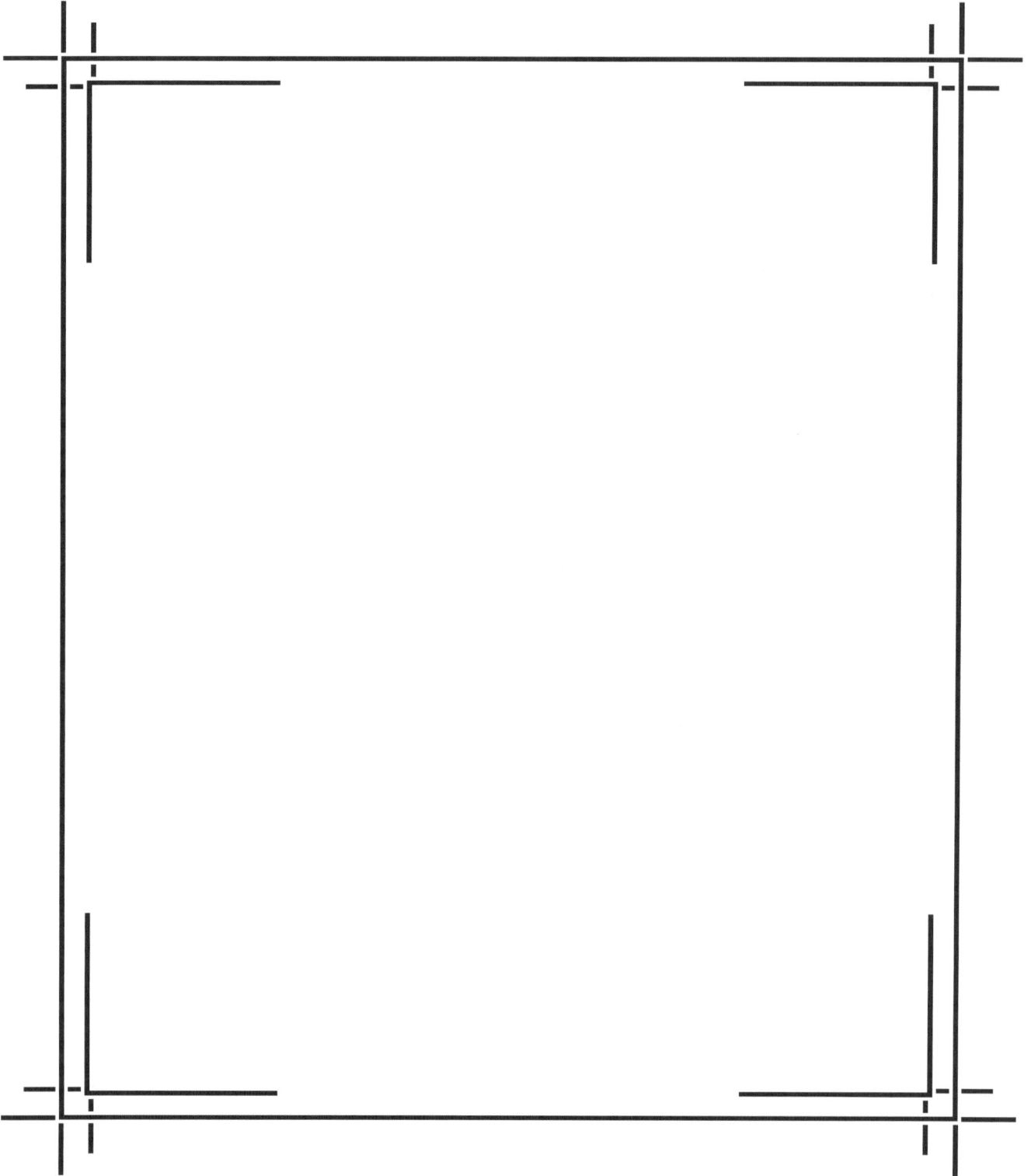

Your canvas...

It is _____ _____, _____
Month   Day   Year

Today, we...

_____
_____
_____
_____
_____

We will always remember...

_____
_____
_____
_____
_____
_____

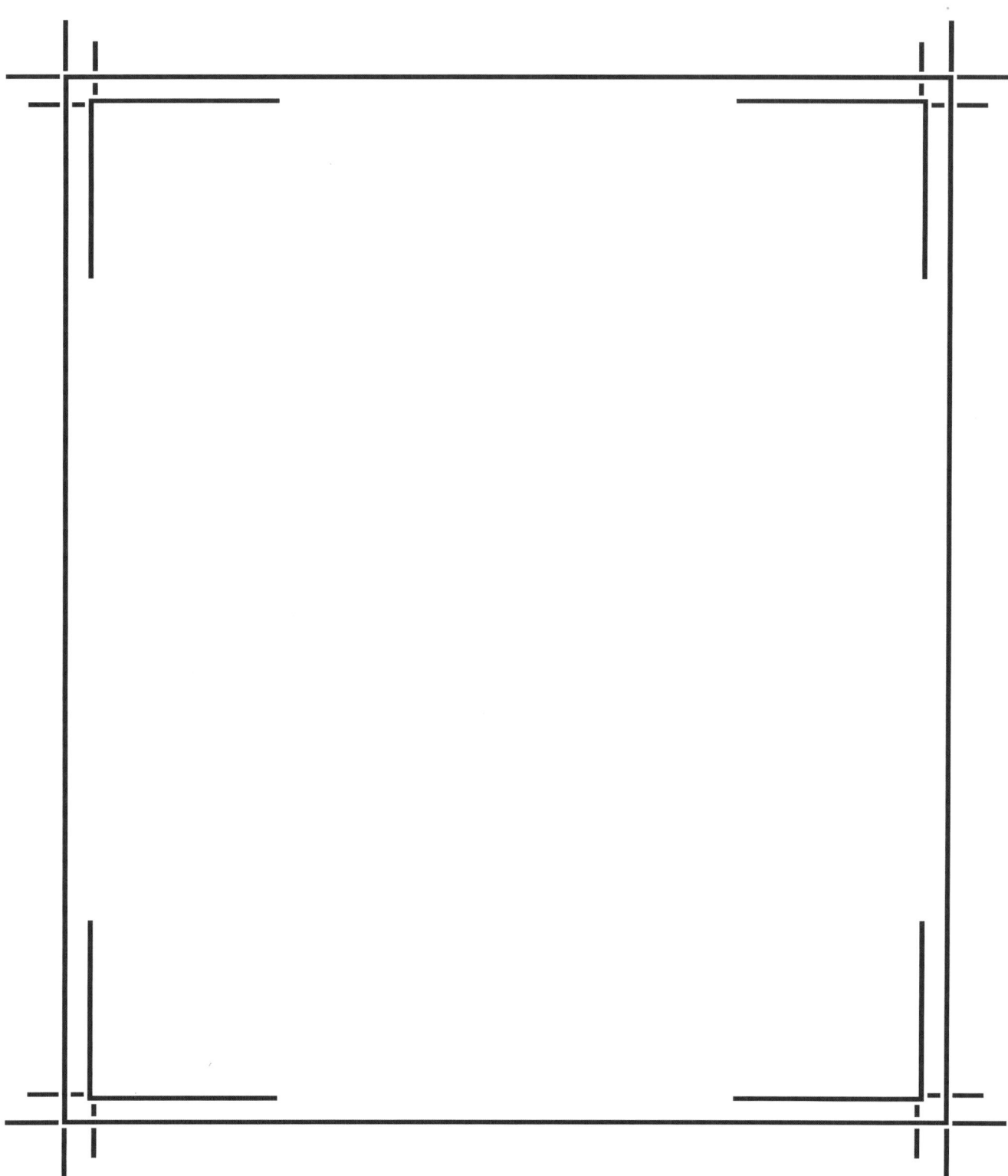

Your canvas...

It is _____ ___, ____
Month   Day   Year

Today, we...

_____
_____
_____
_____
_____

We will always remember...

_____
_____
_____
_____
_____
_____

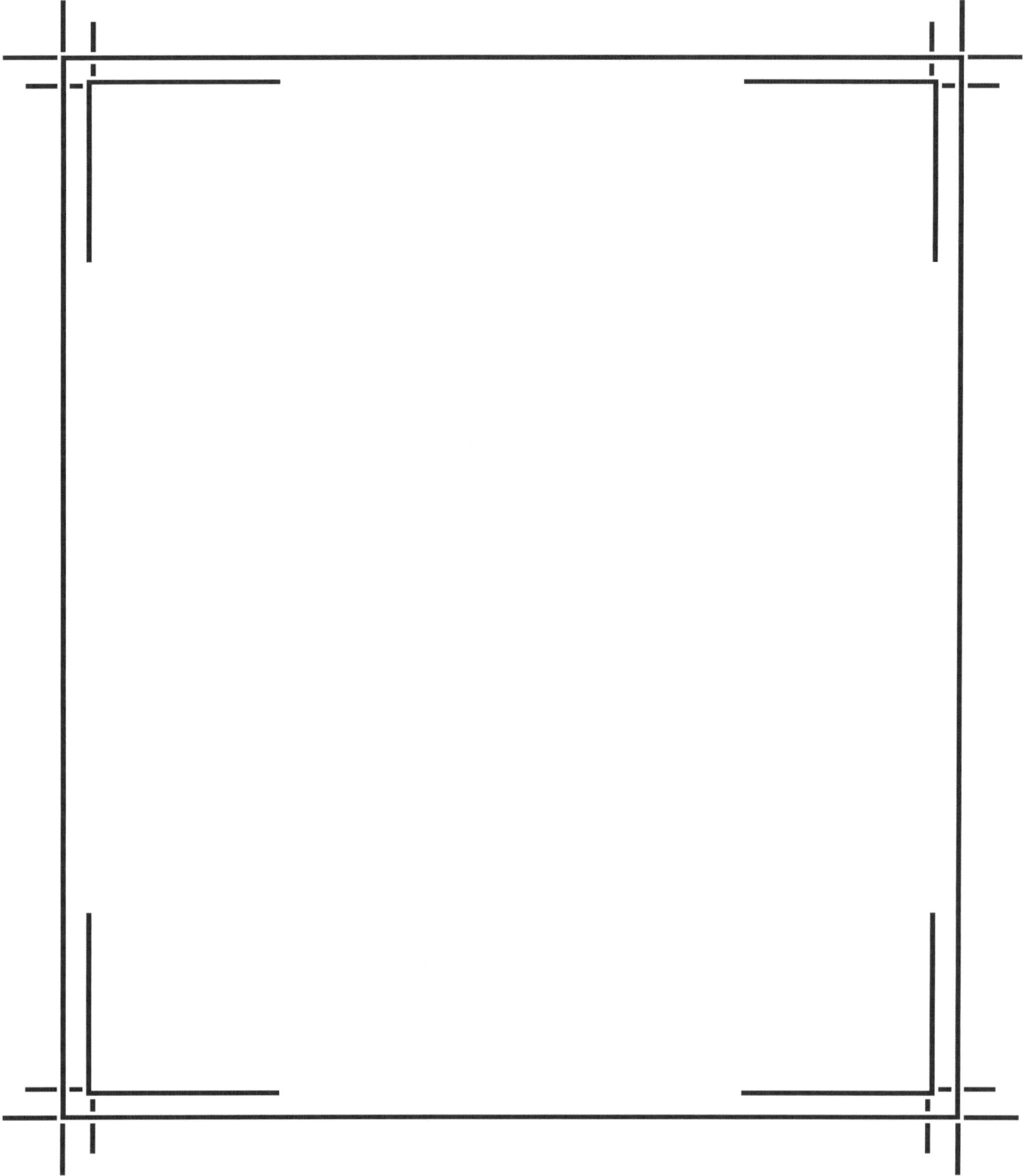

Your canvas...

It is _____ ___, _____

Today, we...

_____

_____

_____

_____

_____

_____

We will always remember...

_____

_____

_____

_____

_____

_____

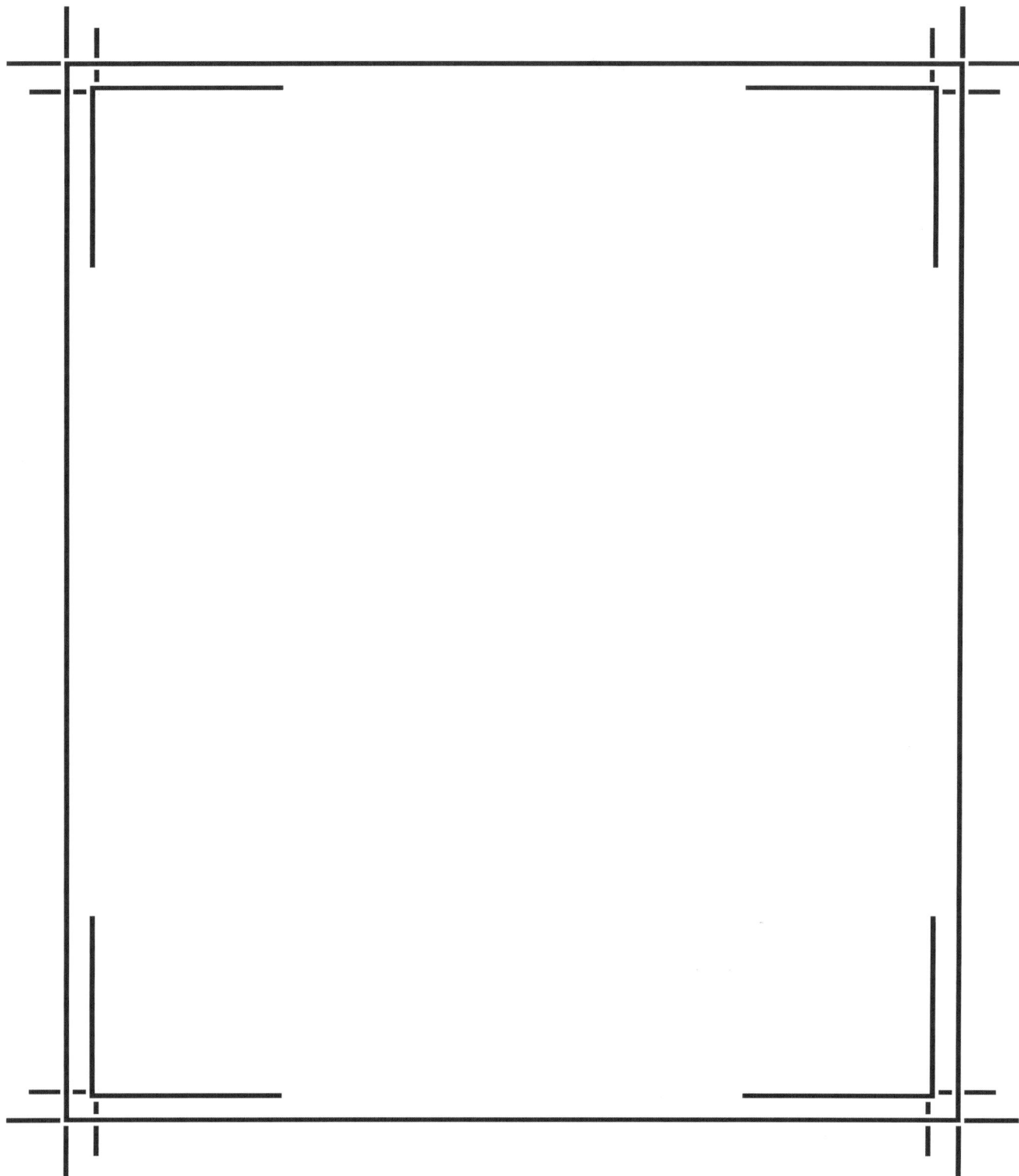

Your canvas...

It is _____ ___, _____
Month   Day   Year

Today, we...

_____

_____

_____

_____

_____

_____

We will always remember...

_____

_____

_____

_____

_____

_____

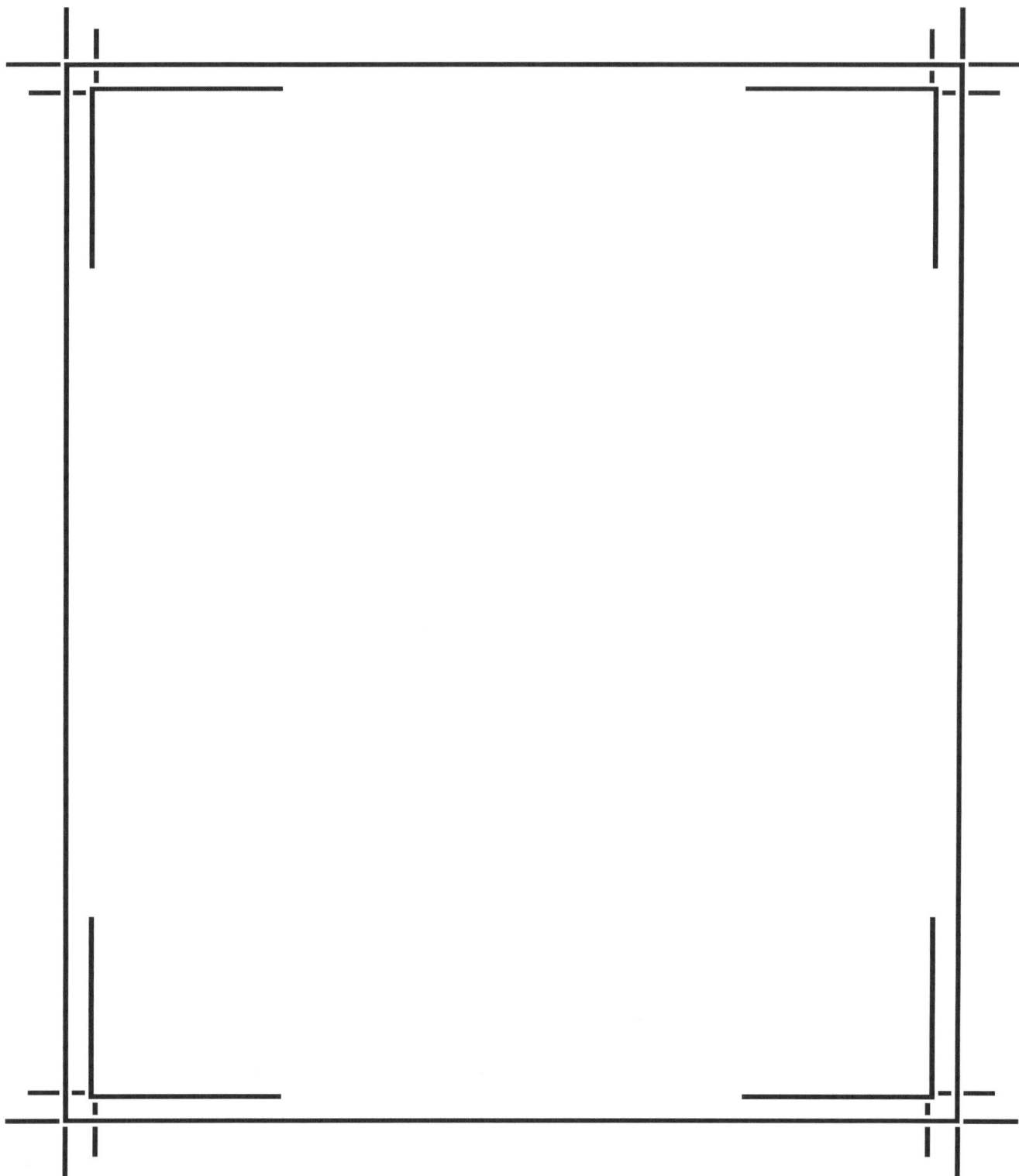

Your canvas...

It is _____ ____, ____
Month   Day   Year

Today, we...

_____

_____

_____

_____

_____

We will always remember...

_____

_____

_____

_____

_____

_____

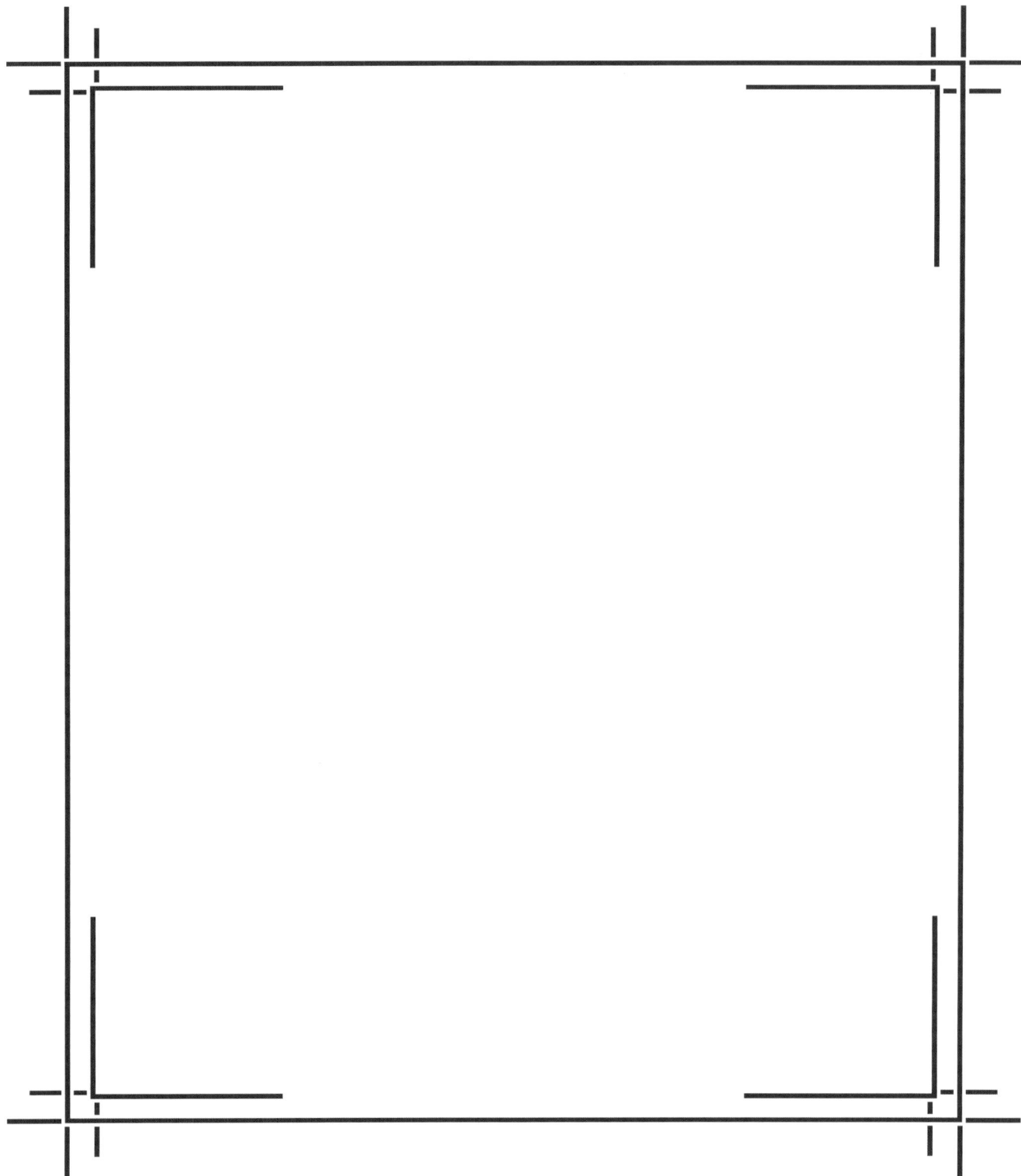

Your canvas...

It is _____ ___, ____
Month   Day   Year

Today, we...

_____

_____

_____

_____

_____

We will always remember...

_____

_____

_____

_____

_____

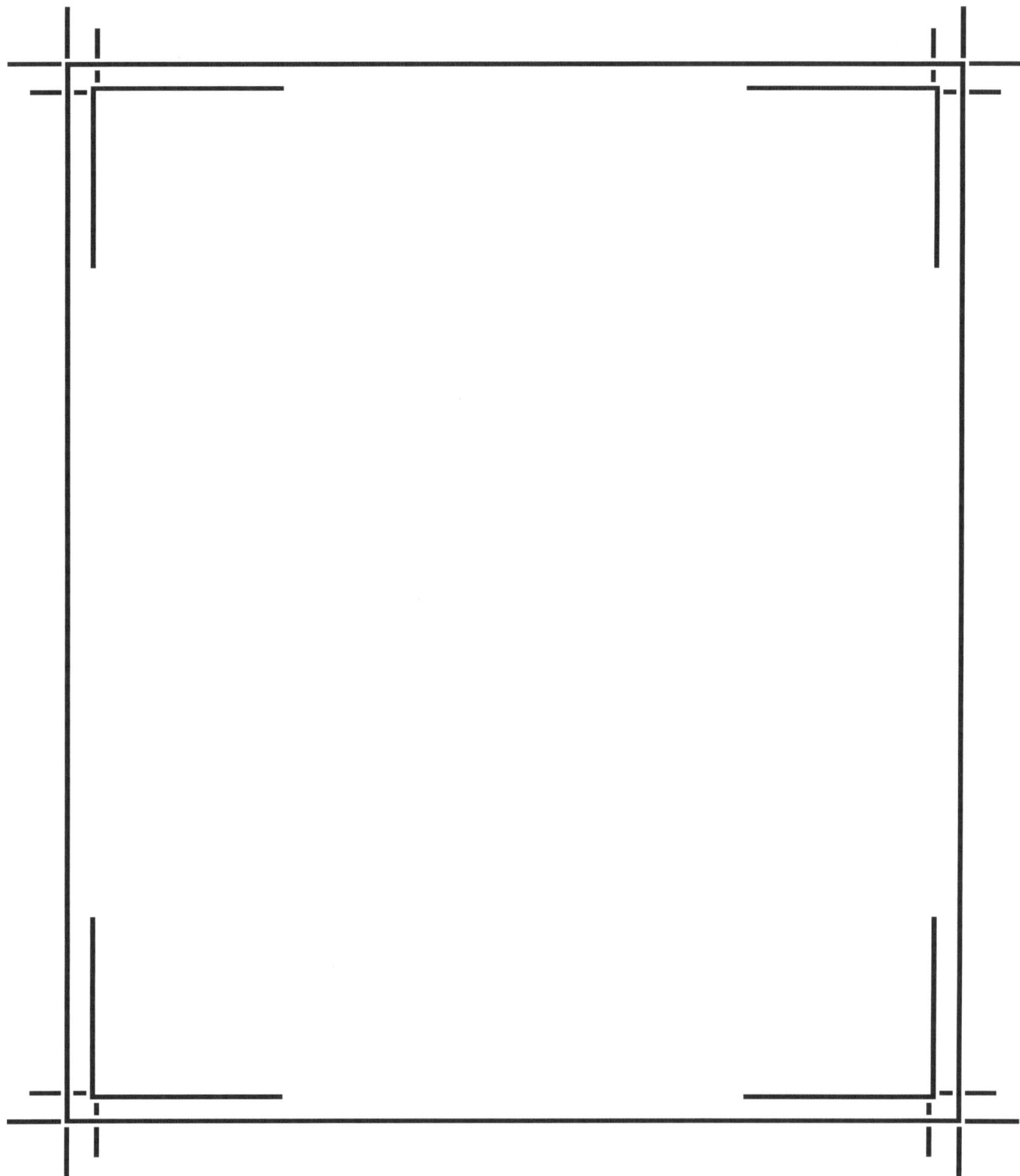

Your canvas...

It is _____ ___, ____
Month   Day   Year

Today, we...

_____

_____

_____

_____

_____

We will always remember...

_____

_____

_____

_____

_____

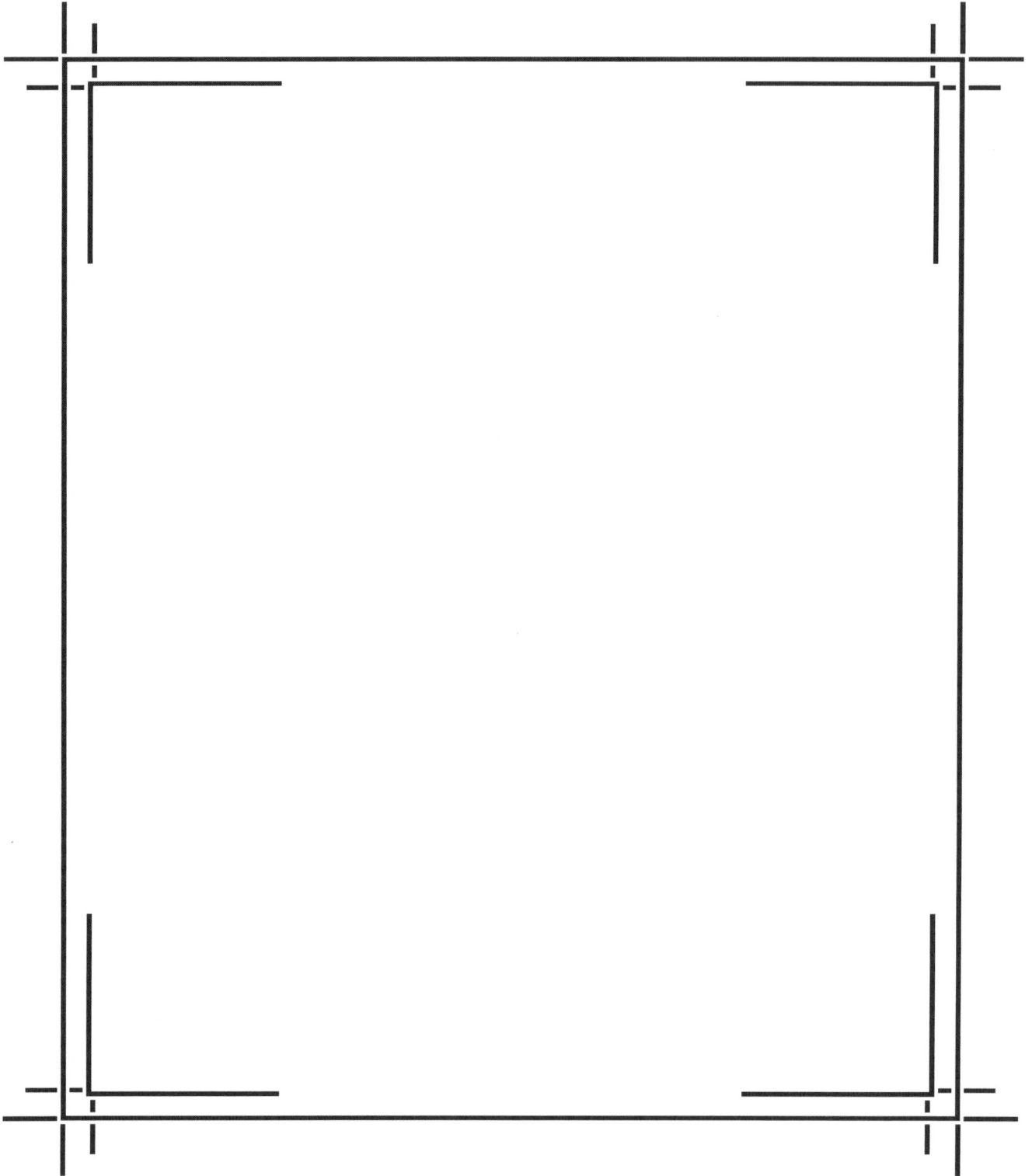

Your canvas...

It is

Month   Day   Year

Today, we...

_____

_____

_____

_____

_____

_____

We will always remember...

_____

_____

_____

_____

_____

_____

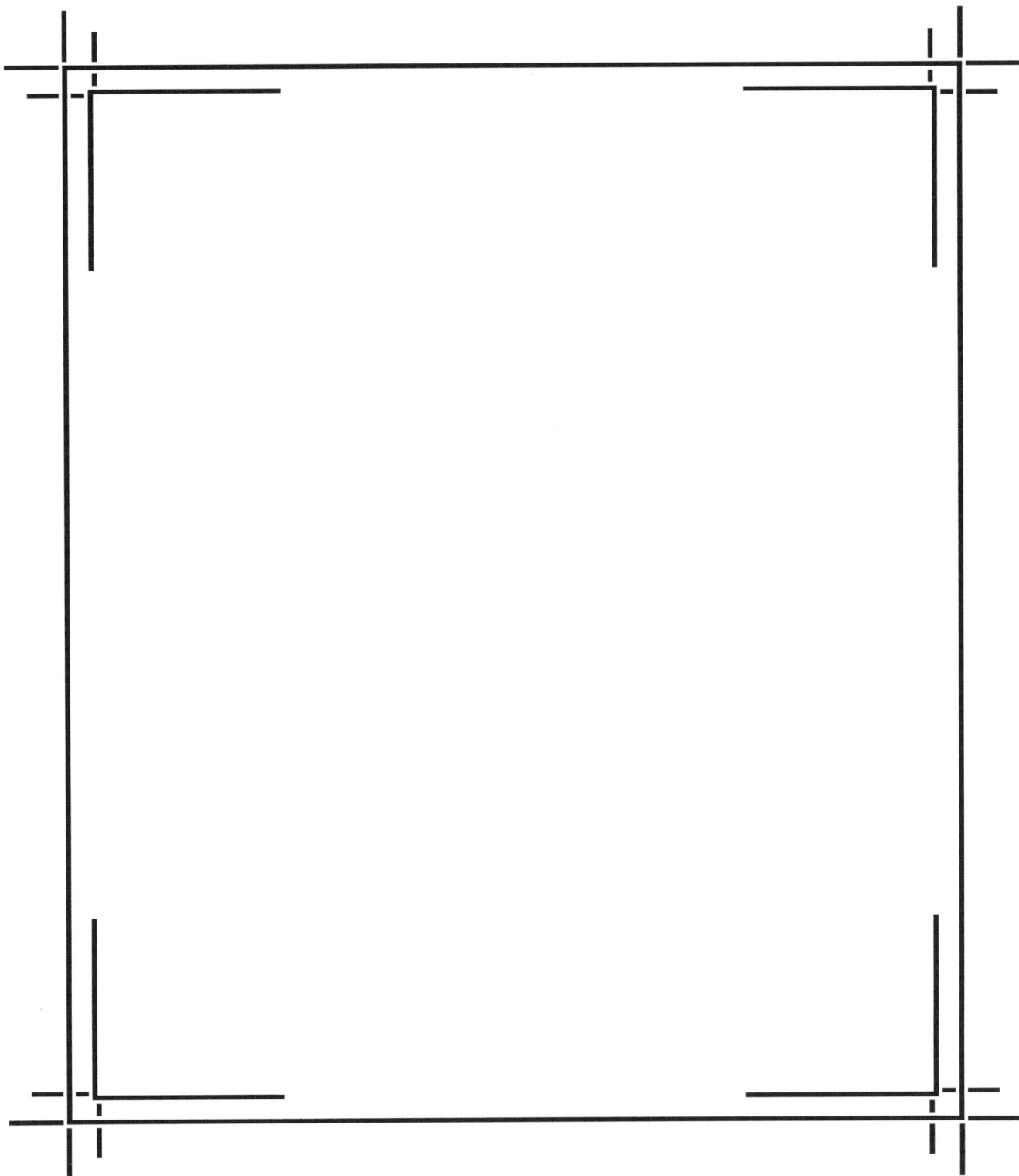

Your canvas...

It is _____ ___, _____

Today, we...

_____

_____

_____

_____

_____

_____

We will always remember...

_____

_____

_____

_____

_____

_____

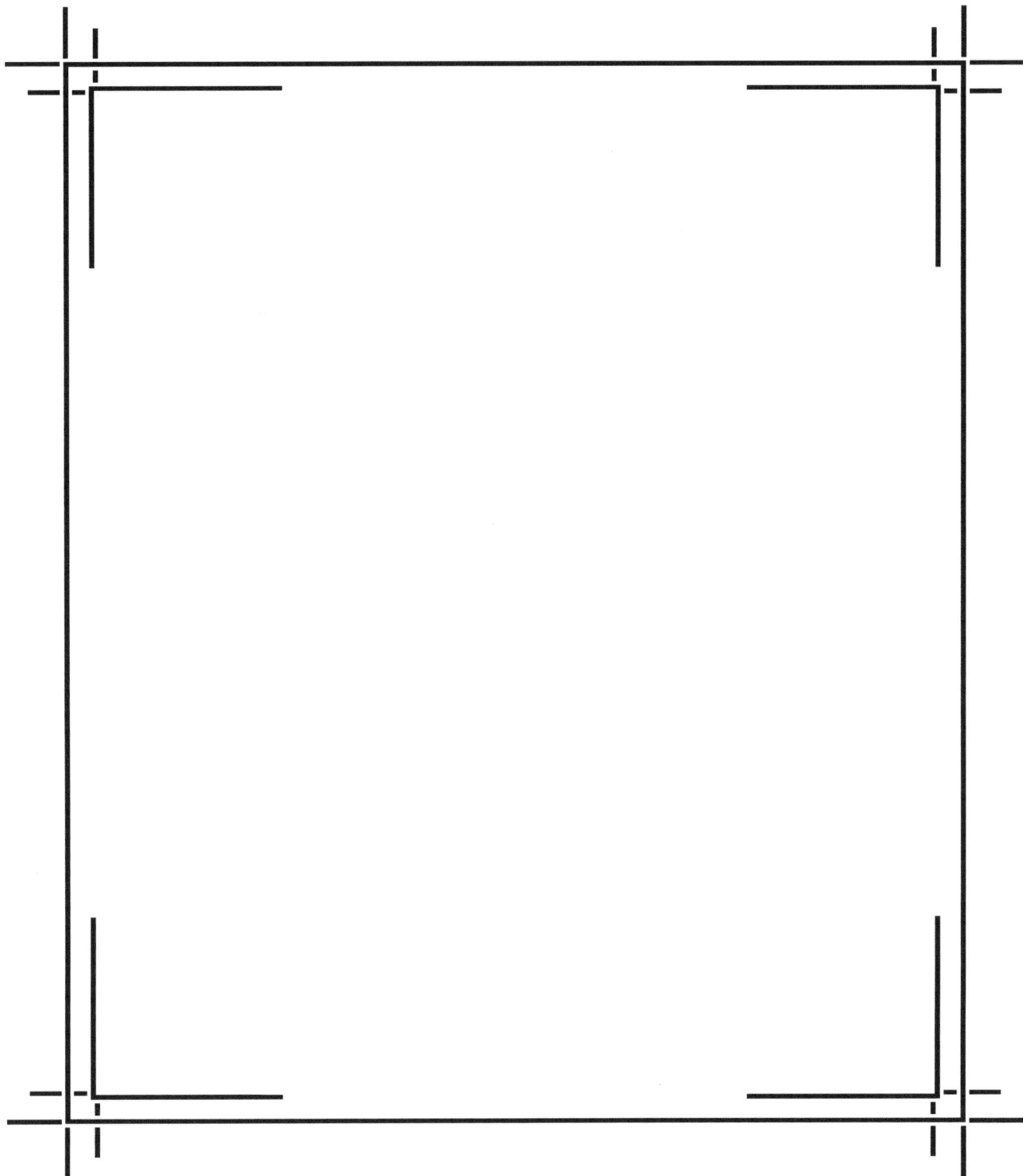

Your canvas...

It is _____ ___, ____
Month   Day   Year

Today, we...

_____

_____

_____

_____

_____

We will always remember...

_____

_____

_____

_____

_____

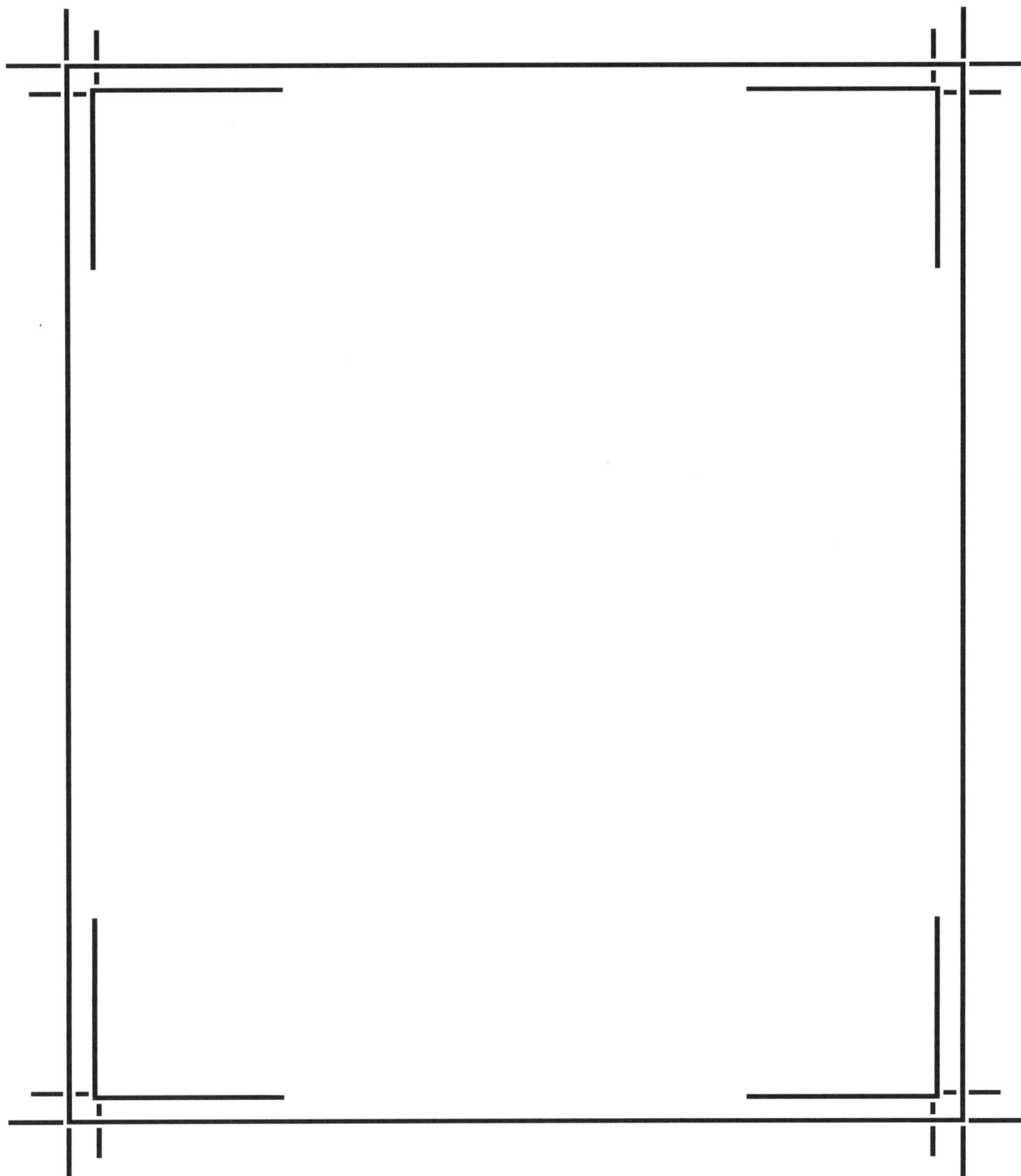

Your canvas...

It is _____ ____, ____

Month   Day   Year

Today, we...

_____

_____

_____

_____

_____

_____

We will always remember...

_____

_____

_____

_____

_____

_____

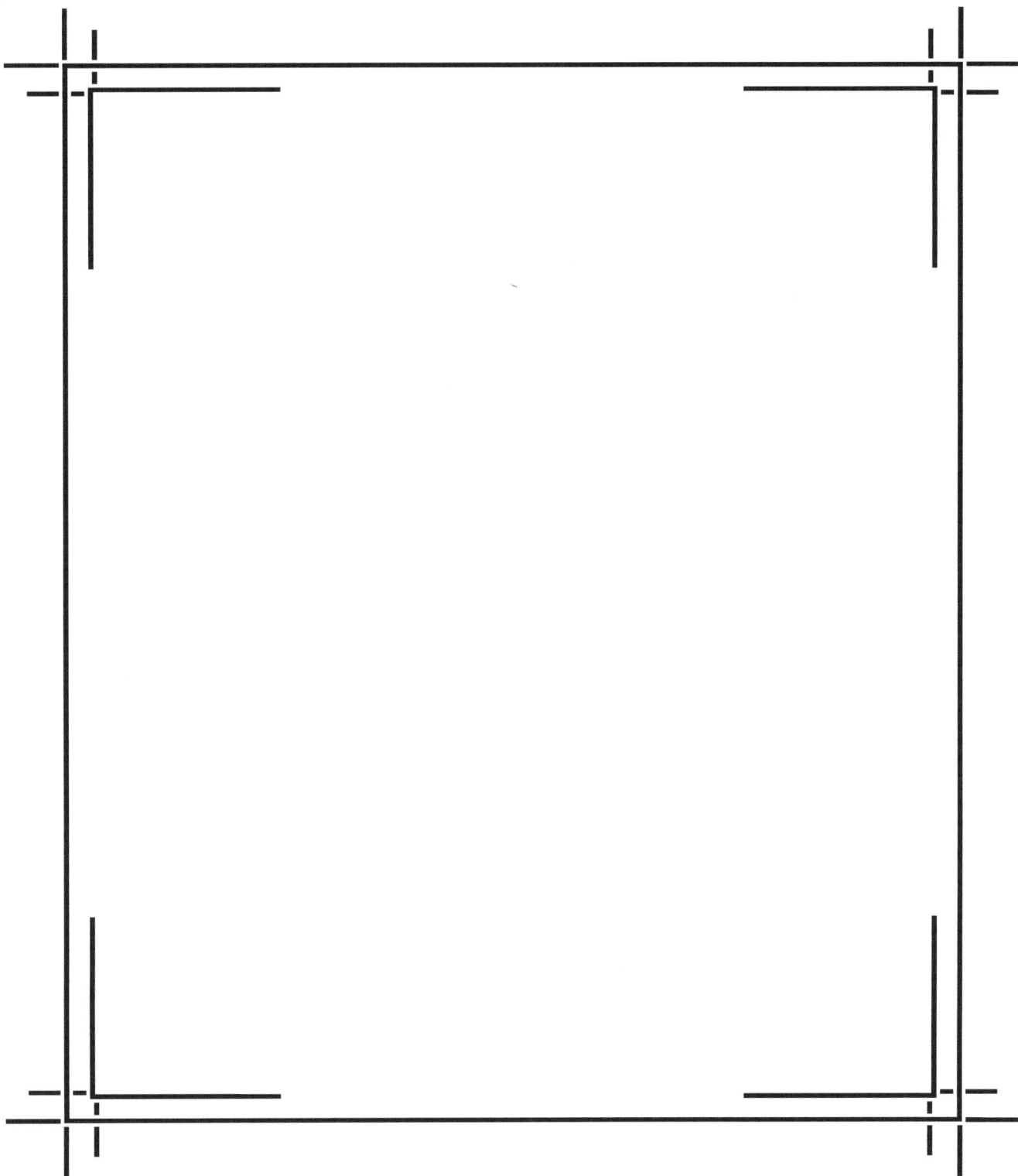

Your canvas...

It is _____ ___, ____
Month Day Year

Today, we...

_____

_____

_____

_____

_____

_____

We will always remember...

_____

_____

_____

_____

_____

_____

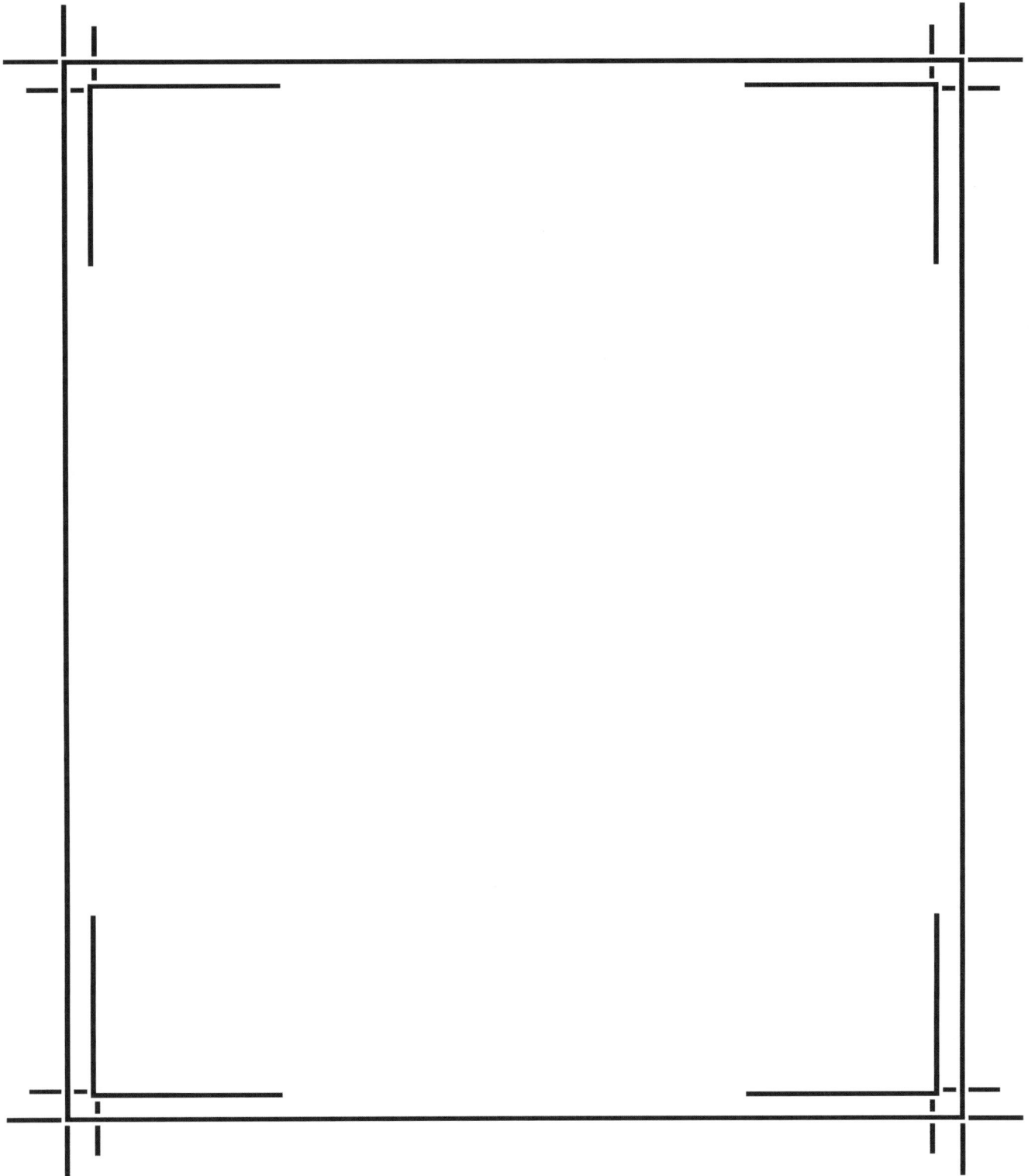

Your canvas...

It is _____ ____ , ____
                                    Month   Day   Year

Today, we...

_____

_____

_____

_____

_____

We will always remember...

_____

_____

_____

_____

_____

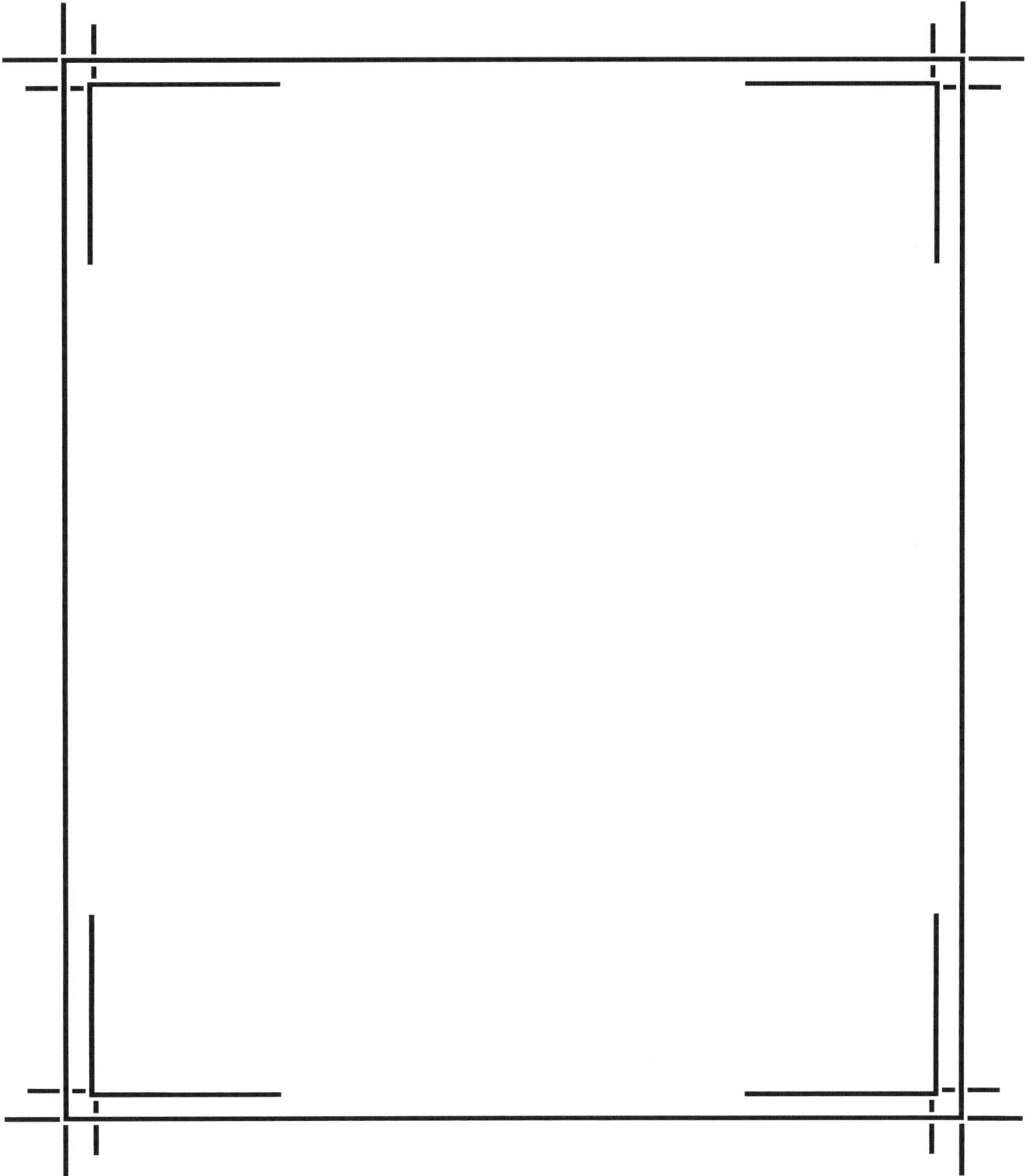

Your canvas...

It is _____ _____, _____
Month   Day   Year

Today, we...

_____

_____

_____

_____

_____

We will always remember...

_____

_____

_____

_____

_____

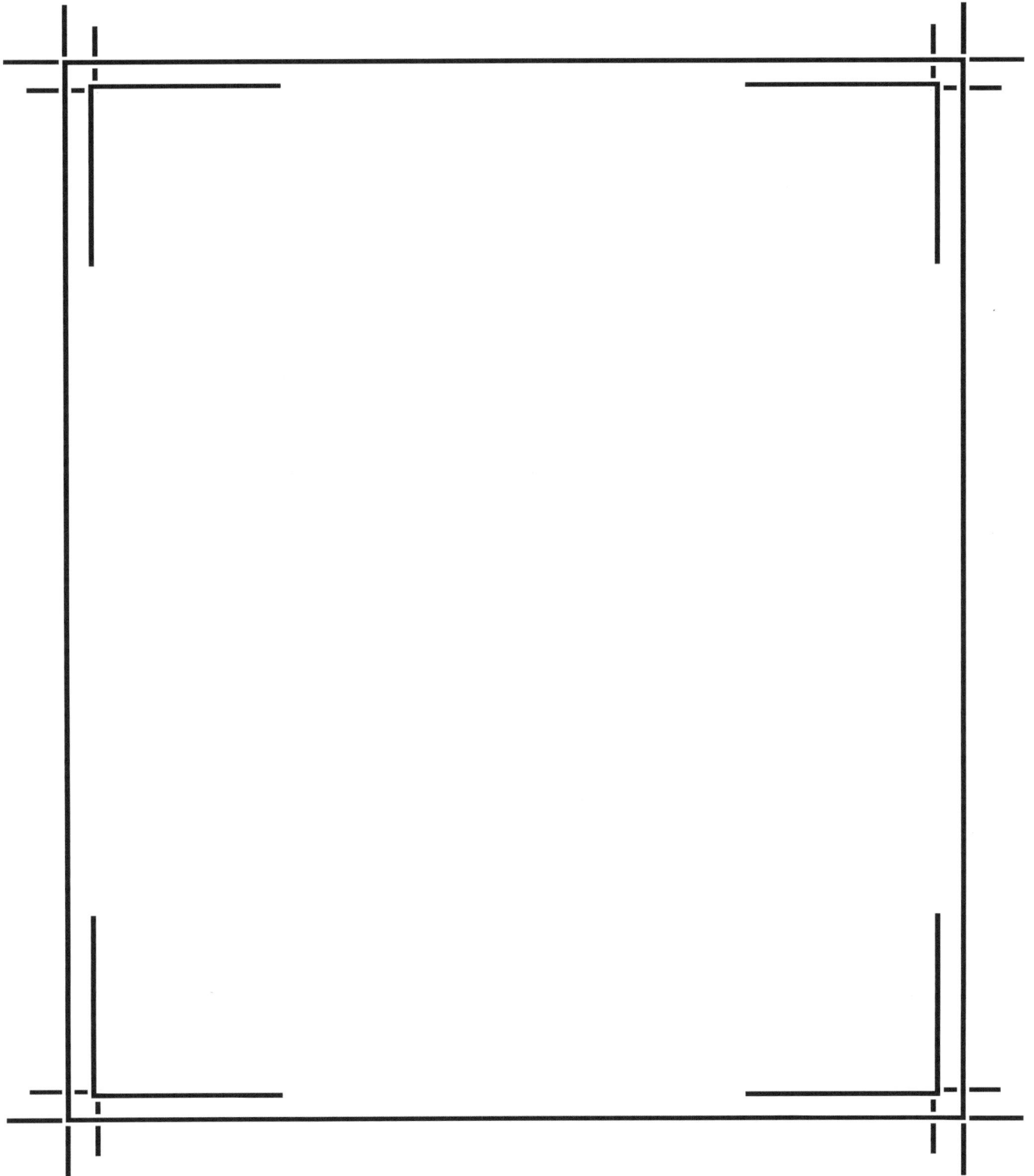

Your canvas...

It is _____ _____, _____
Month · Day · Year

Today, we...

_____
_____
_____
_____
_____
_____

We will always remember...

_____
_____
_____
_____
_____
_____

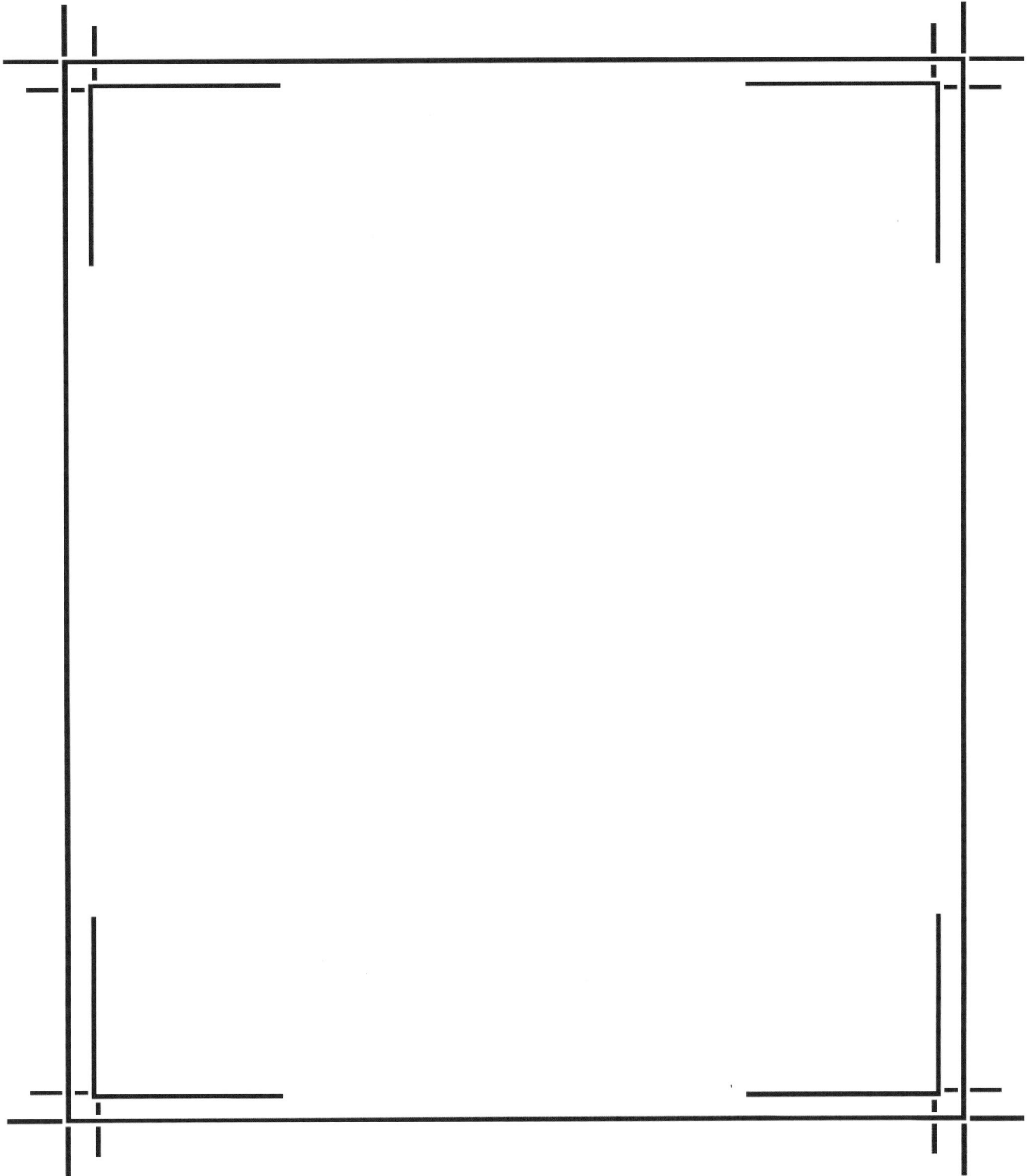

Your canvas...

It is

Today, we...

_____
_____
_____
_____
_____

We will always remember...

_____
_____
_____
_____
_____

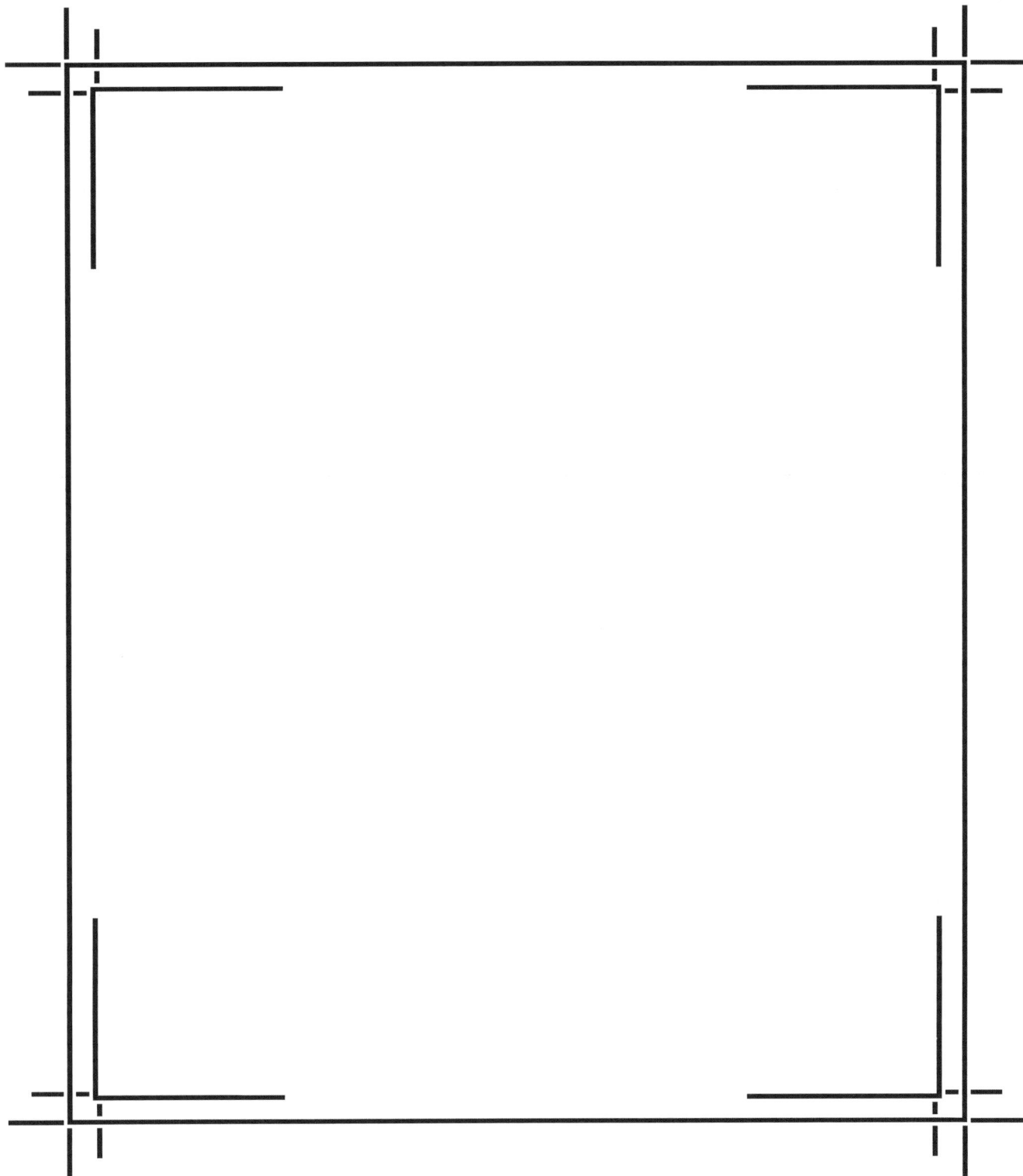

Your canvas...

It is _____ _____, _____
Month   Day   Year

Today, we...

_____

_____

_____

_____

_____

We will always remember...

_____

_____

_____

_____

_____

_____

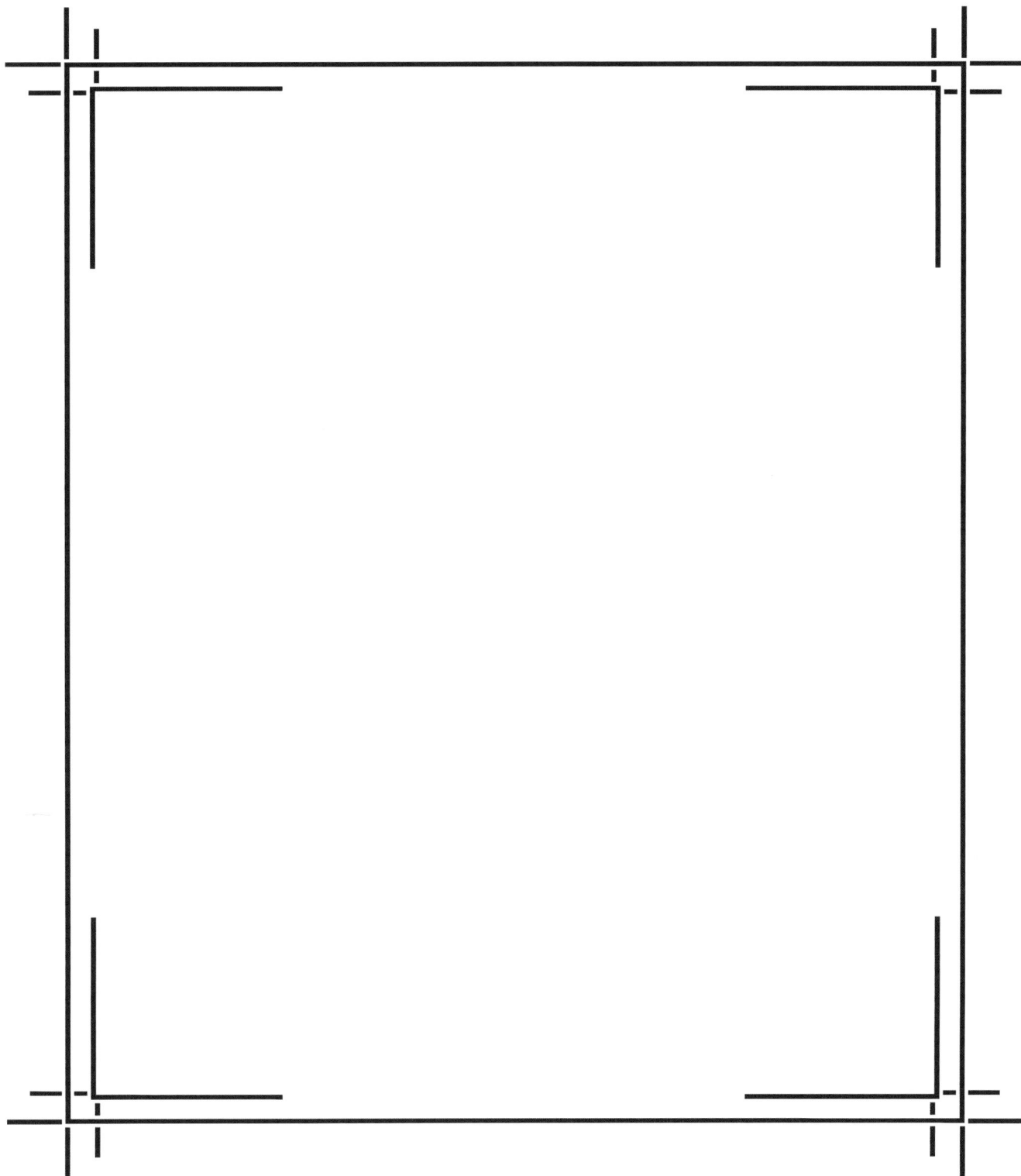

Your canvas...

It is _____ _____, _____
Month   Day   Year

Today, we...

_____

_____

_____

_____

_____

We will always remember...

_____

_____

_____

_____

_____

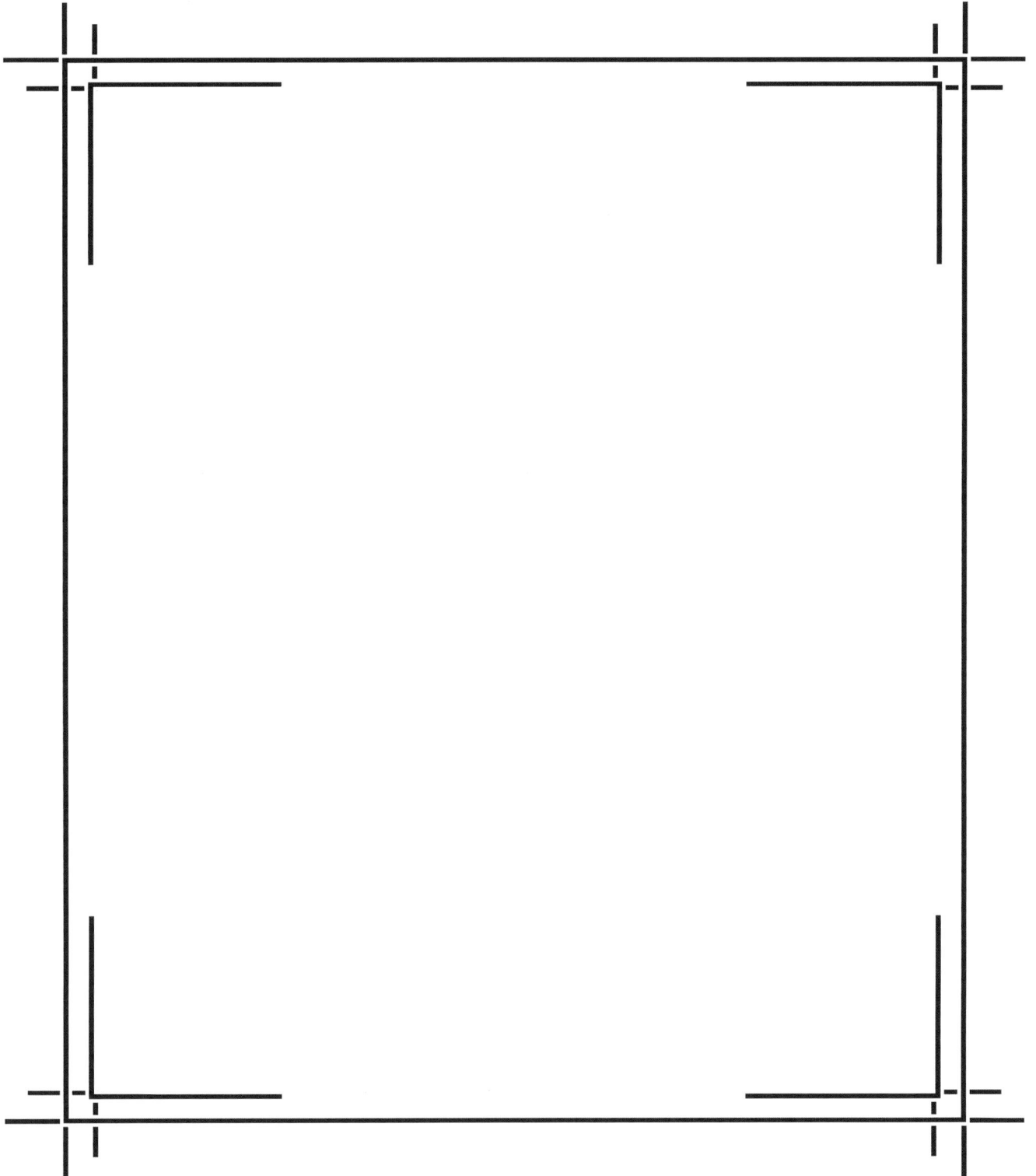

Your canvas...

It is _____ _____, ____
Month   Day   Year

Today, we...

_____

_____

_____

_____

_____

We will always remember...

_____

_____

_____

_____

_____

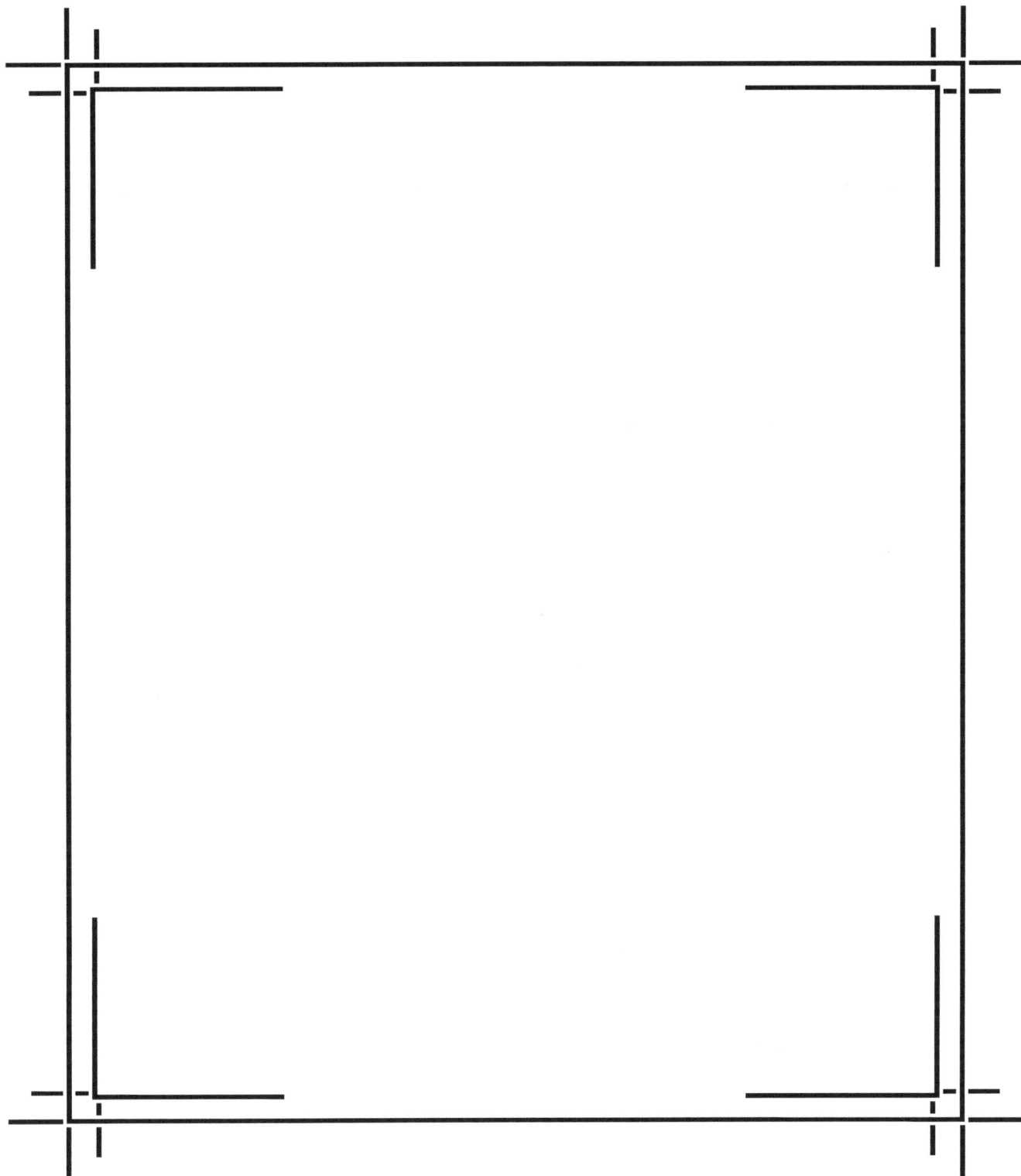

Your canvas...

It is _____ ___, ____
　　　　　　　　Month　　Day　　Year

Today, we...

_____

_____

_____

_____

_____

_____

We will always remember...

_____

_____

_____

_____

_____

_____

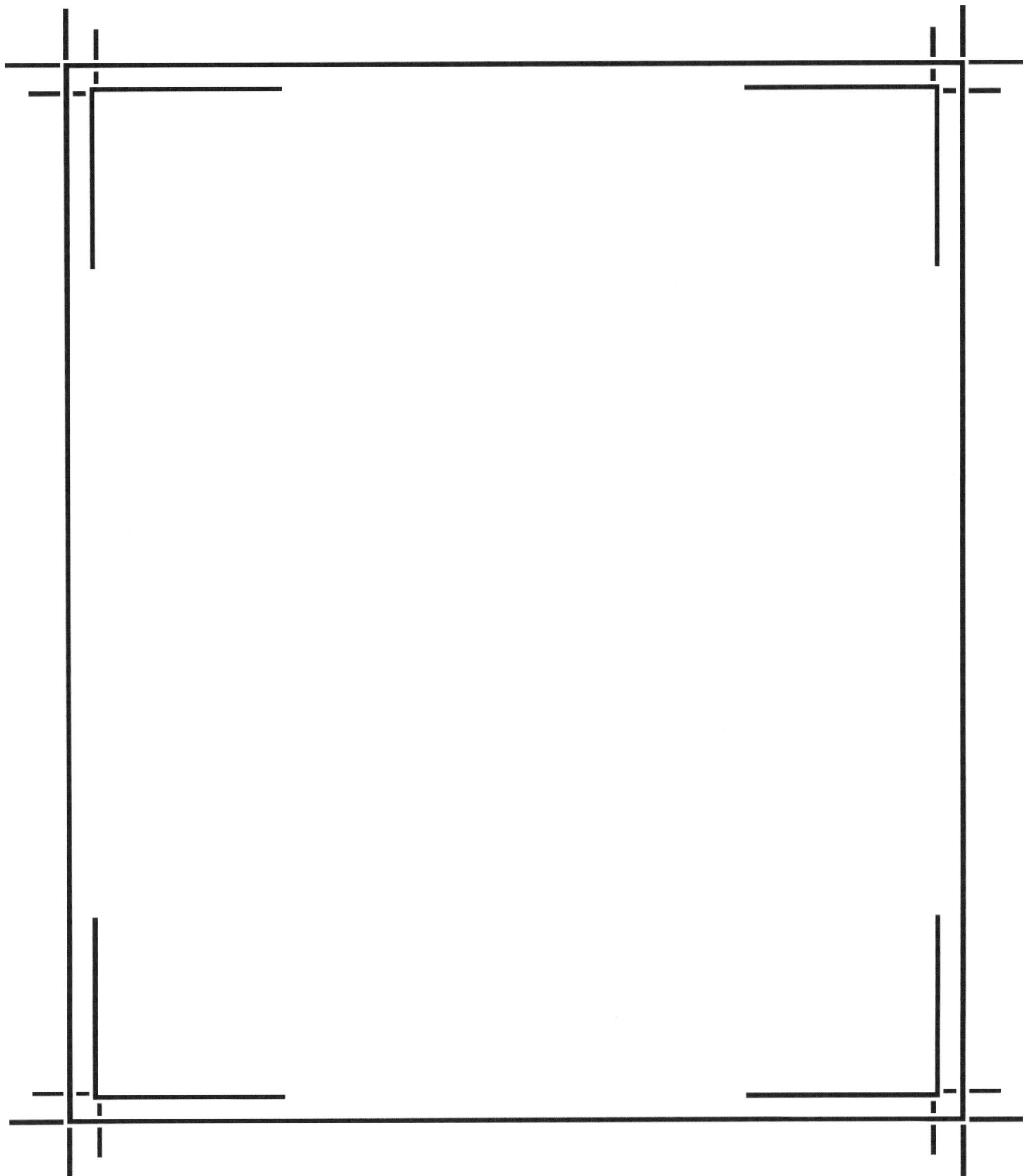

Your canvas...

It is _____ ___, ____

Today, we...

_____

_____

_____

_____

_____

We will always remember...

_____

_____

_____

_____

_____

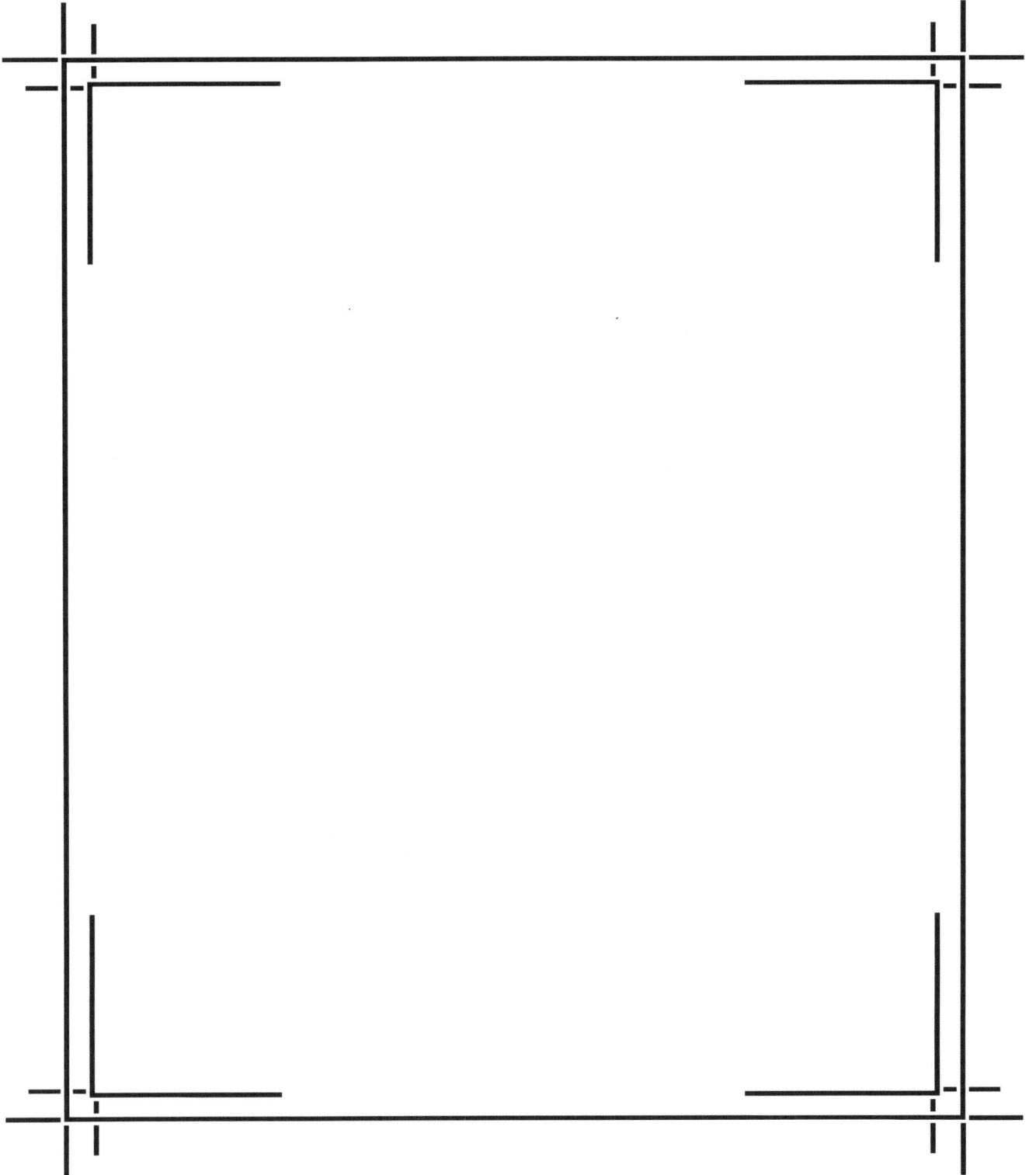

Your canvas...

It is _____ ____, ____

Today, we...

_____

_____

_____

_____

_____

_____

We will always remember...

_____

_____

_____

_____

_____

_____

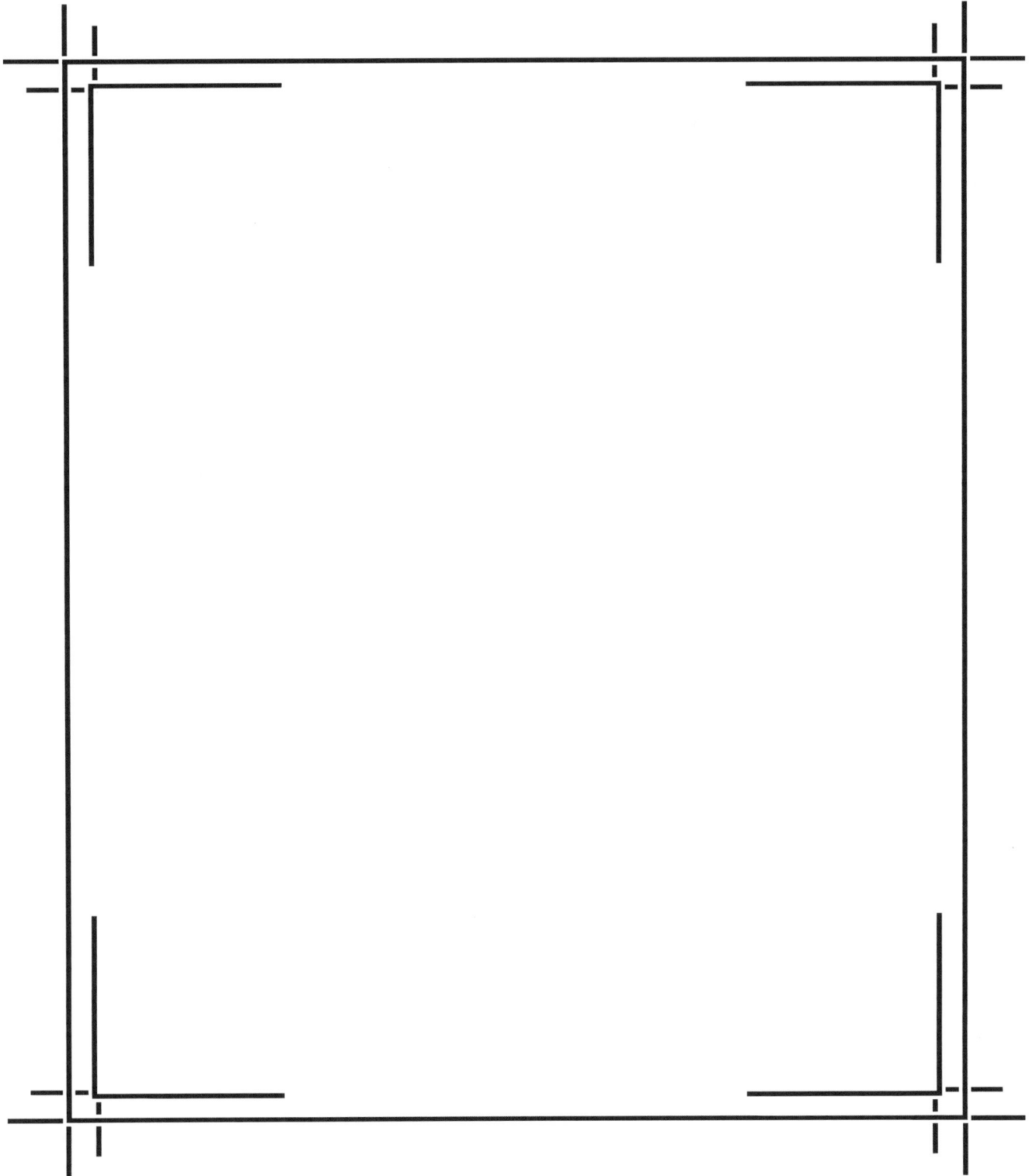

Your canvas...

It is _____ ____, _____

Today, we...

_____

_____

_____

_____

_____

We will always remember...

_____

_____

_____

_____

_____

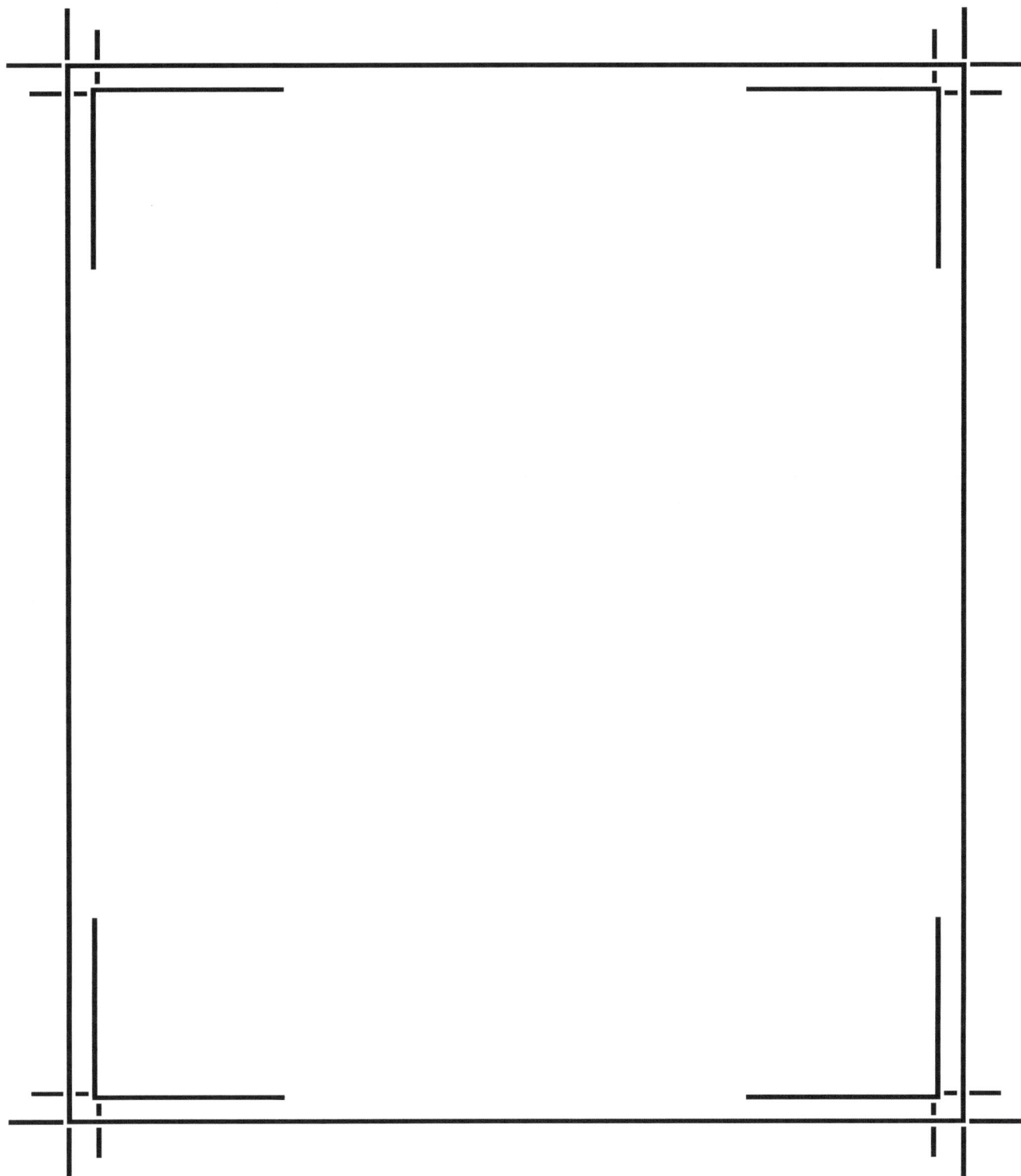

Your canvas...

It is _____ ___, ___
Month   Day   Year

Today, we...
_____
_____
_____
_____
_____
_____

We will always remember...
_____
_____
_____
_____
_____

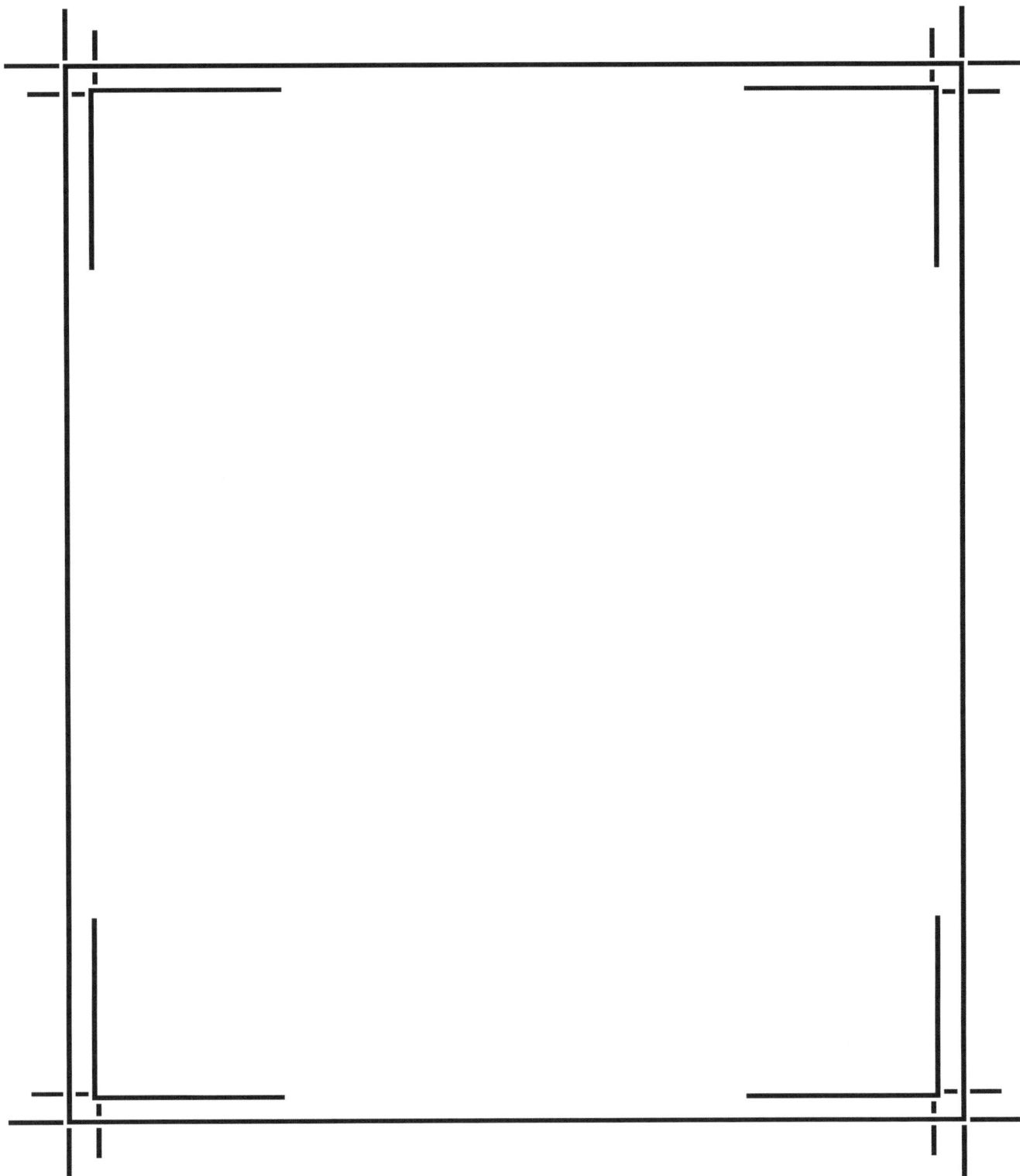

Your canvas...

It is _____ ____, ____
Month   Day   Year

Today, we...

_____

_____

_____

_____

_____

We will always remember...

_____

_____

_____

_____

_____

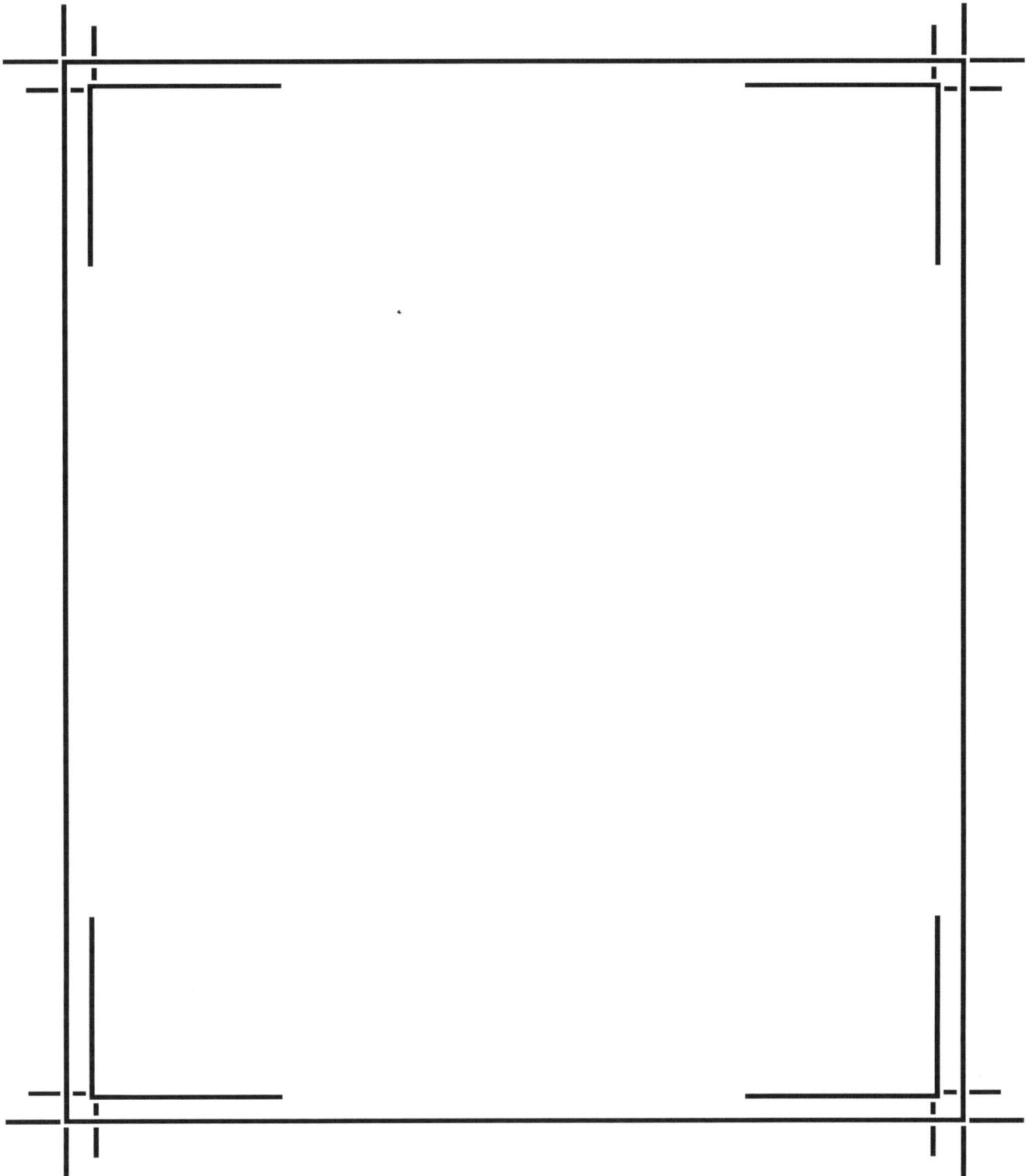

Your canvas...

It is _____ ___, ____
Month   Day   Year

Today, we...

_____

_____

_____

_____

_____

We will always remember...

_____

_____

_____

_____

_____

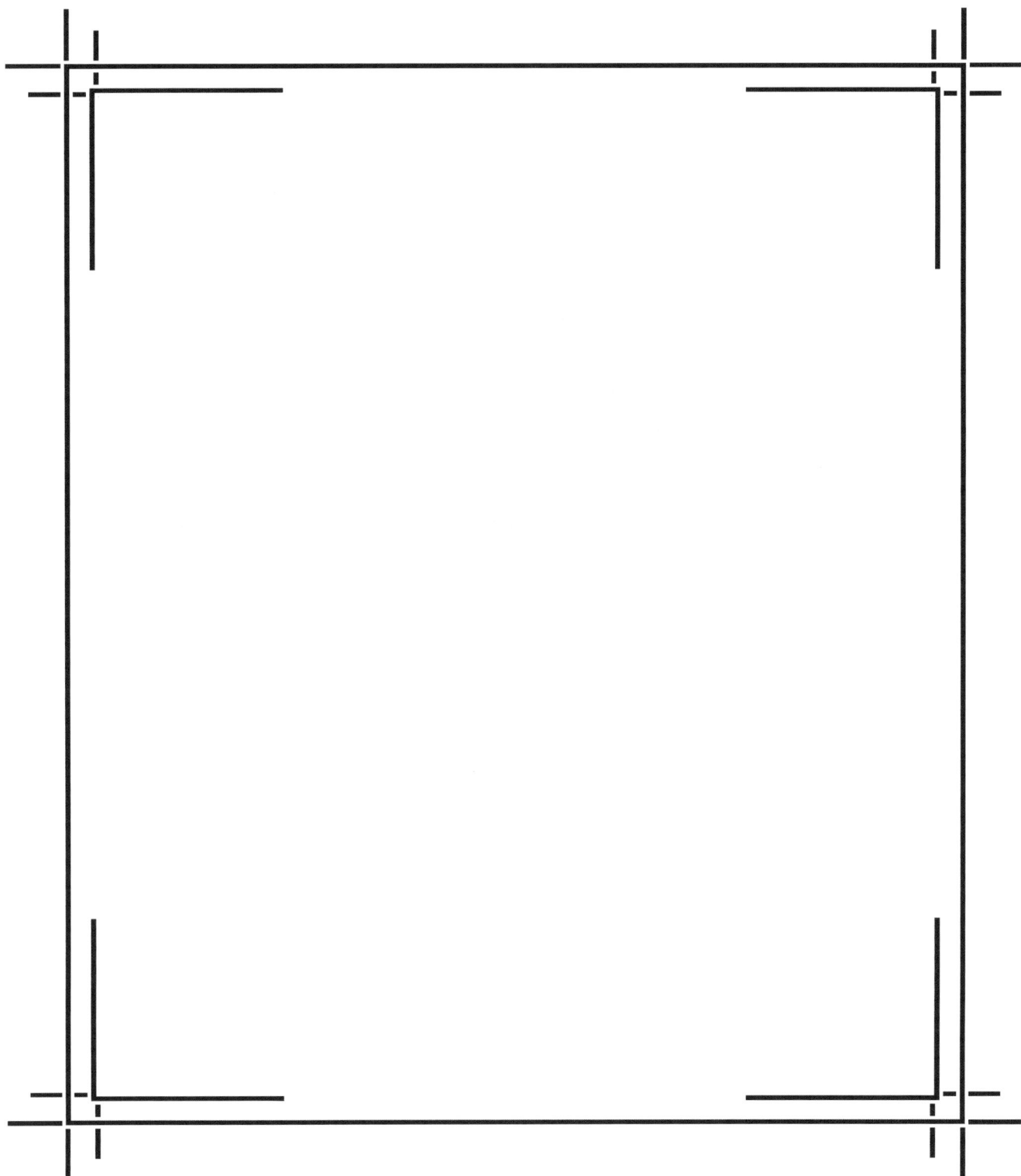

Your canvas...

It is _____ ___, ____
Month   Day   Year

Today, we...

_____

_____

_____

_____

_____

We will always remember...

_____

_____

_____

_____

_____

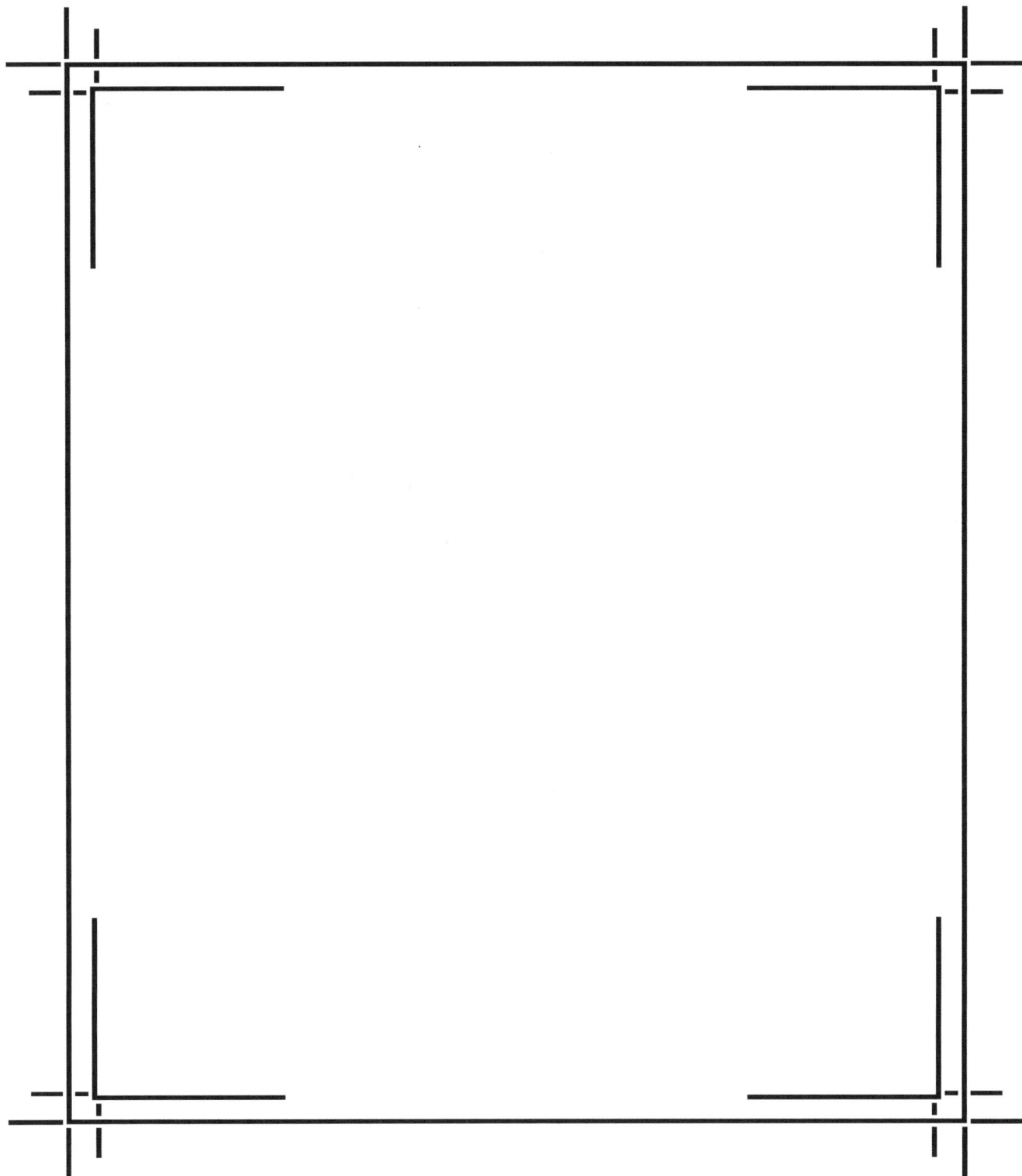

Your canvas...

It is _____ ___, _____

Today, we...

_____

_____

_____

_____

_____

_____

We will always remember...

_____

_____

_____

_____

_____

_____

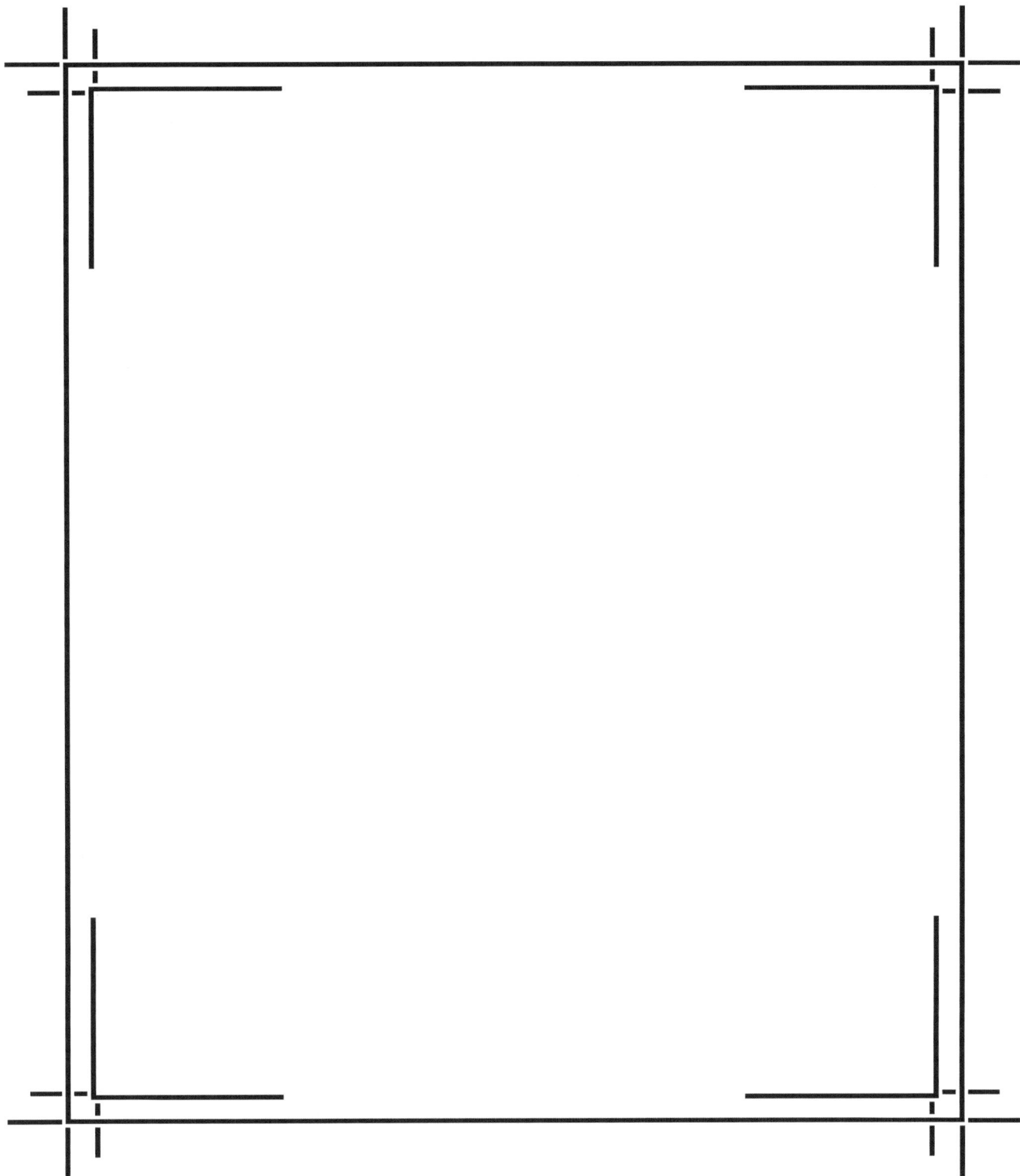

Your canvas...

It is _____ ___, ___
Month   Day   Year

Today, we...

_____

_____

_____

_____

_____

We will always remember...

_____

_____

_____

_____

_____

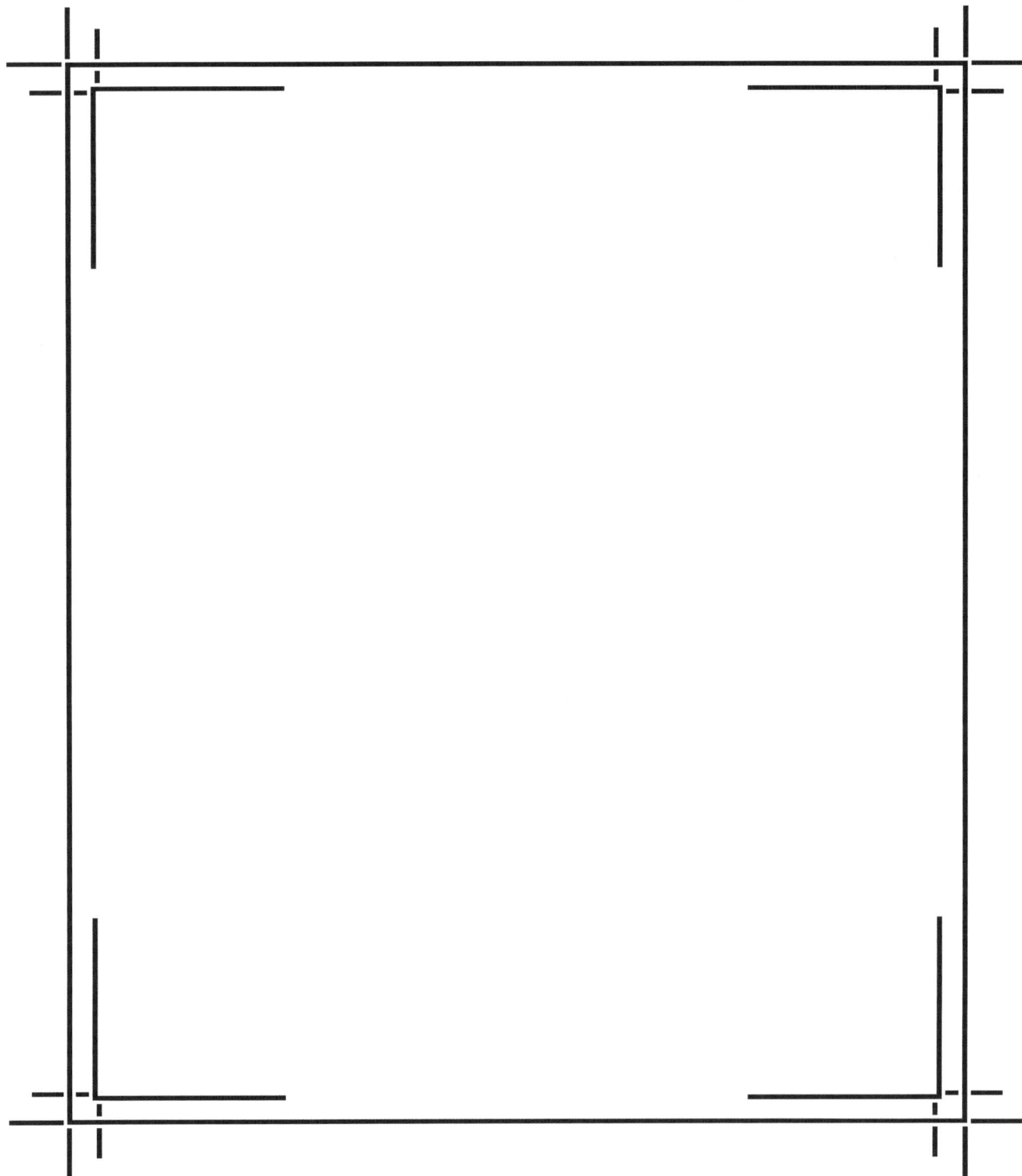

Your canvas...

It is _____ _____ , _____
Month   Day   Year

Today, we...

_____

_____

_____

_____

_____

_____

We will always remember...

_____

_____

_____

_____

_____

_____

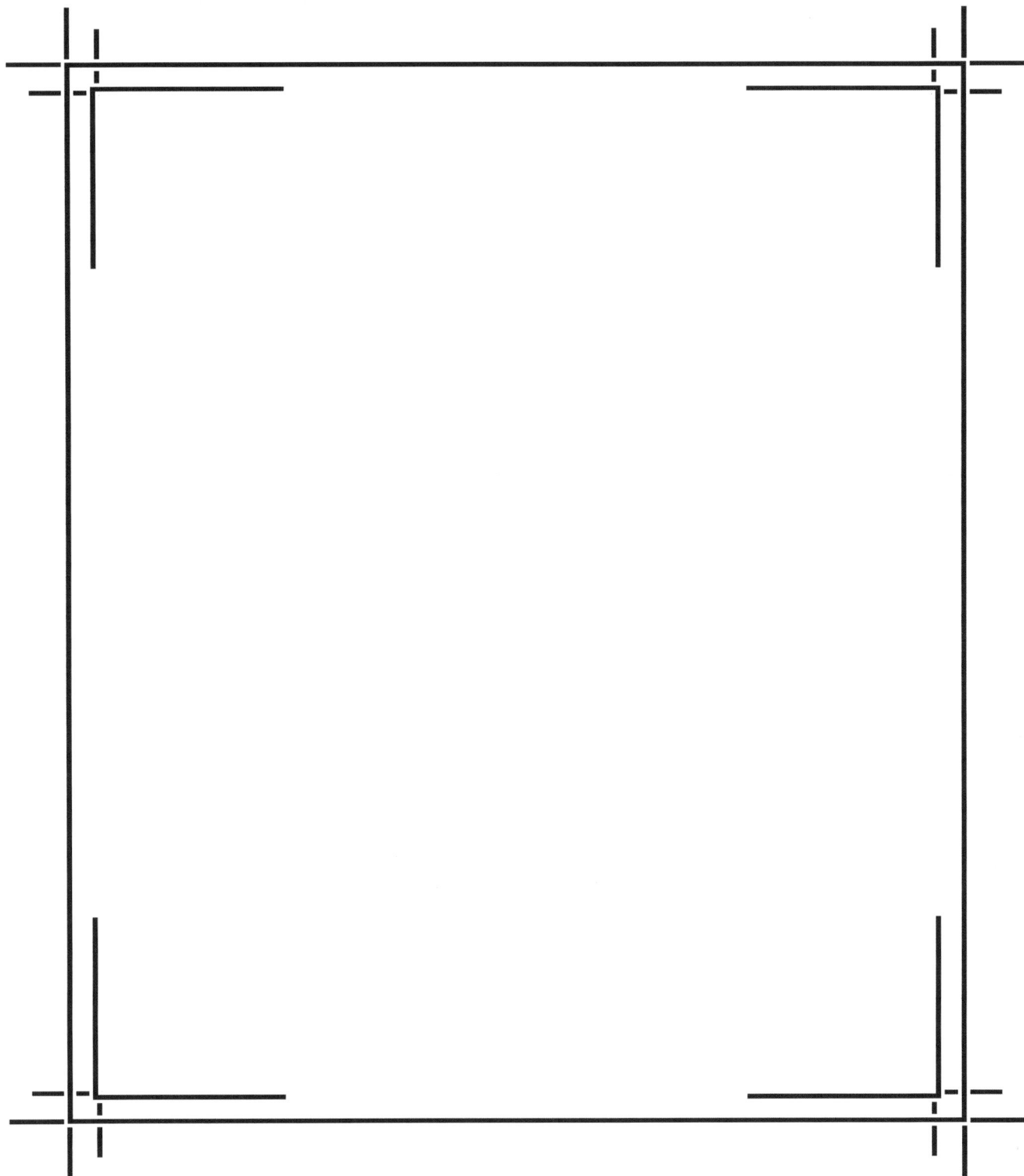

Your canvas...

It is _____ ___, _____
Month   Day   Year

Today, we...

_____

_____

_____

_____

_____

_____

We will always remember...

_____

_____

_____

_____

_____

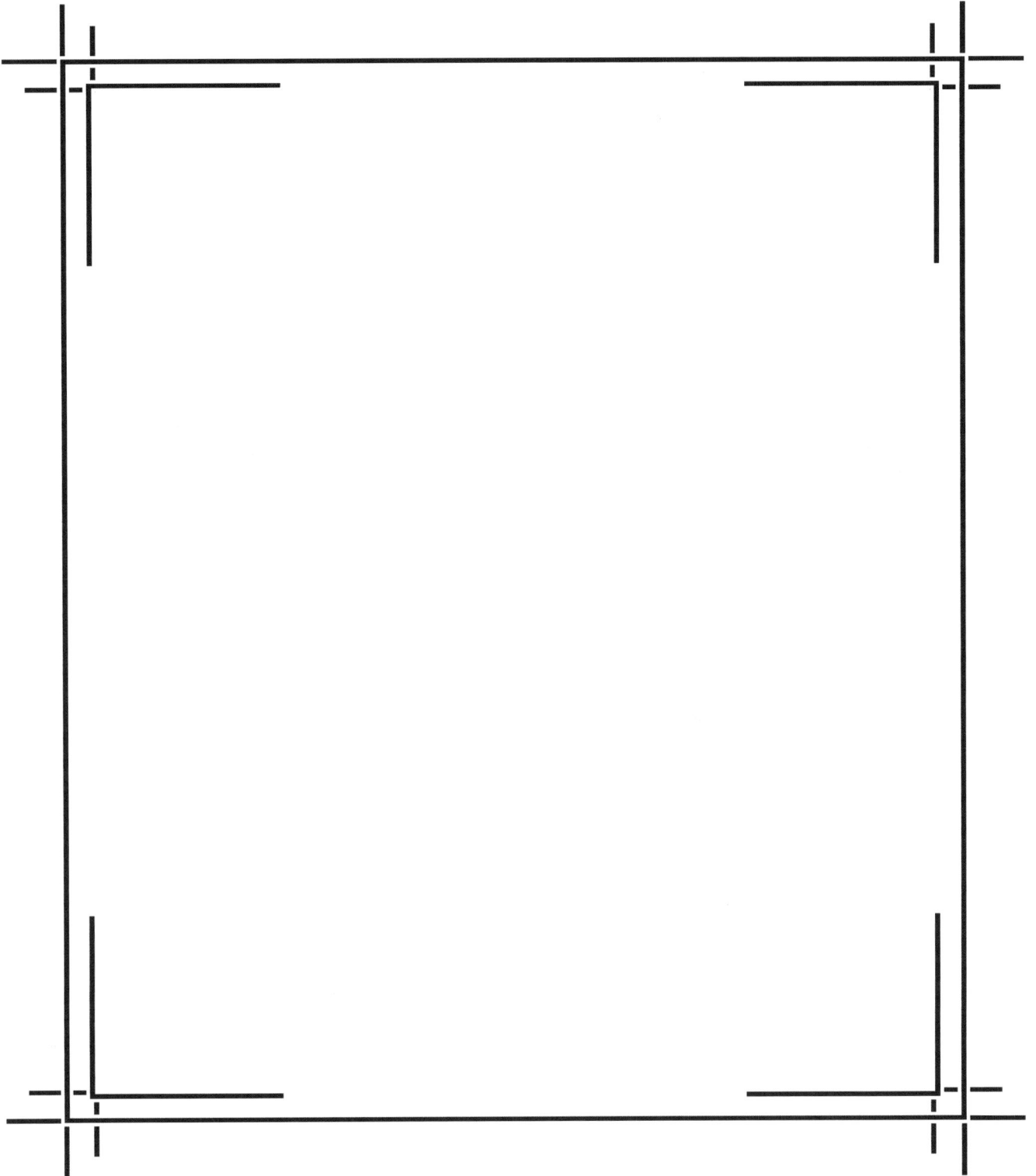

Your canvas...

It is _____ ___, _____
Month   Day   Year

Today, we...

_____

_____

_____

_____

_____

We will always remember...

_____

_____

_____

_____

_____

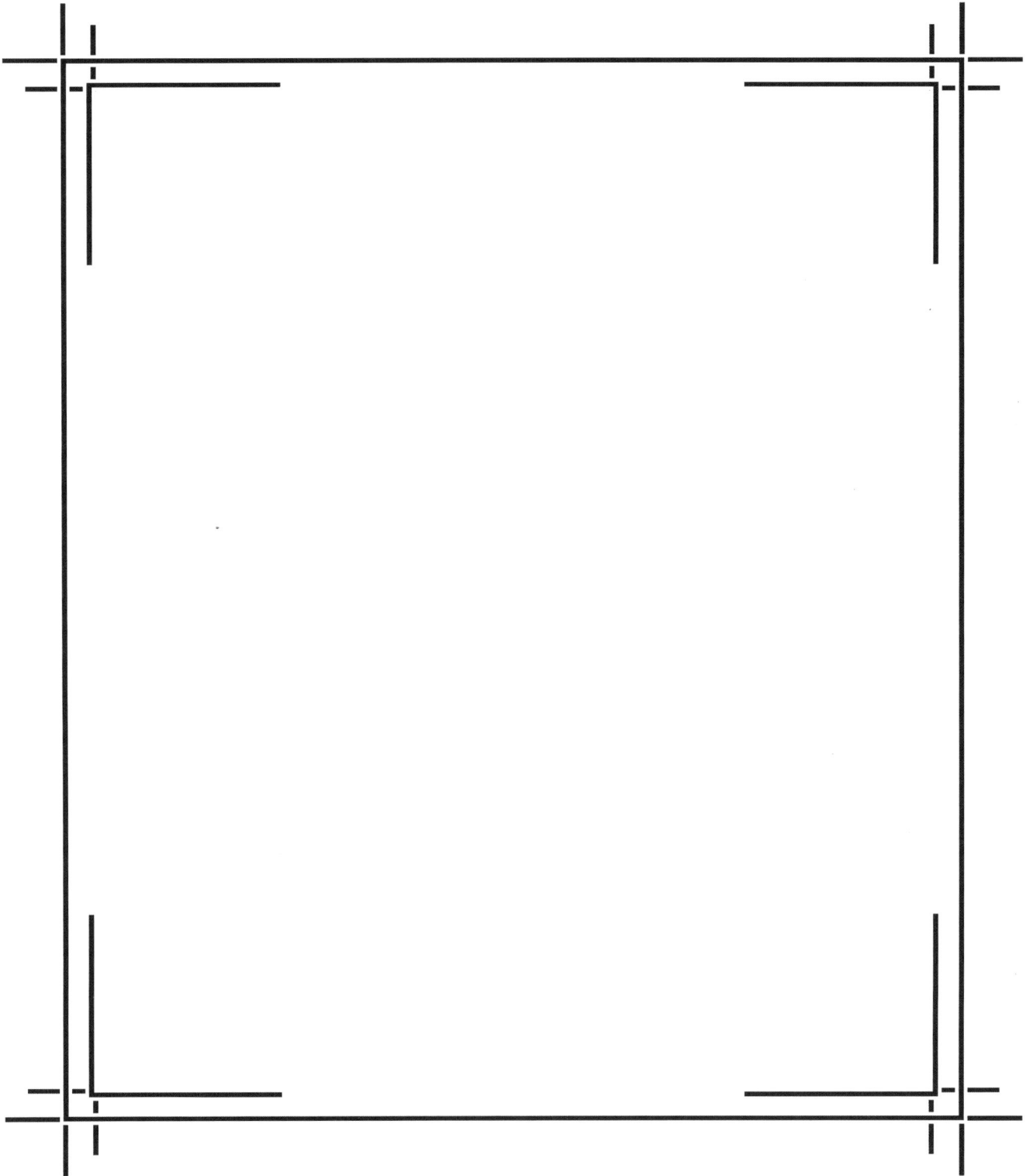

Your canvas...

It is _____ ___, ____
Month   Day   Year

Today, we...

_____

_____

_____

_____

_____

We will always remember...

_____

_____

_____

_____

_____

_____

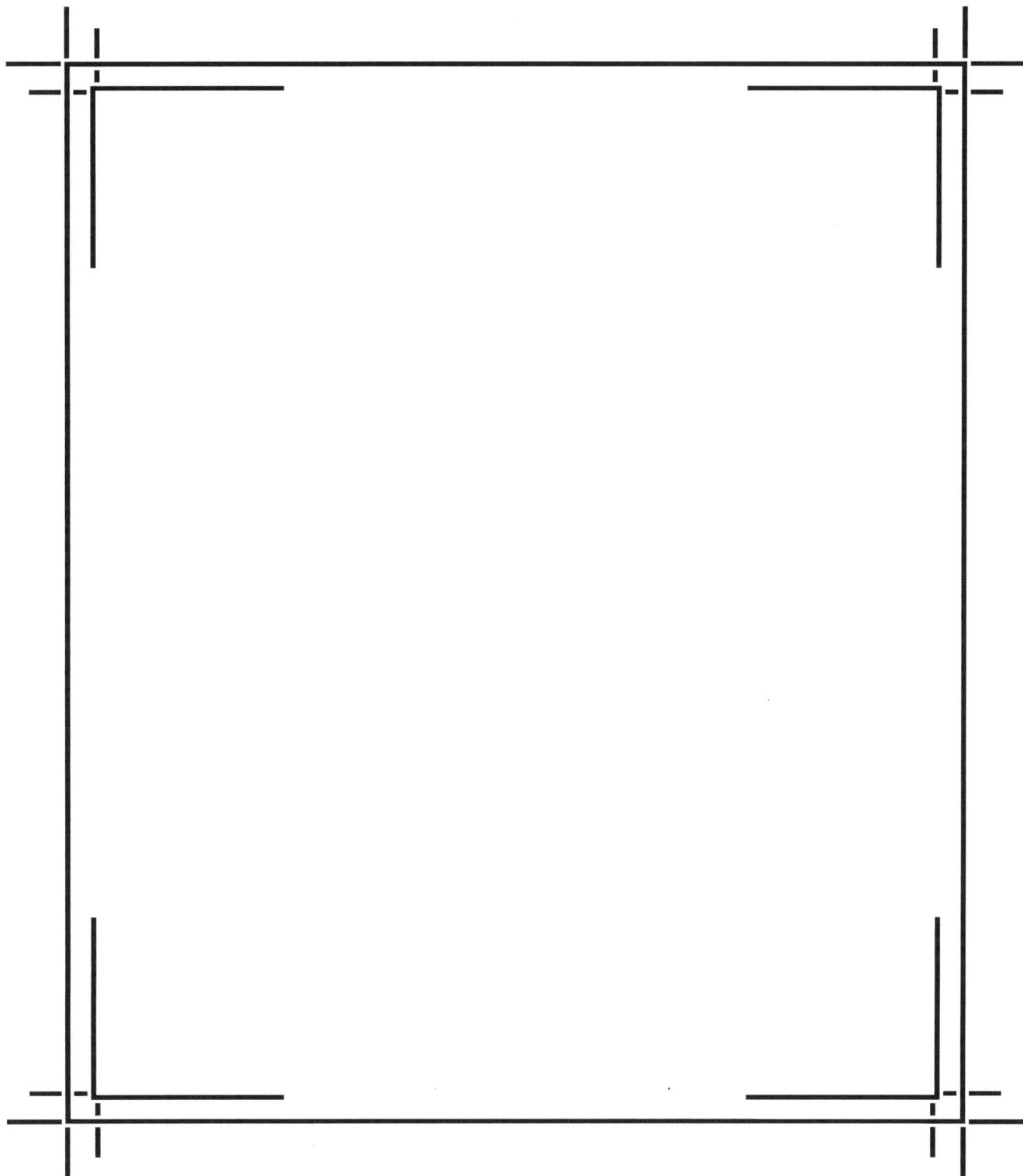

Your canvas...

It is _____ _____, _____
Month   Day   Year

Today, we...

_____

_____

_____

_____

_____

_____

We will always remember...

_____

_____

_____

_____

_____

_____

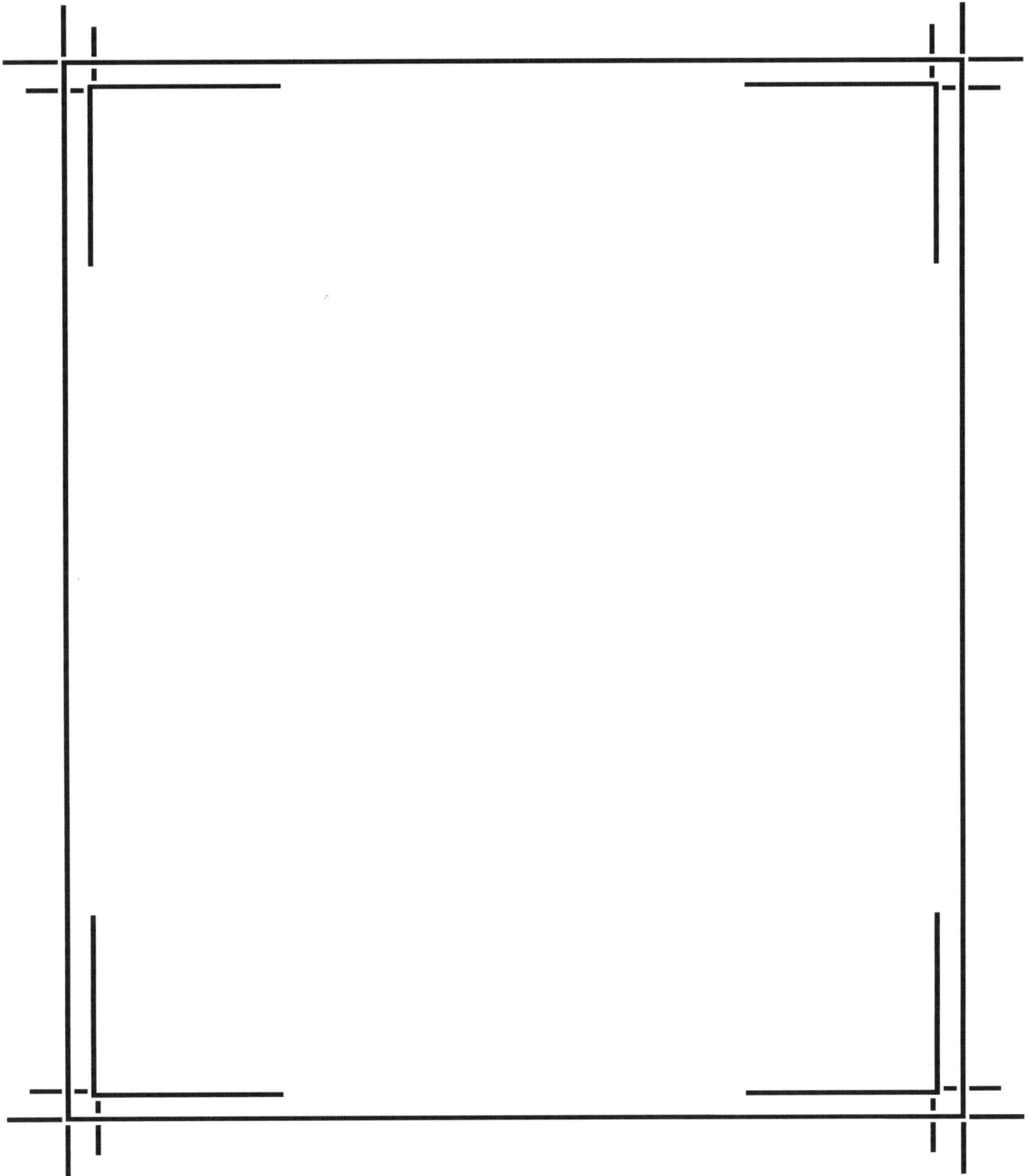

Your canvas...

It is _____ ____, ____
Month   Day   Year

Today, we...

_____

_____

_____

_____

_____

We will always remember...

_____

_____

_____

_____

_____

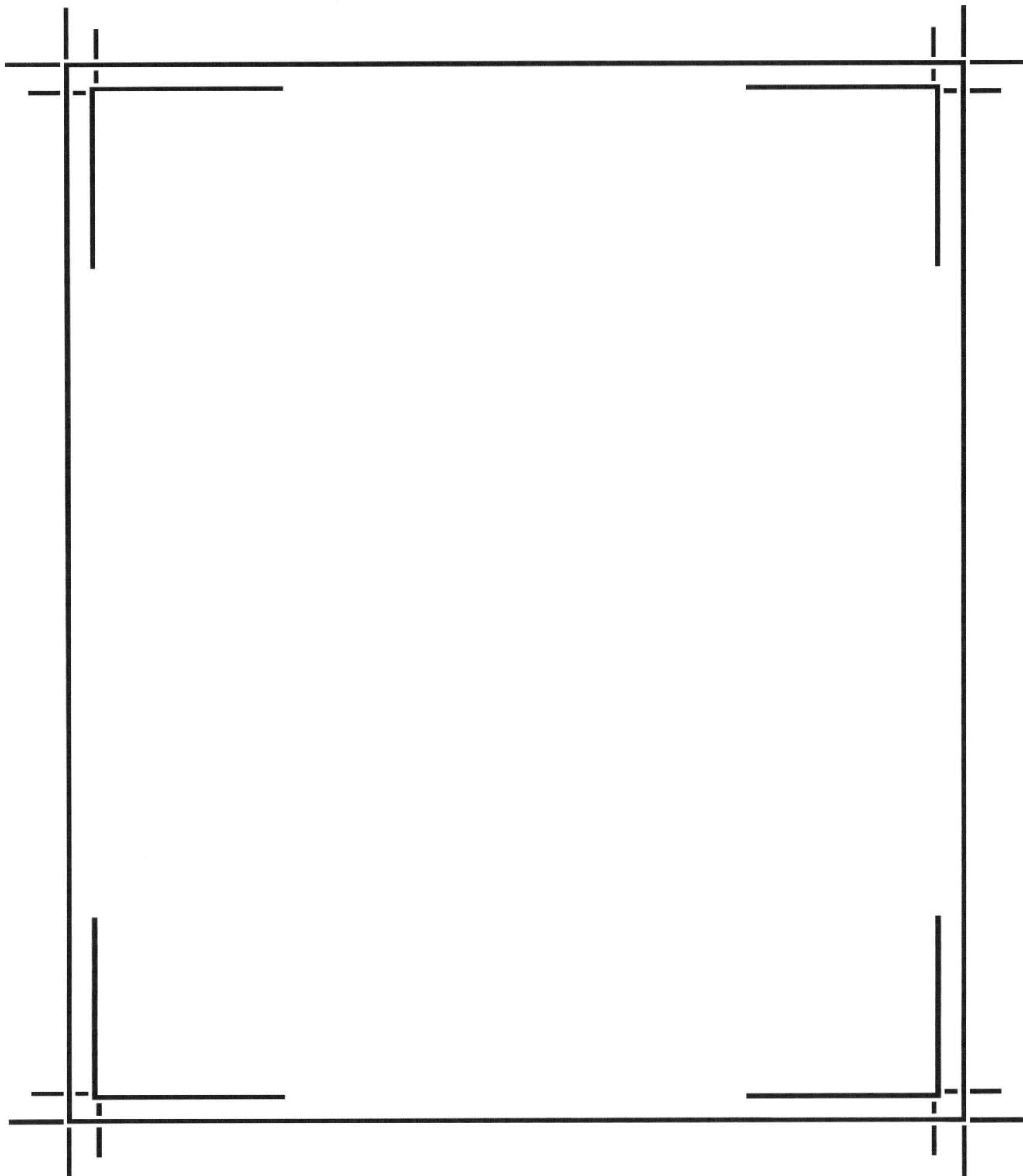

Your canvas...

It is _____ _____, _____

Today, we...

_____

_____

_____

_____

_____

We will always remember...

_____

_____

_____

_____

_____

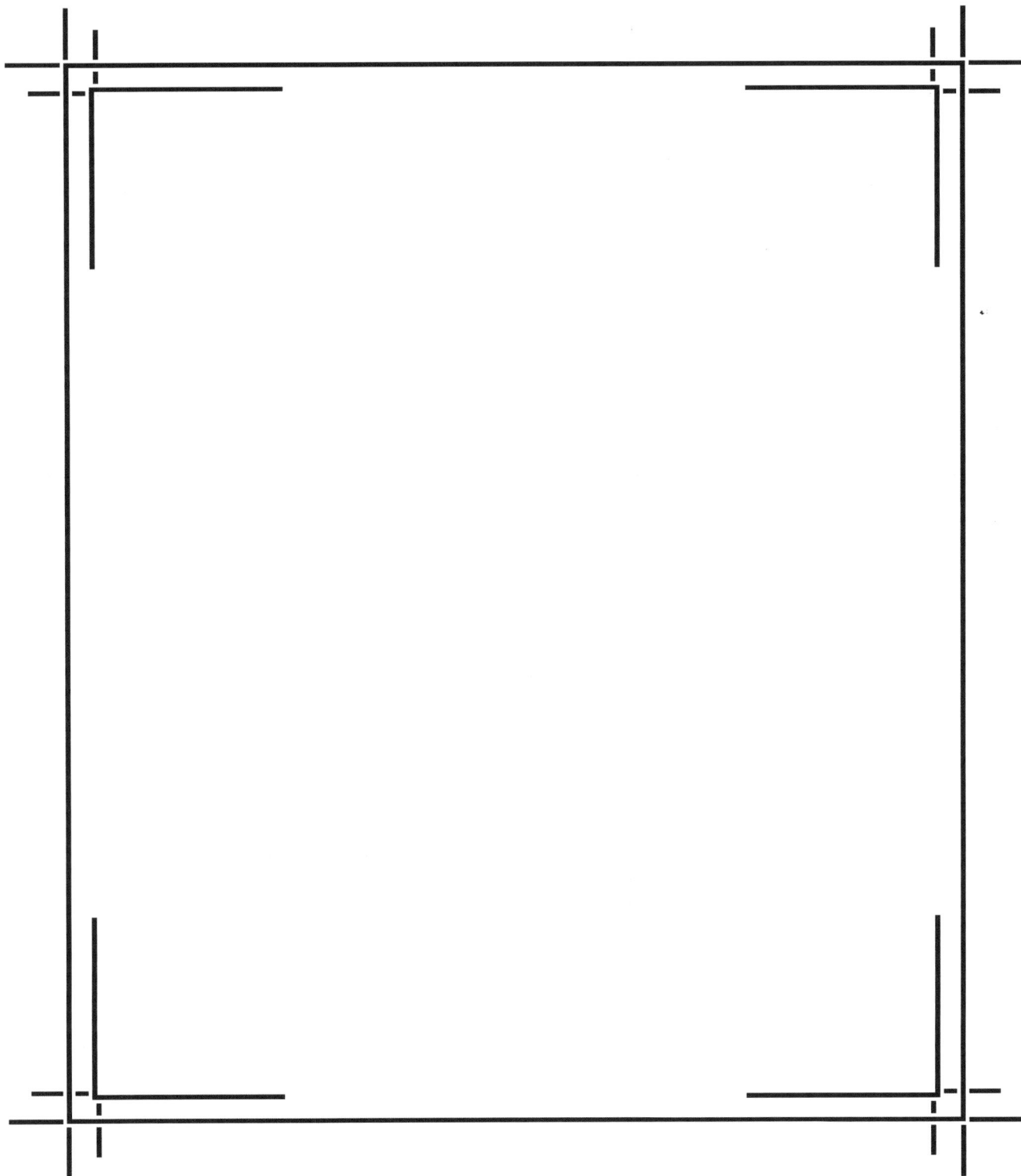

Your canvas...

It is

Month   Day ,   Year

Today, we...

_____

_____

_____

_____

_____

We will always remember...

_____

_____

_____

_____

_____

_____

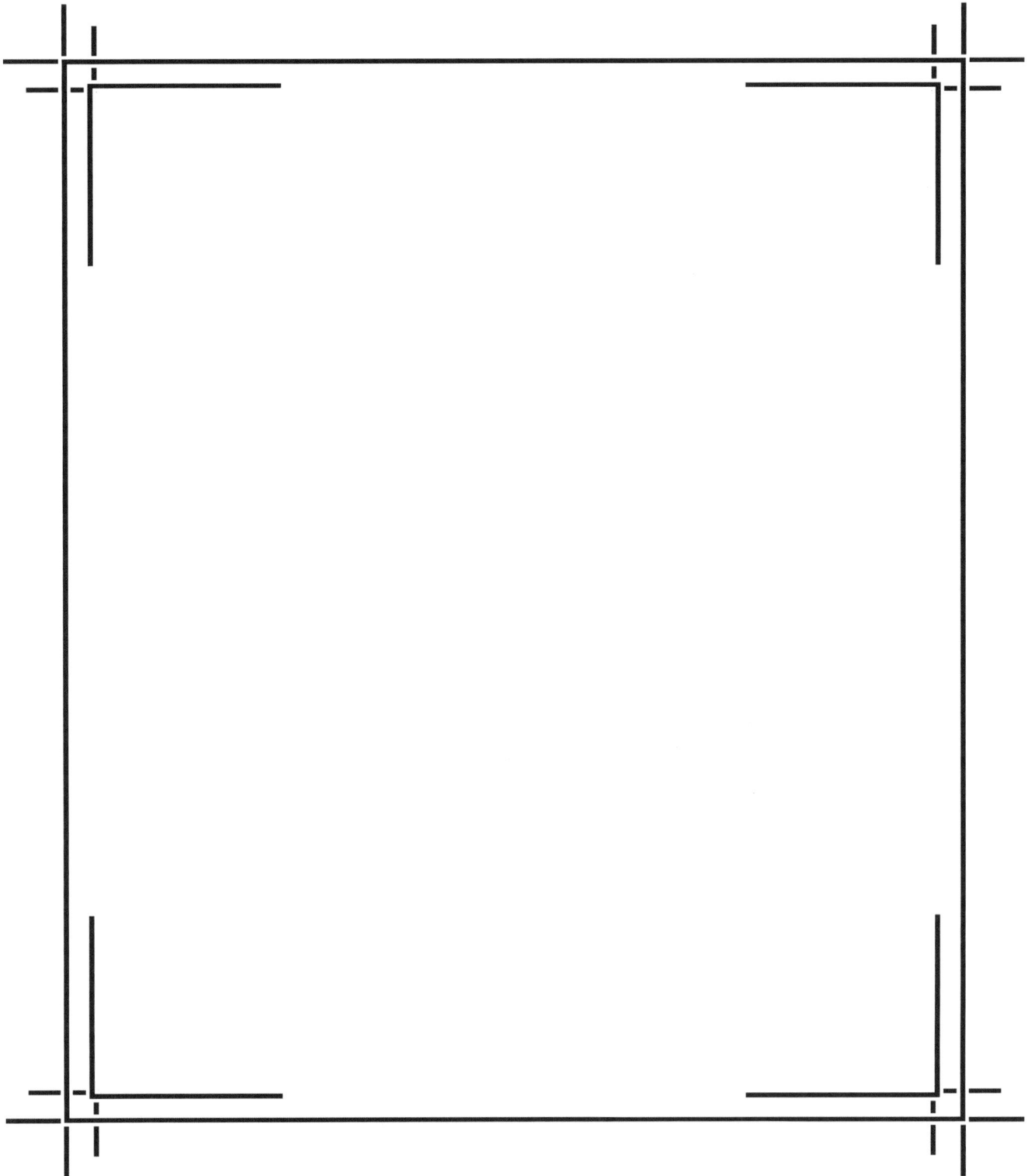

Your canvas...

It is _____ _____, _____
Month   Day   Year

Today, we...

_____
_____
_____
_____
_____

We will always remember...

_____
_____
_____
_____
_____
_____

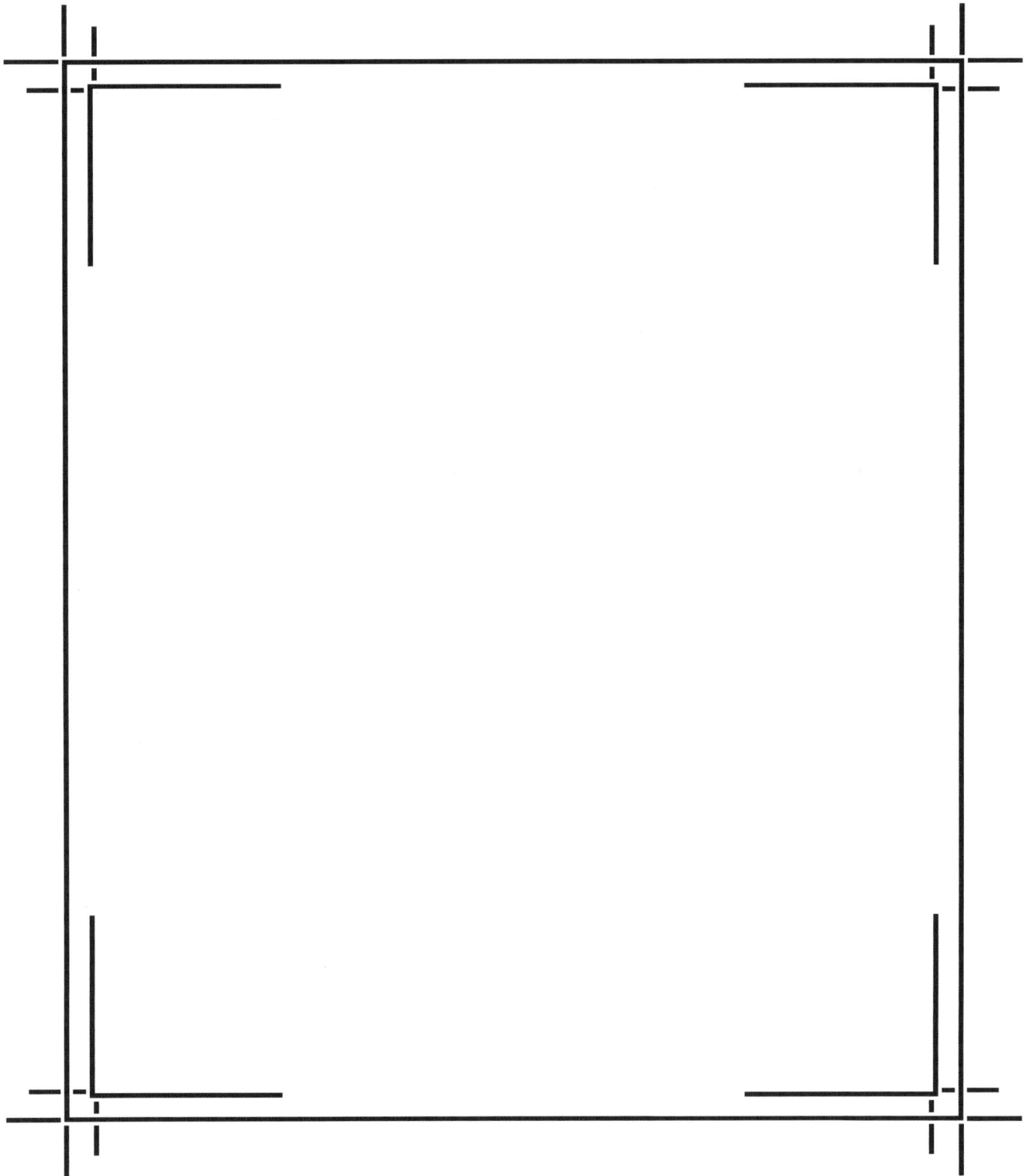

Your canvas...

It is _____ ___, ___

Today, we...

_____

_____

_____

_____

_____

_____

We will always remember...

_____

_____

_____

_____

_____

_____

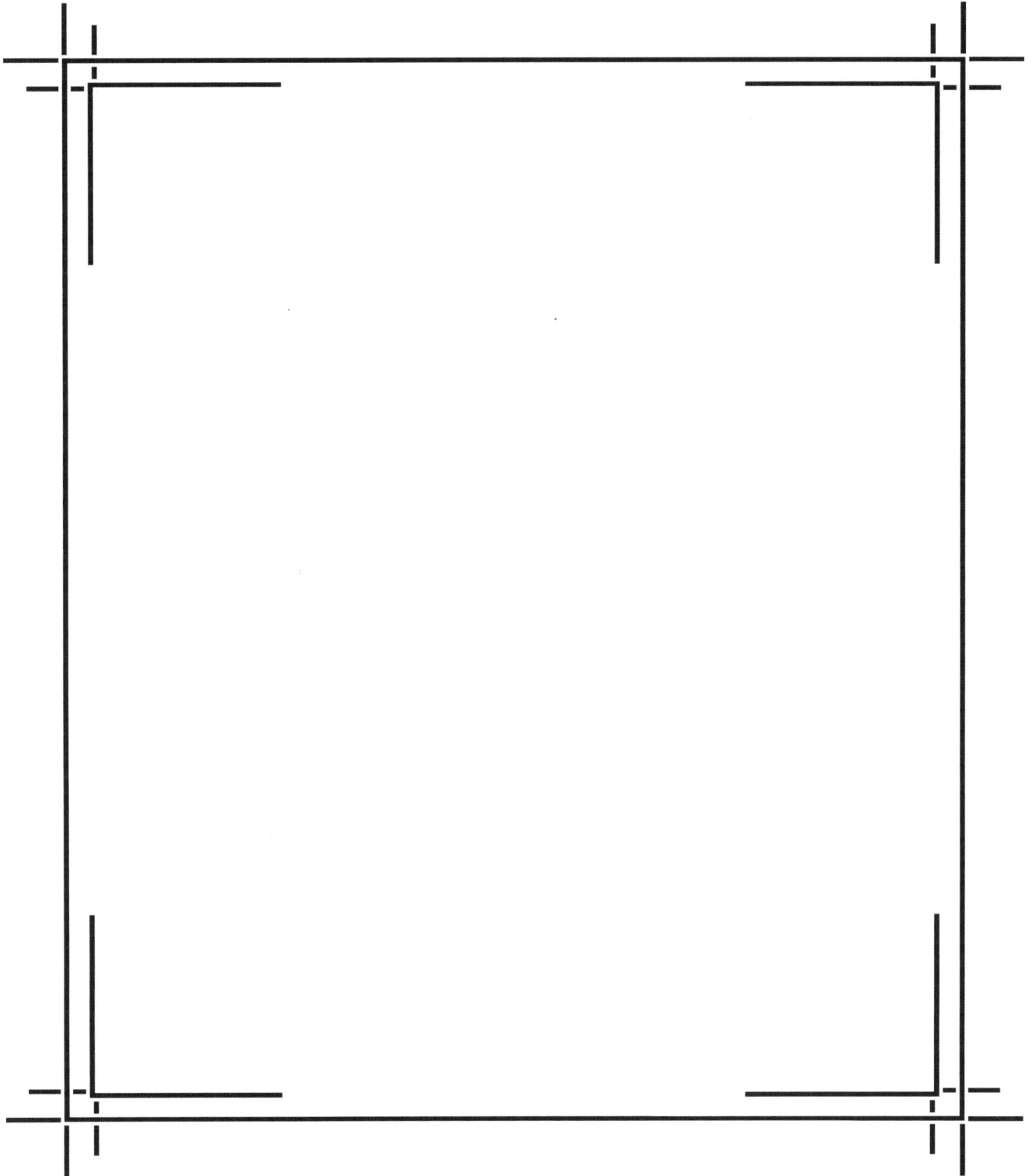

Your canvas...

It is _____ _____, _____
Month   Day   Year

Today, we...

_____

_____

_____

_____

_____

_____

We will always remember...

_____

_____

_____

_____

_____

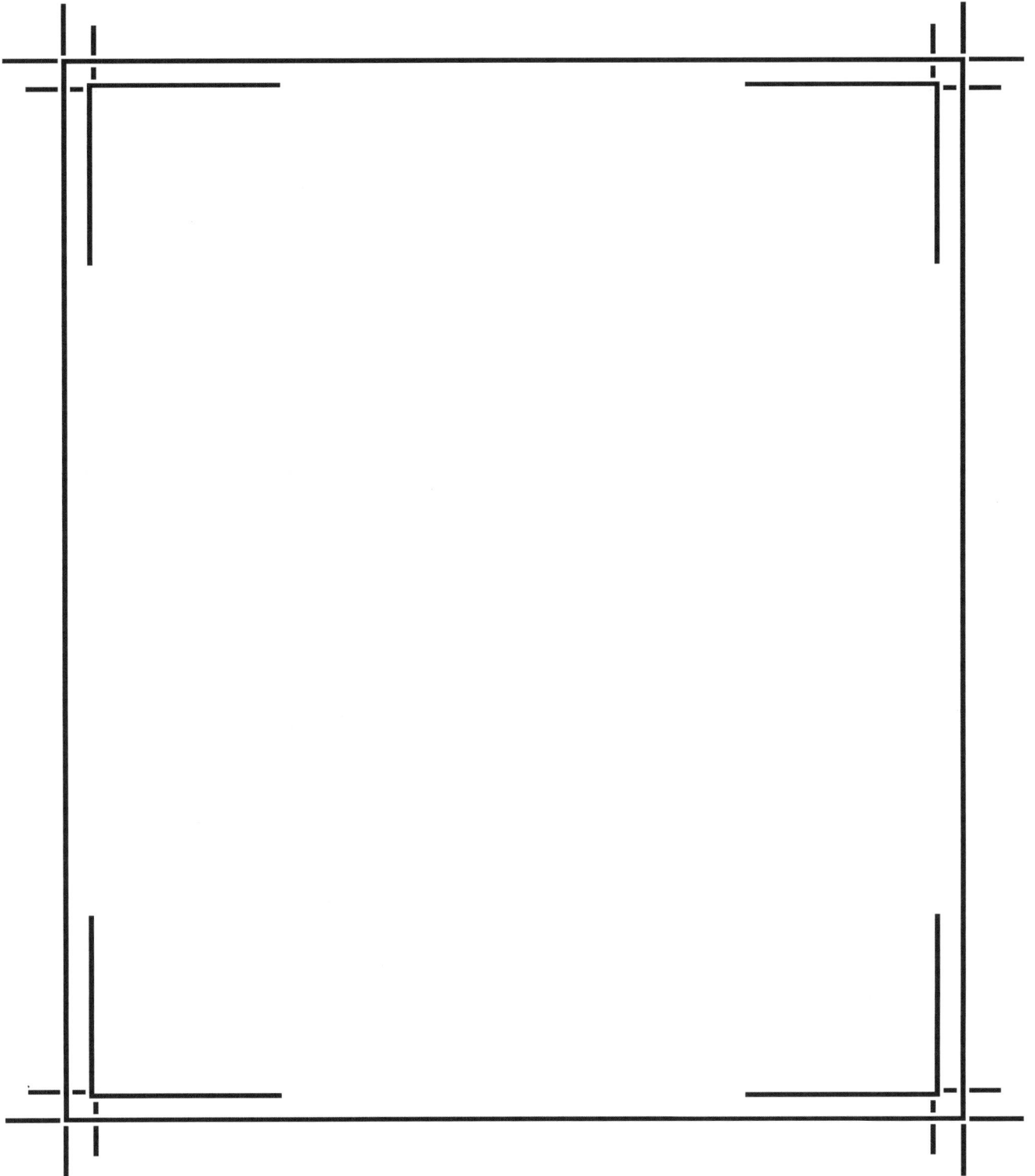

Your canvas...

It is _____ ___, _____
Month   Day ,   Year

Today, we...

_____

_____

_____

_____

_____

We will always remember...

_____

_____

_____

_____

_____

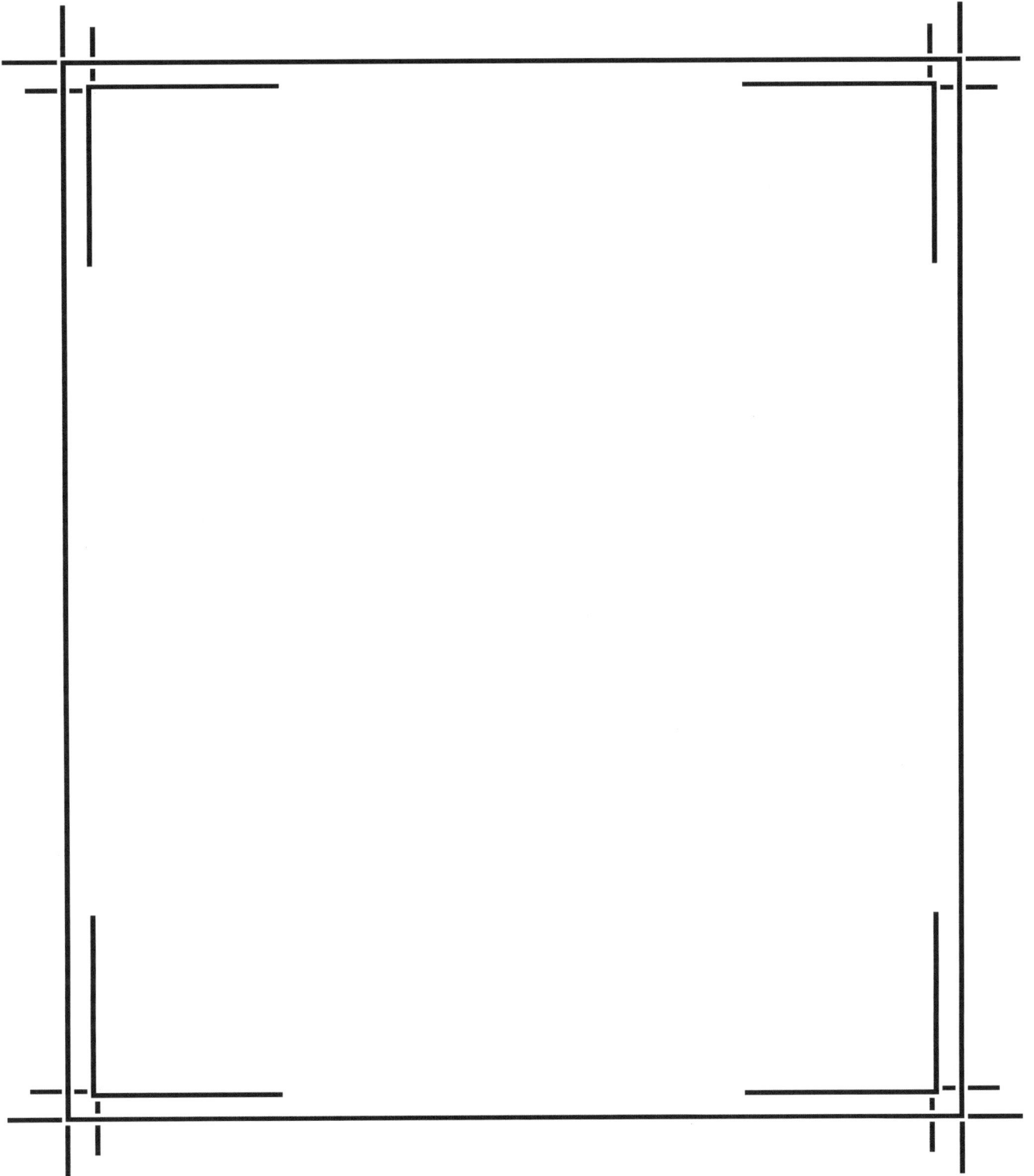

Your canvas...

It is _____ _____, _____

Today, we...

_____

_____

_____

_____

_____

We will always remember...

_____

_____

_____

_____

_____

_____

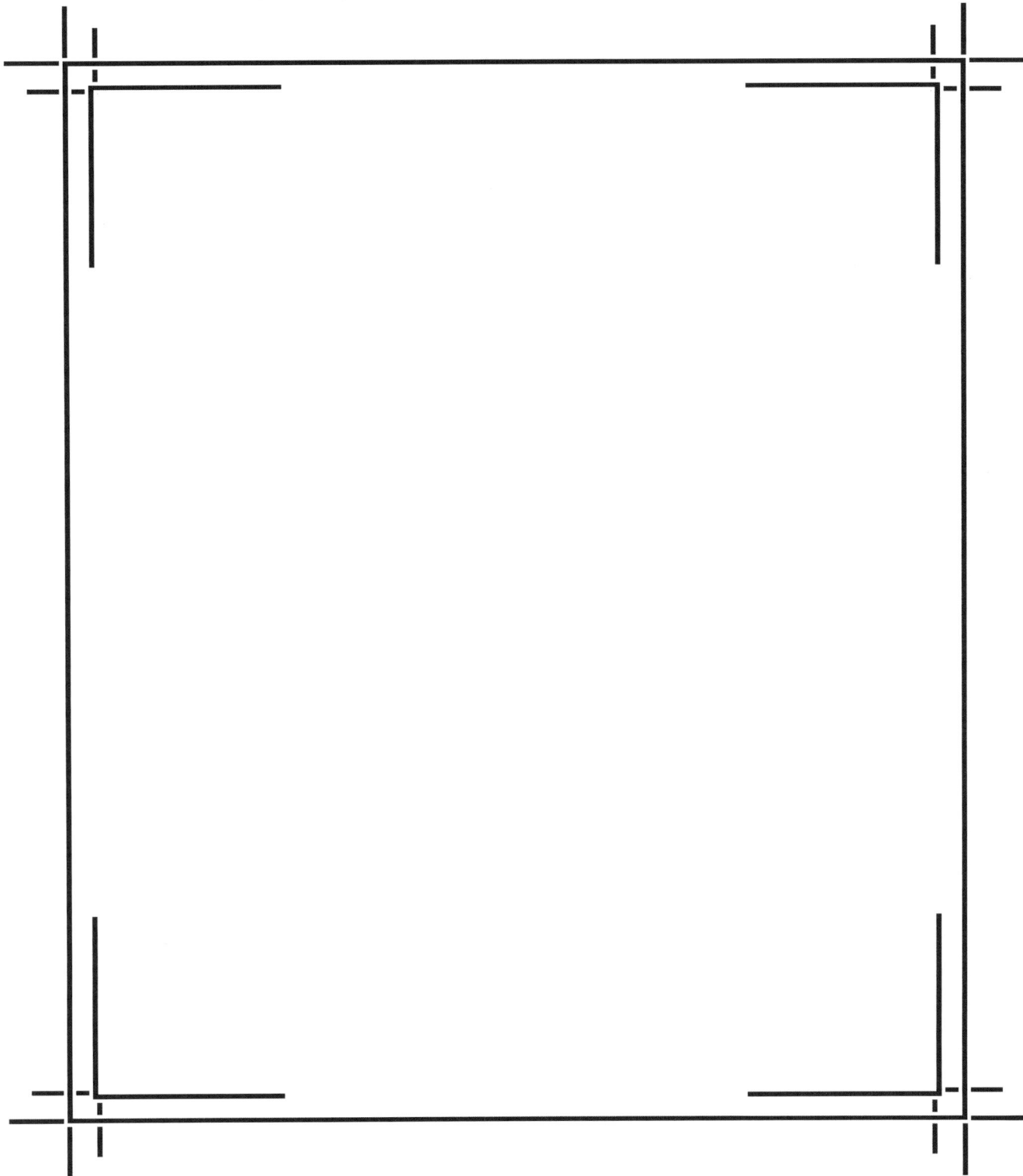

Your canvas...

It is

Month   Day   Year

Today, we...

_____

_____

_____

_____

_____

We will always remember...

_____

_____

_____

_____

_____

_____

Your canvas...

It is _____ ___, _____
Month   Day ,   Year

Today, we...

_____

_____

_____

_____

_____

_____

We will always remember...

_____

_____

_____

_____

_____

_____

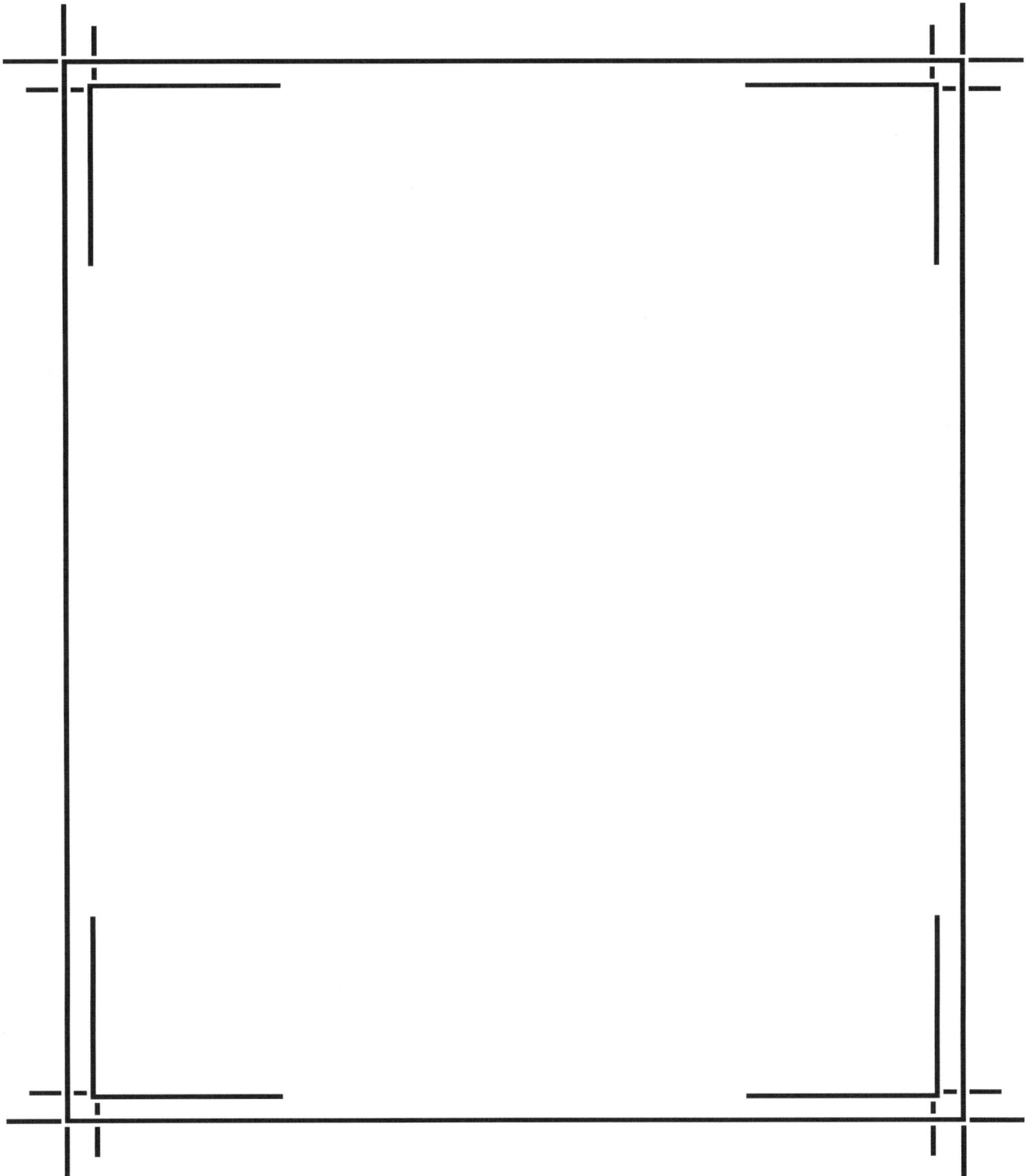

Your canvas...

It is _____ ___, ____
Month   Day   Year

Today, we...
_____
_____
_____
_____
_____

We will always remember...
_____
_____
_____
_____
_____

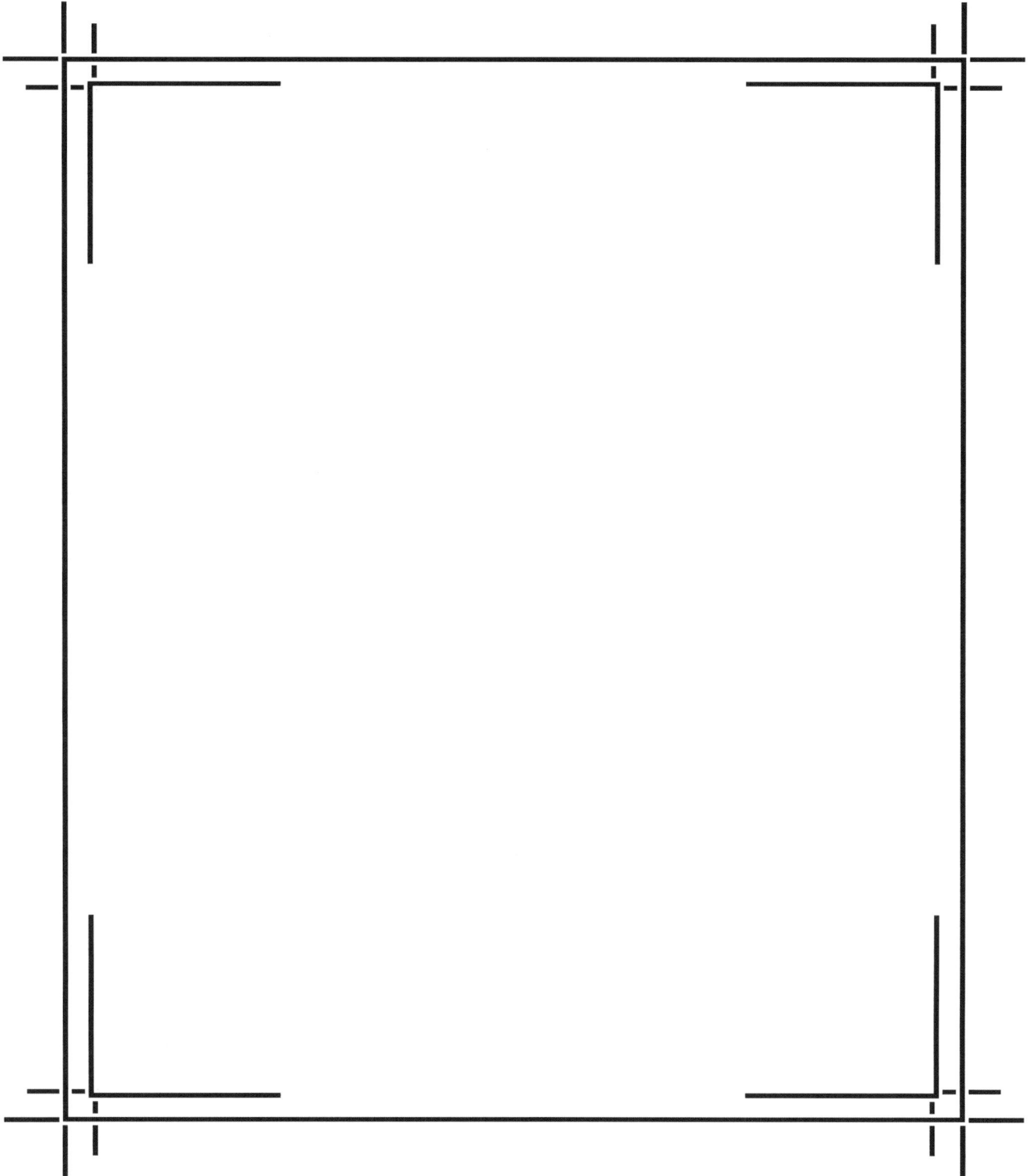

Your canvas...

It is _____ ___, ___
Month   Day   Year

Today, we...

_____

_____

_____

_____

_____

We will always remember...

_____

_____

_____

_____

_____

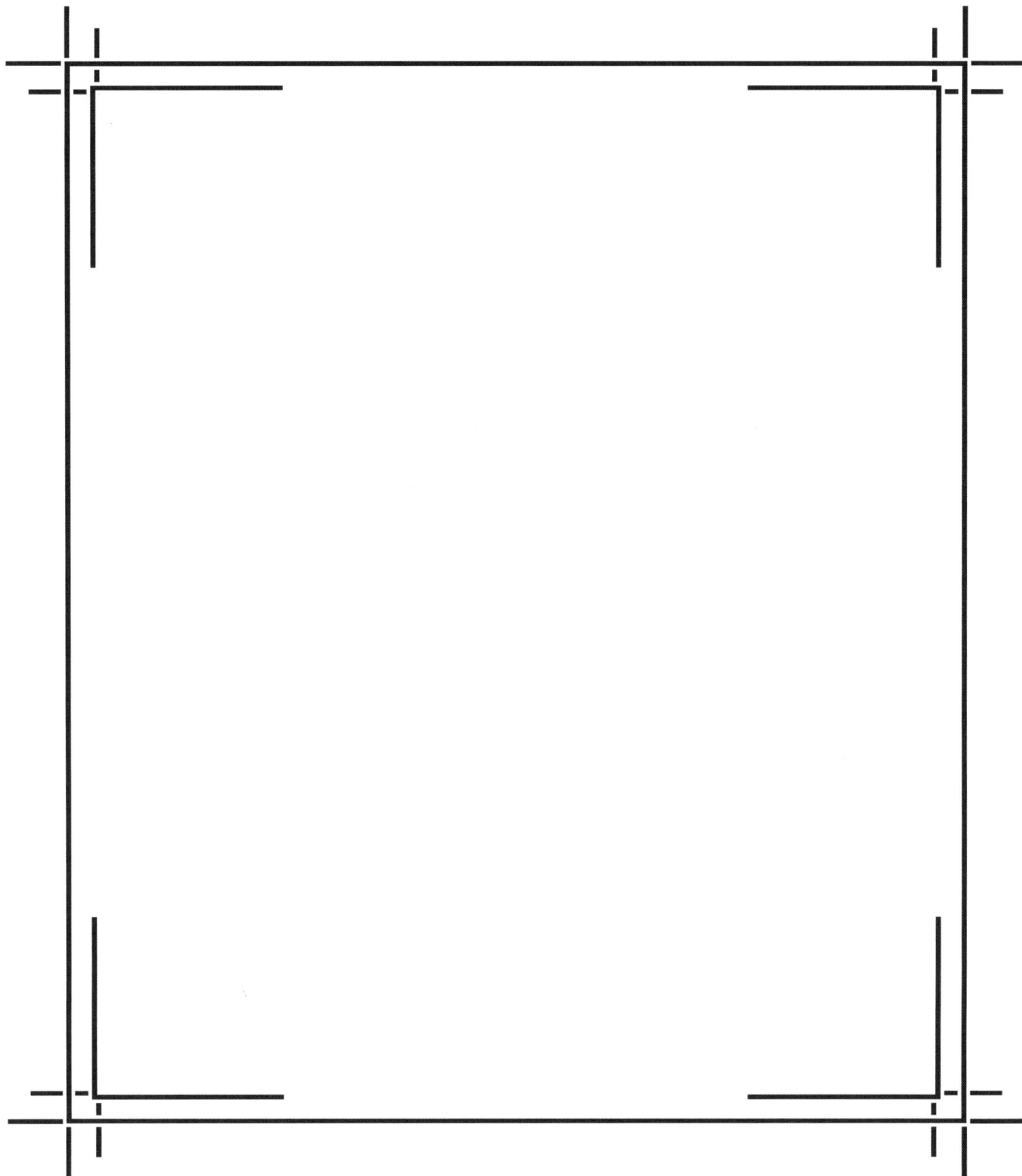

Your canvas...

It is _____ ___, ___
Month   Day   Year

Today, we...

_____

_____

_____

_____

_____

_____

We will always remember...

_____

_____

_____

_____

_____

_____

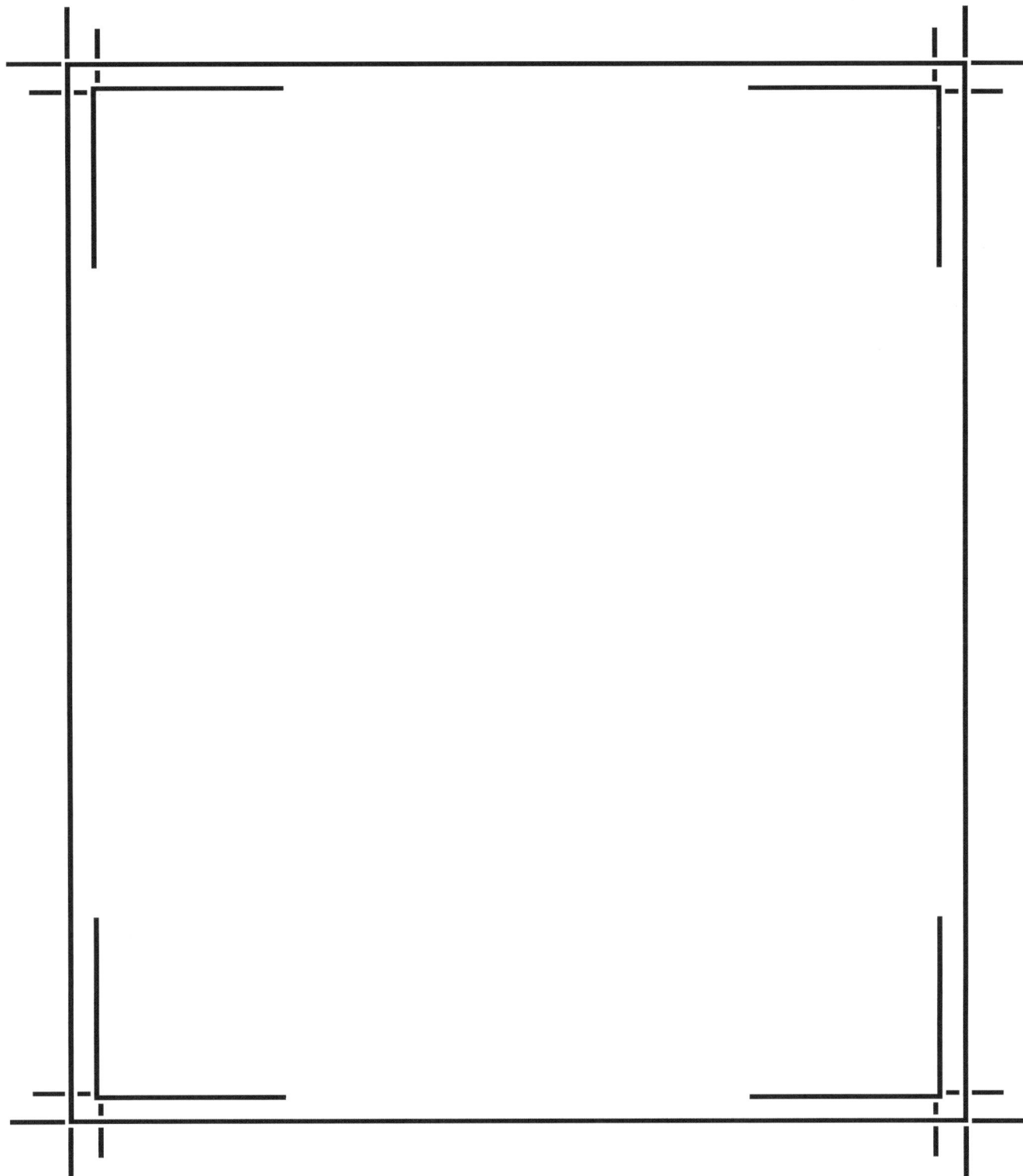

Your canvas...

It is _____ ___, _____
Month   Day   Year

Today, we...

_____

_____

_____

_____

_____

We will always remember...

_____

_____

_____

_____

_____

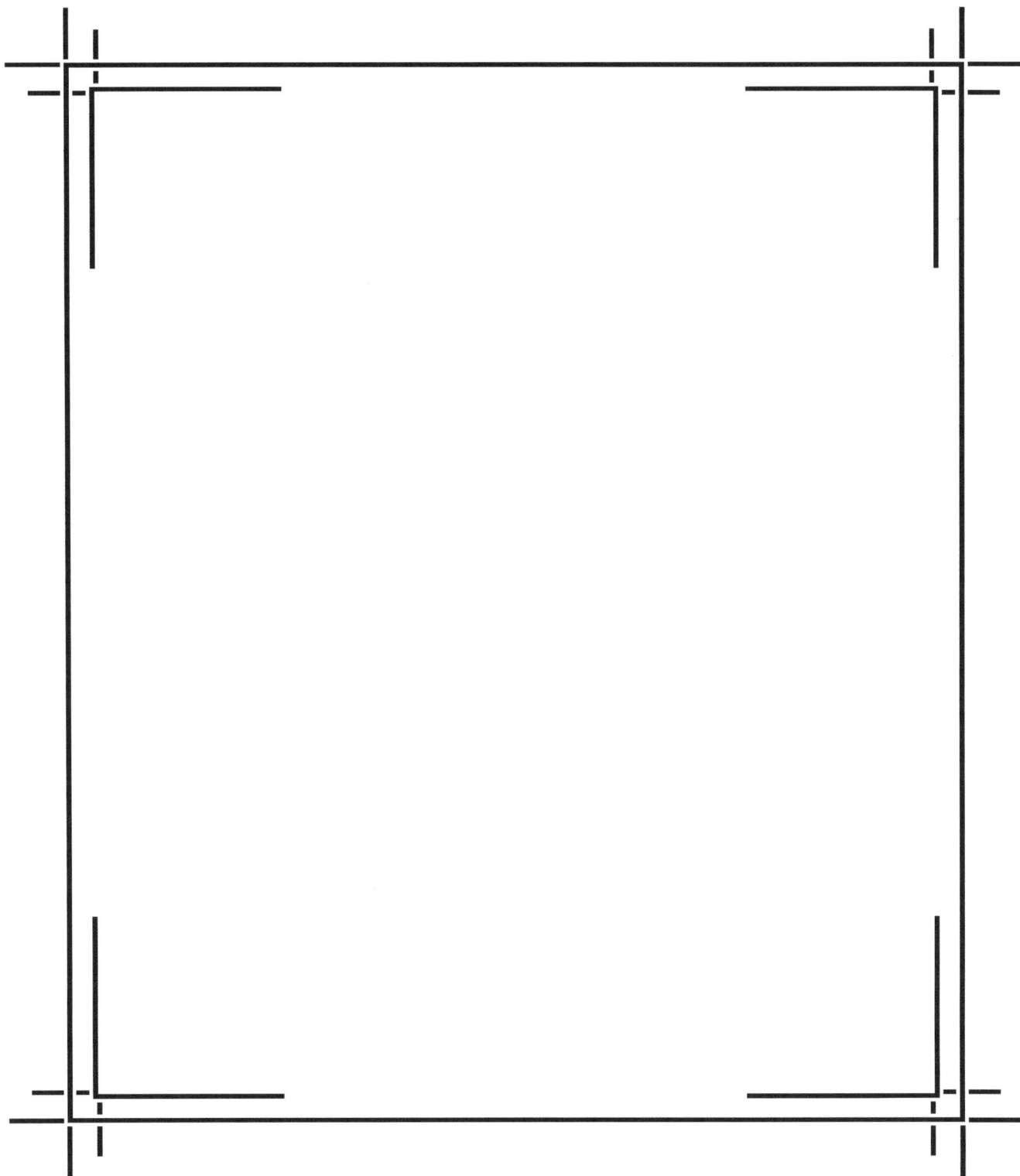

Your canvas...

It is _____ ___, ____
Month   Day   Year

Today, we...

_____

_____

_____

_____

_____

_____

We will always remember...

_____

_____

_____

_____

_____

_____

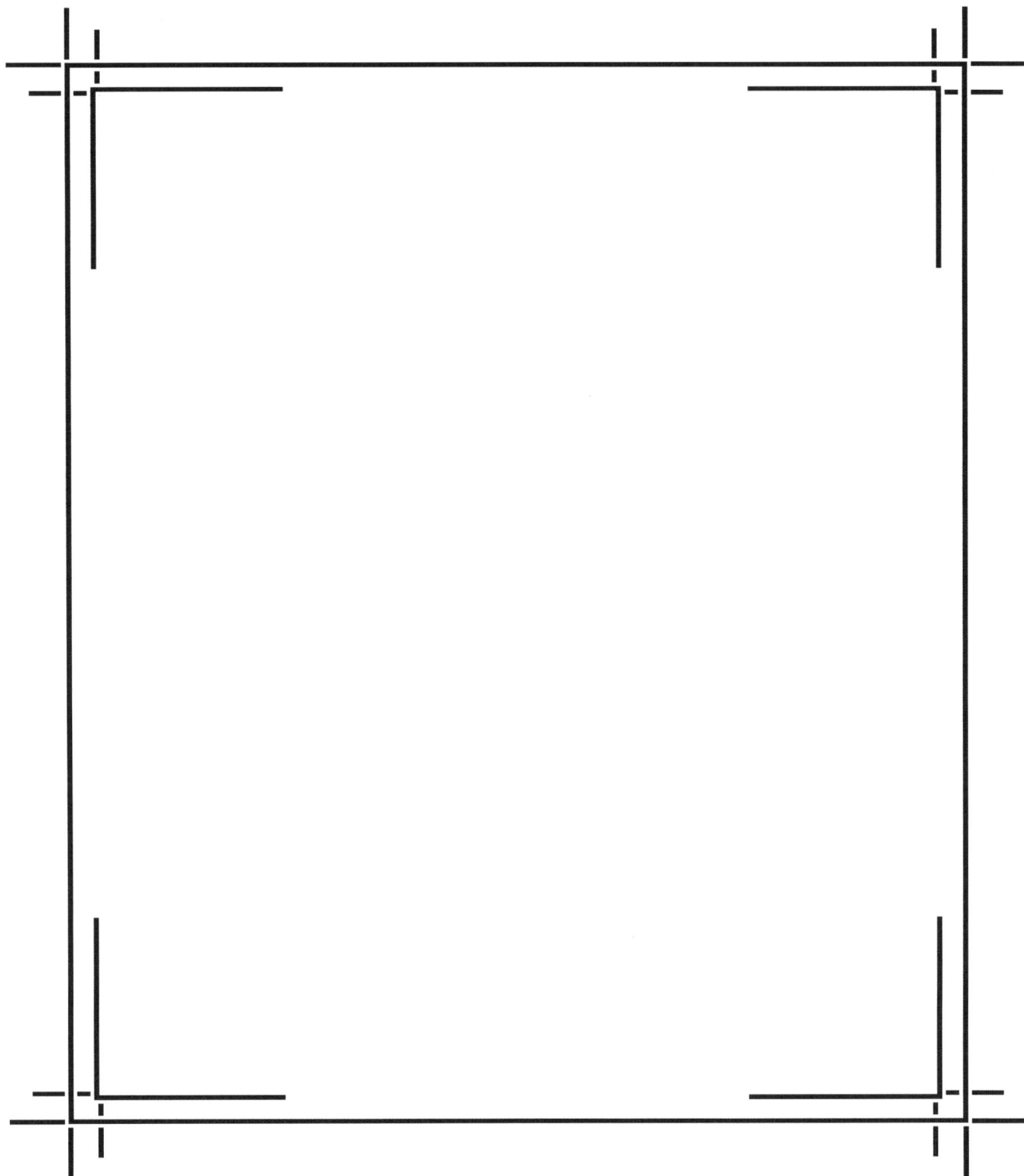

Your canvas...

It is _____ ___, _____
Month   Day   Year

Today, we...

_____
_____
_____
_____
_____

We will always remember...

_____
_____
_____
_____
_____

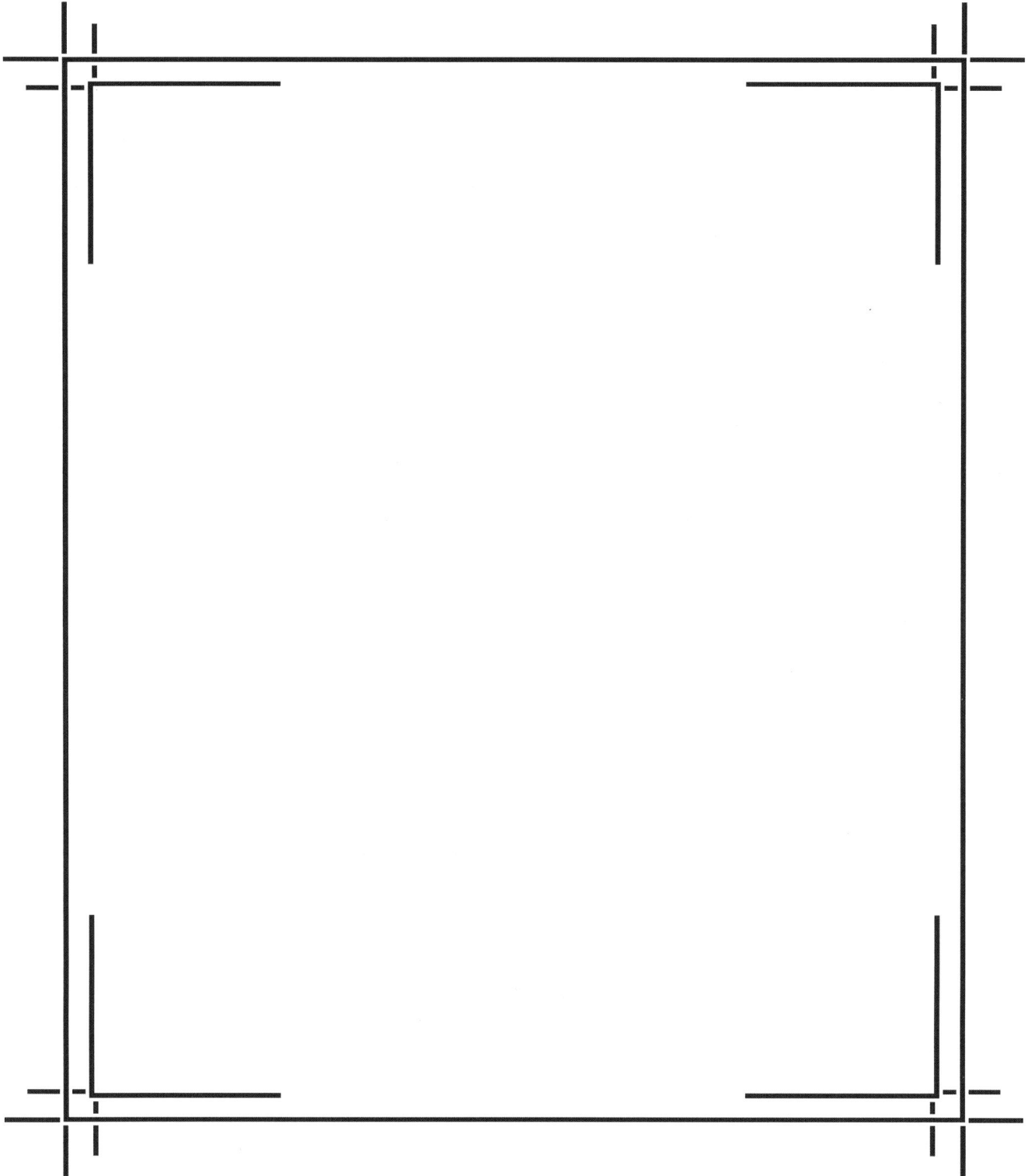

Your canvas...

It is _____ _____, _____
Month   Day   Year

Today, we...

_____

_____

_____

_____

_____

We will always remember...

_____

_____

_____

_____

_____

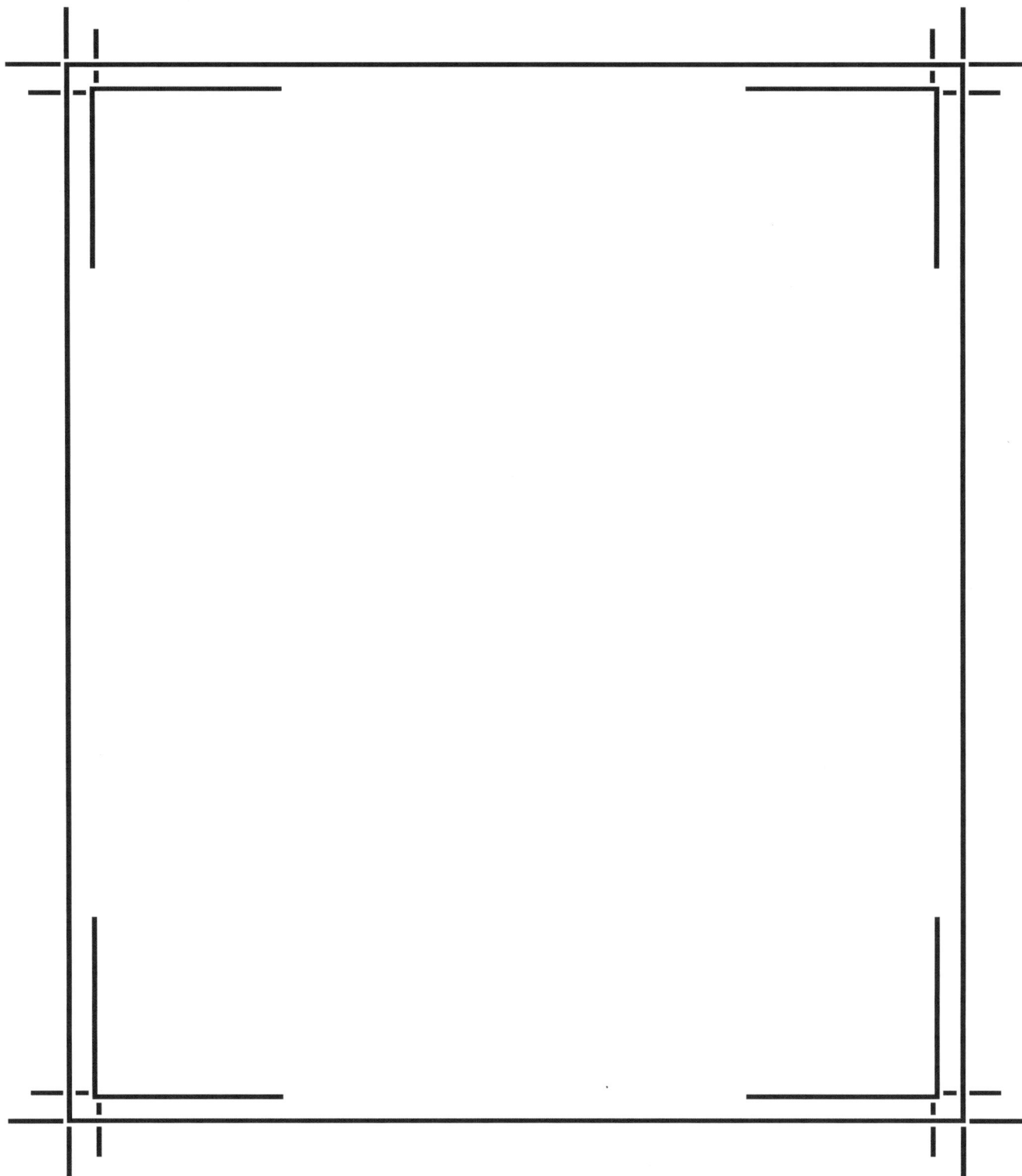

Your canvas...

It is

Month   Day ,   Year

Today, we...

_____

_____

_____

_____

_____

We will always remember...

_____

_____

_____

_____

_____

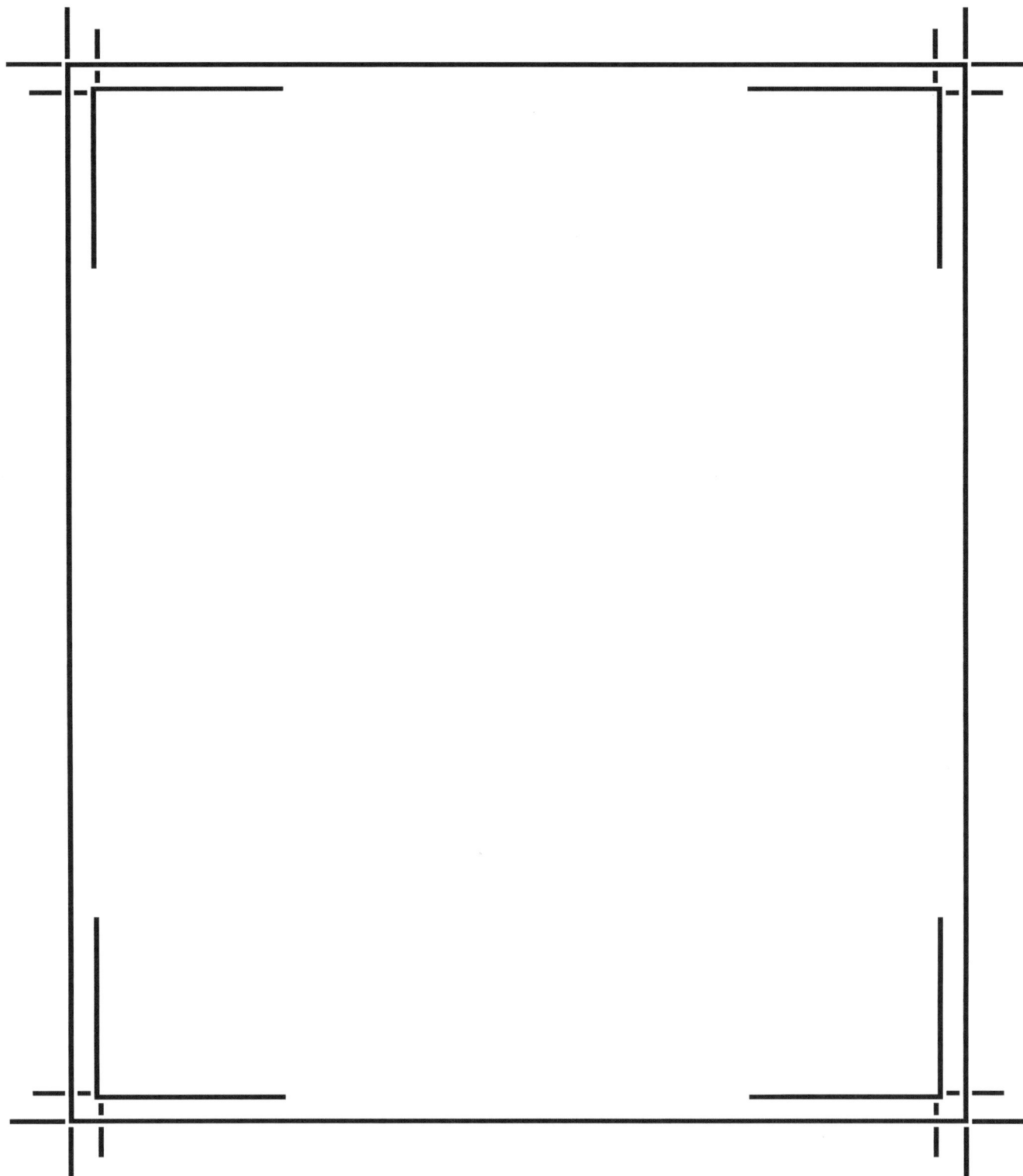

Your canvas...

It is _____ ___ , ____
Month   Day   Year

Today, we...

_____
_____
_____
_____
_____

We will always remember...

_____
_____
_____
_____
_____
_____

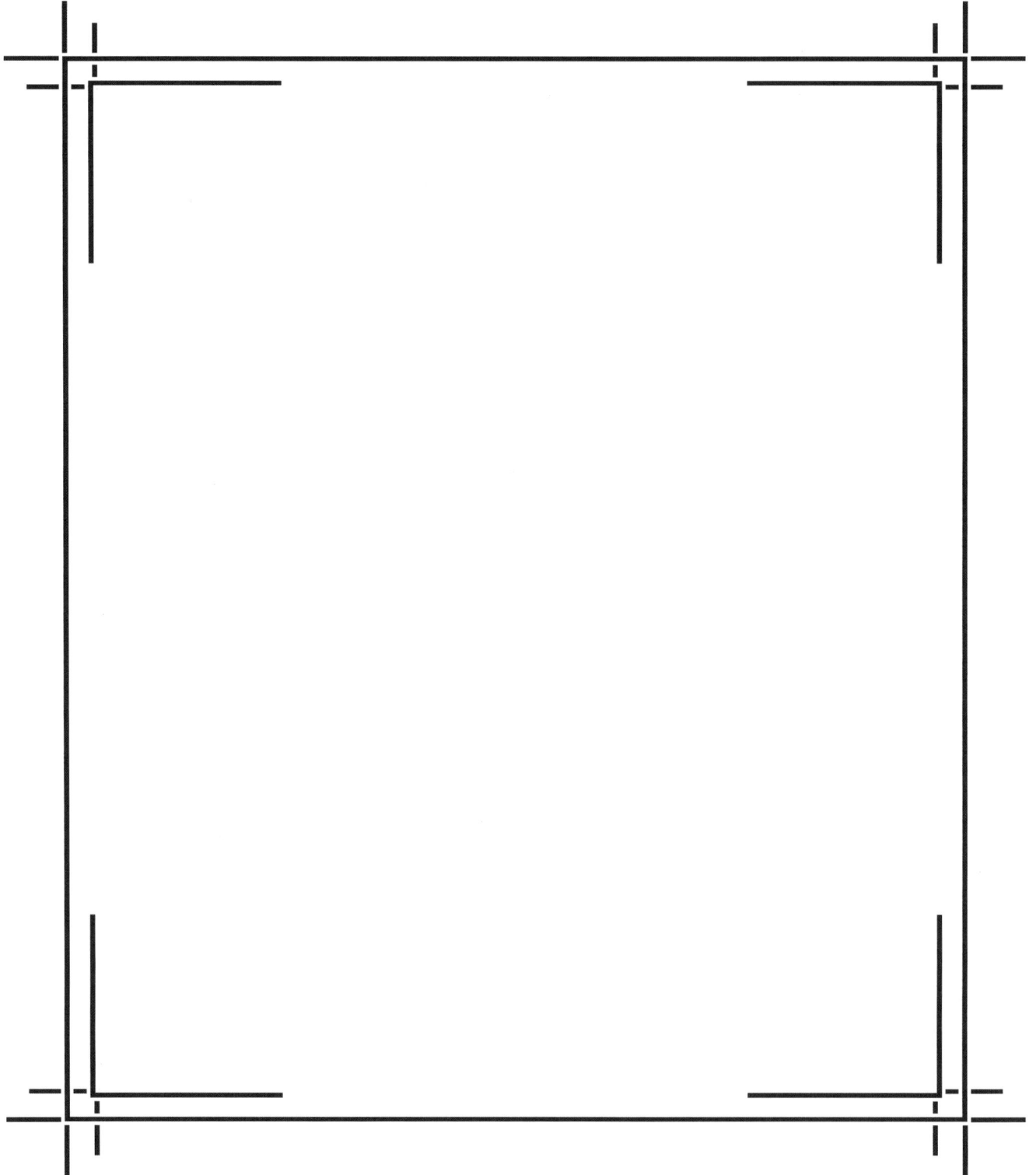

Your canvas...

It is _____ ____, ____
Month   Day   Year

Today, we...

_____

_____

_____

_____

_____

We will always remember...

_____

_____

_____

_____

_____

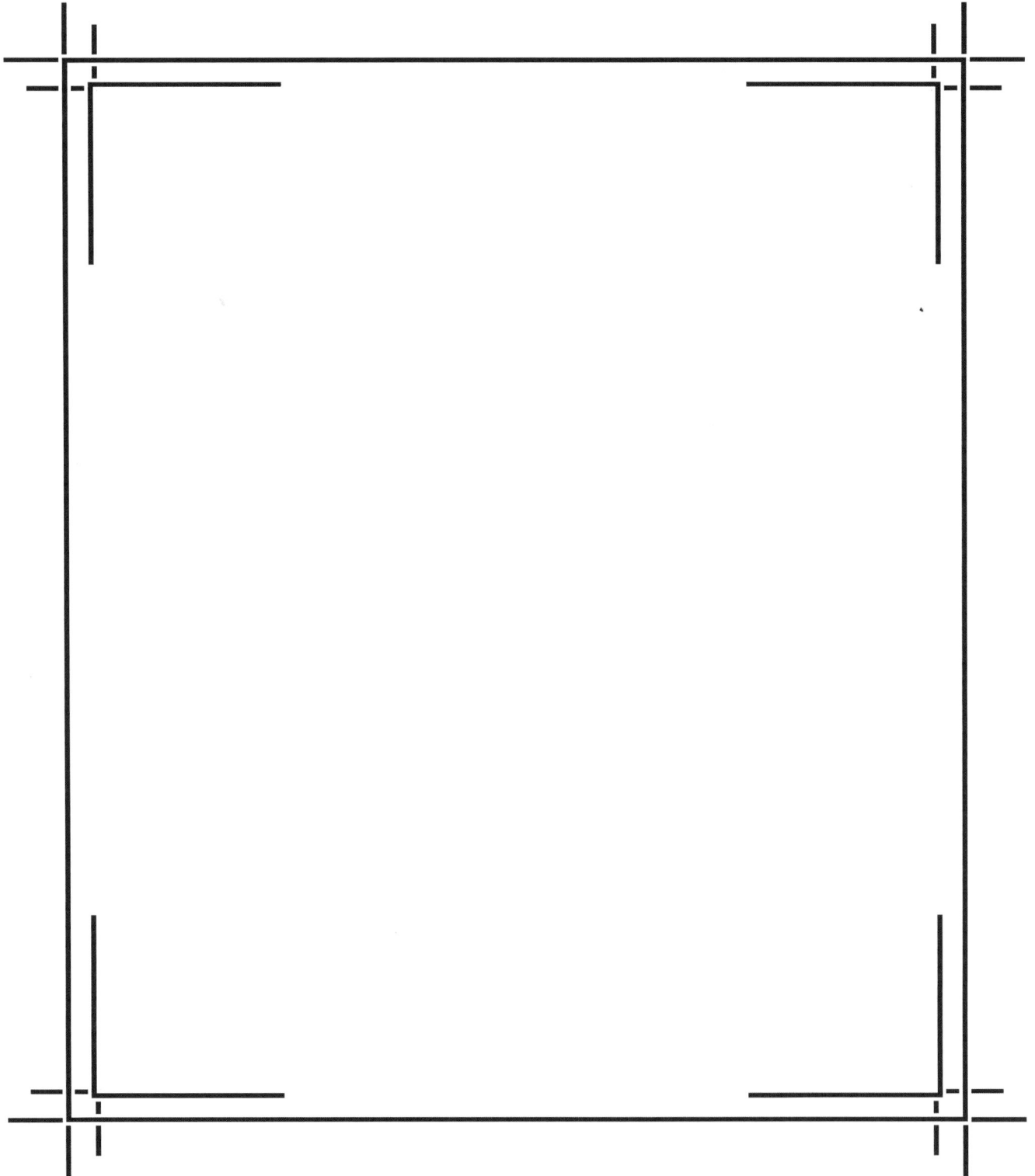

Your canvas...

It is _____ ___, ____
                                Month   Day   Year

Today, we...

_____

_____

_____

_____

_____

_____

We will always remember...

_____

_____

_____

_____

_____

_____

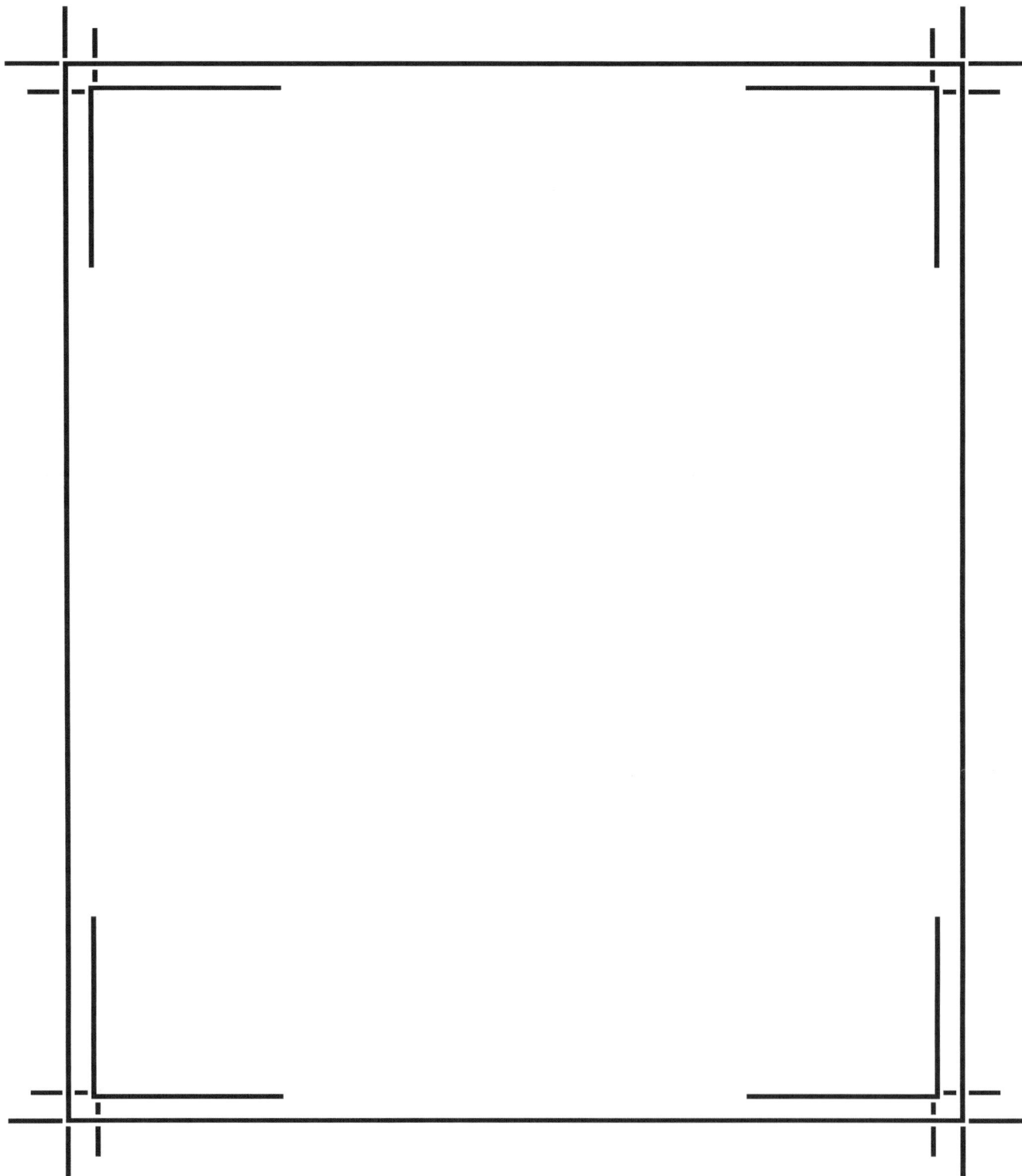

Your canvas...

It is _____ ____ , ____
Month   Day   Year

Today, we...

_____

_____

_____

_____

_____

We will always remember...

_____

_____

_____

_____

_____

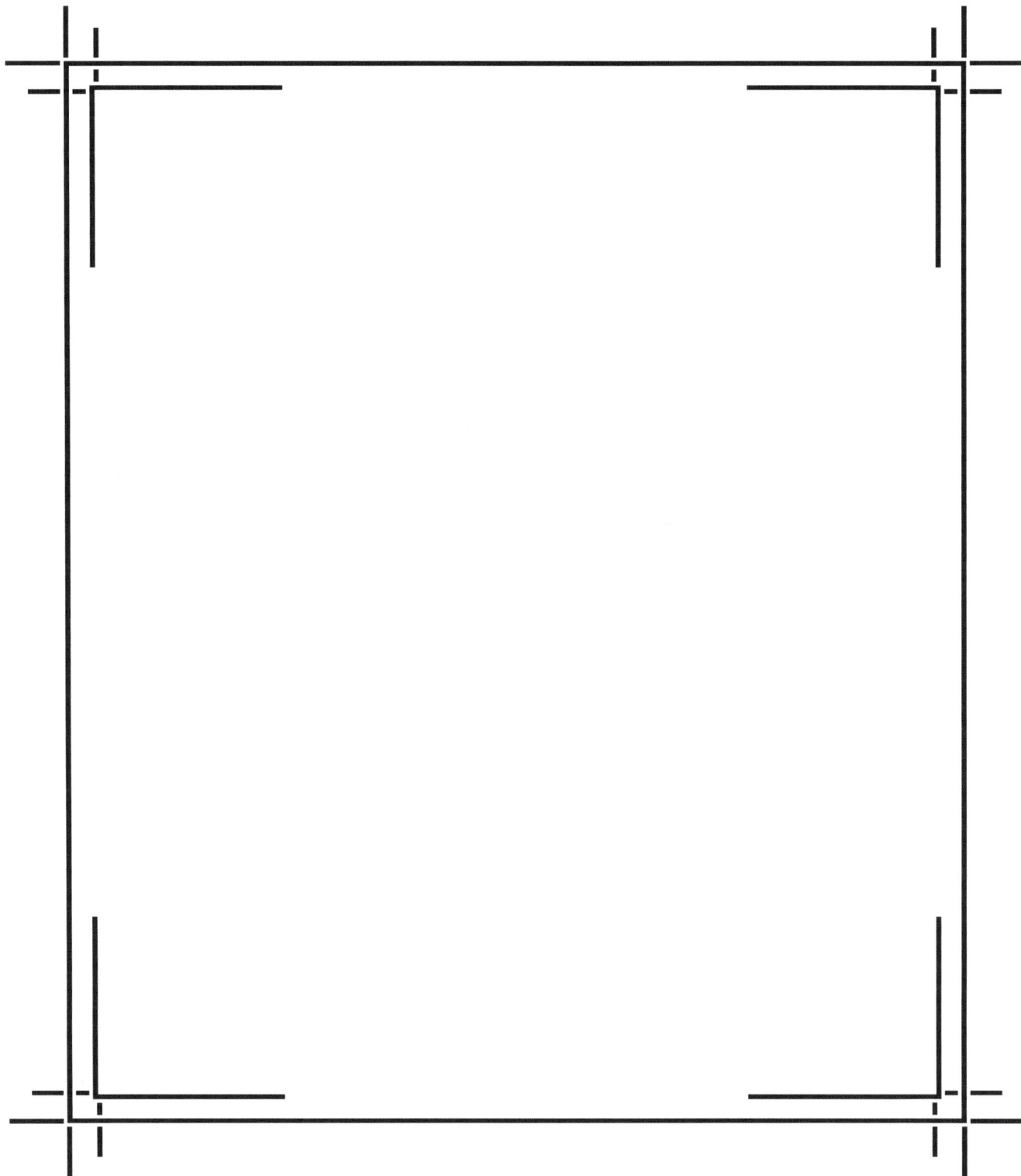

Your canvas...

It is _____ __, _____
Month   Day   Year

Today, we...

_____

_____

_____

_____

_____

We will always remember...

_____

_____

_____

_____

_____

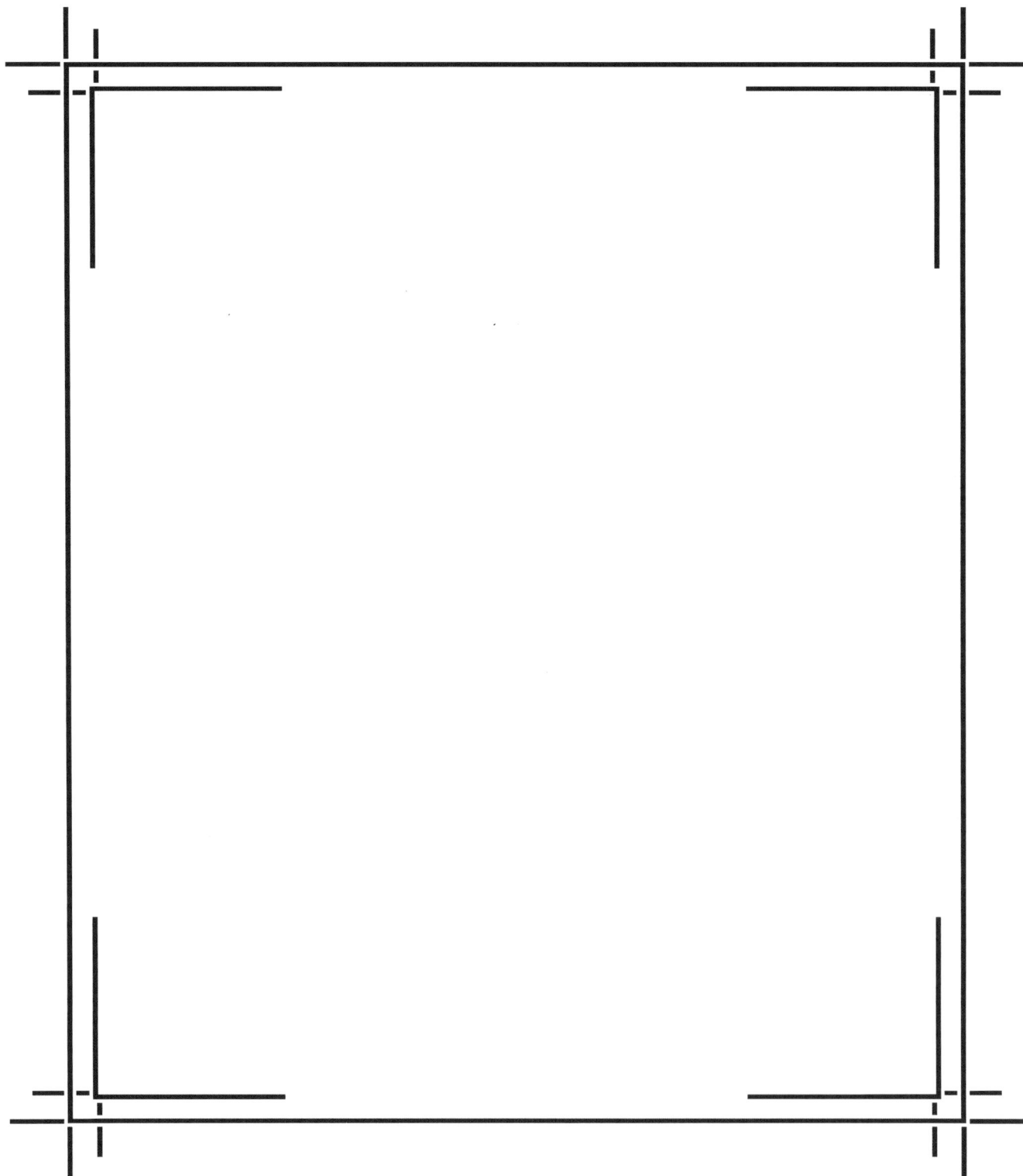

Your canvas...

It is _____ ___, ____
Month   Day   Year

Today, we...

_____

_____

_____

_____

_____

We will always remember...

_____

_____

_____

_____

_____

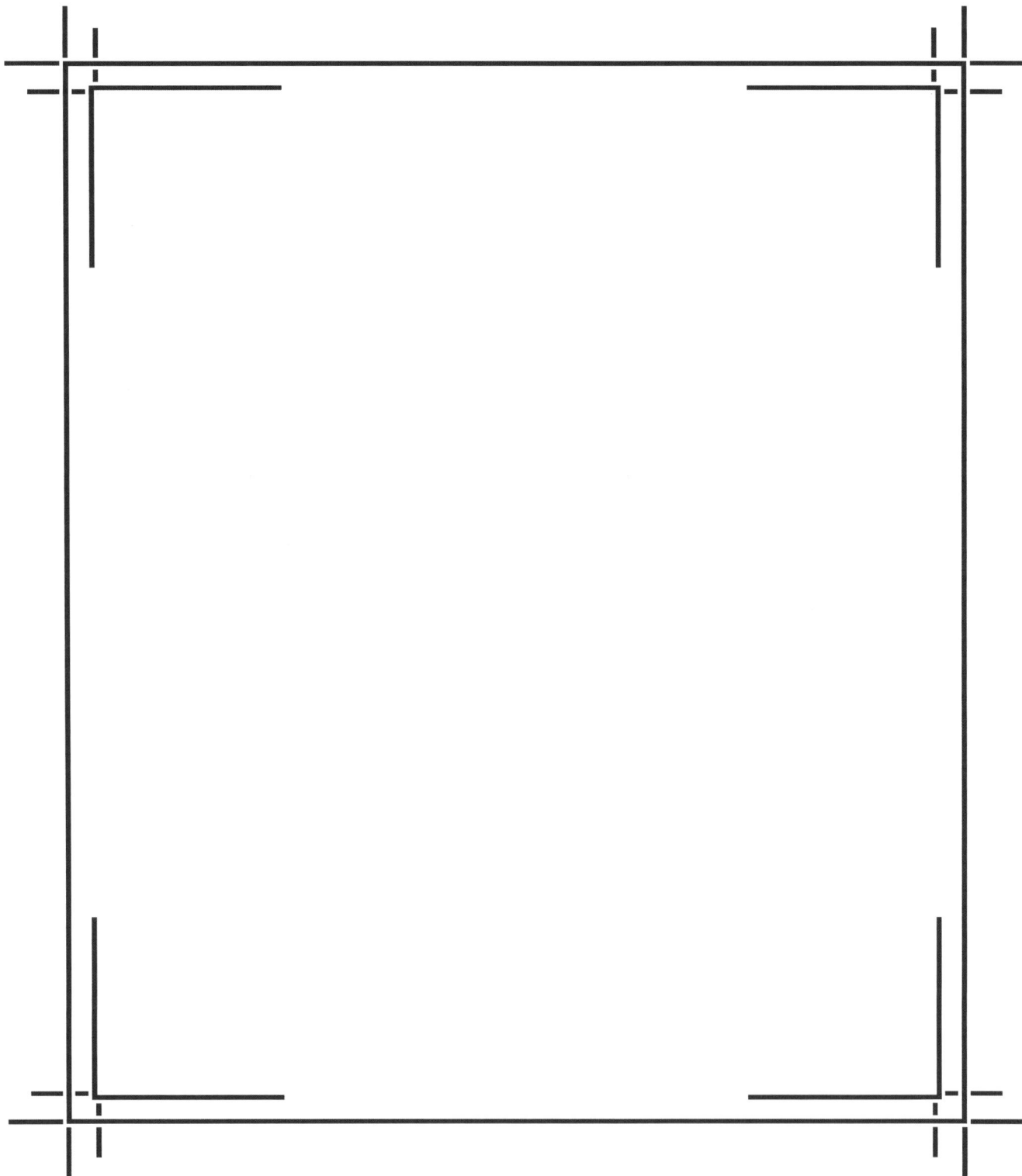

Your canvas...

It is _____ ___, ____
Month   Day   Year

Today, we...

_____

_____

_____

_____

_____

We will always remember...

_____

_____

_____

_____

_____

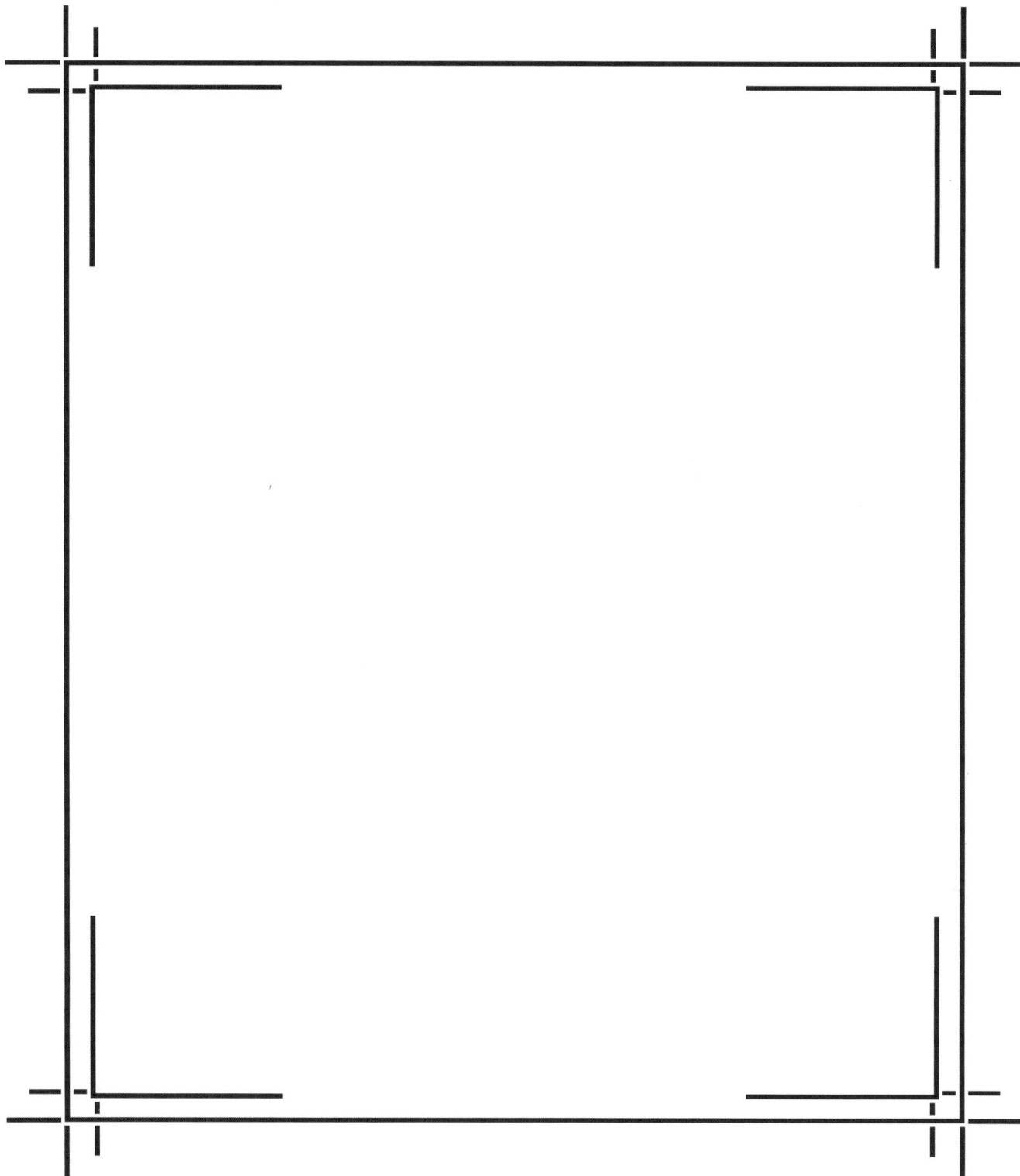

Your canvas...

It is _____ ___ , _____
Month   Day   Year

Today, we...

_____

_____

_____

_____

_____

We will always remember...

_____

_____

_____

_____

_____

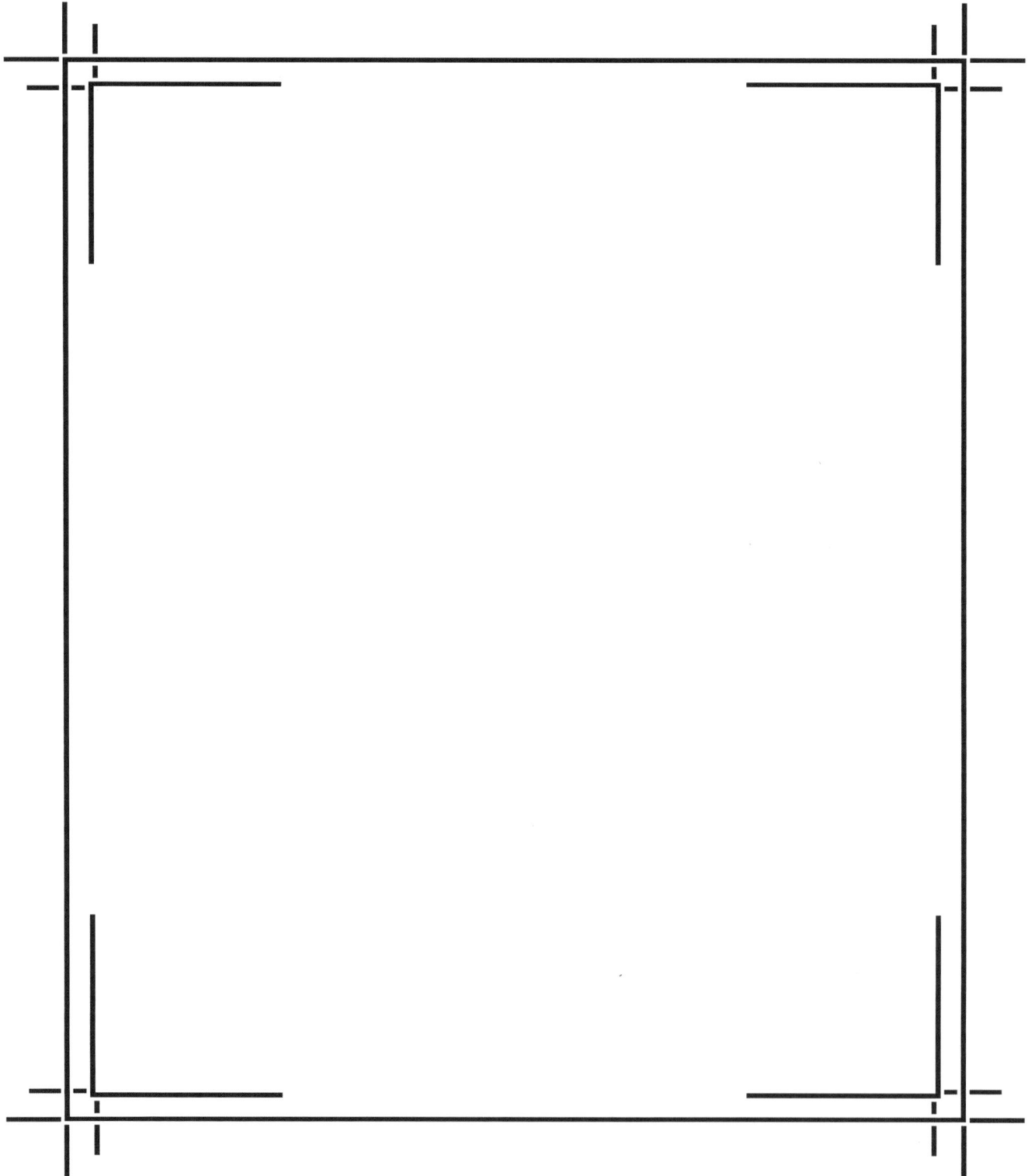

Your canvas...

It is _____ ___, _____
Month Day   Year

Today, we...

_____

_____

_____

_____

_____

We will always remember...

_____

_____

_____

_____

_____

_____

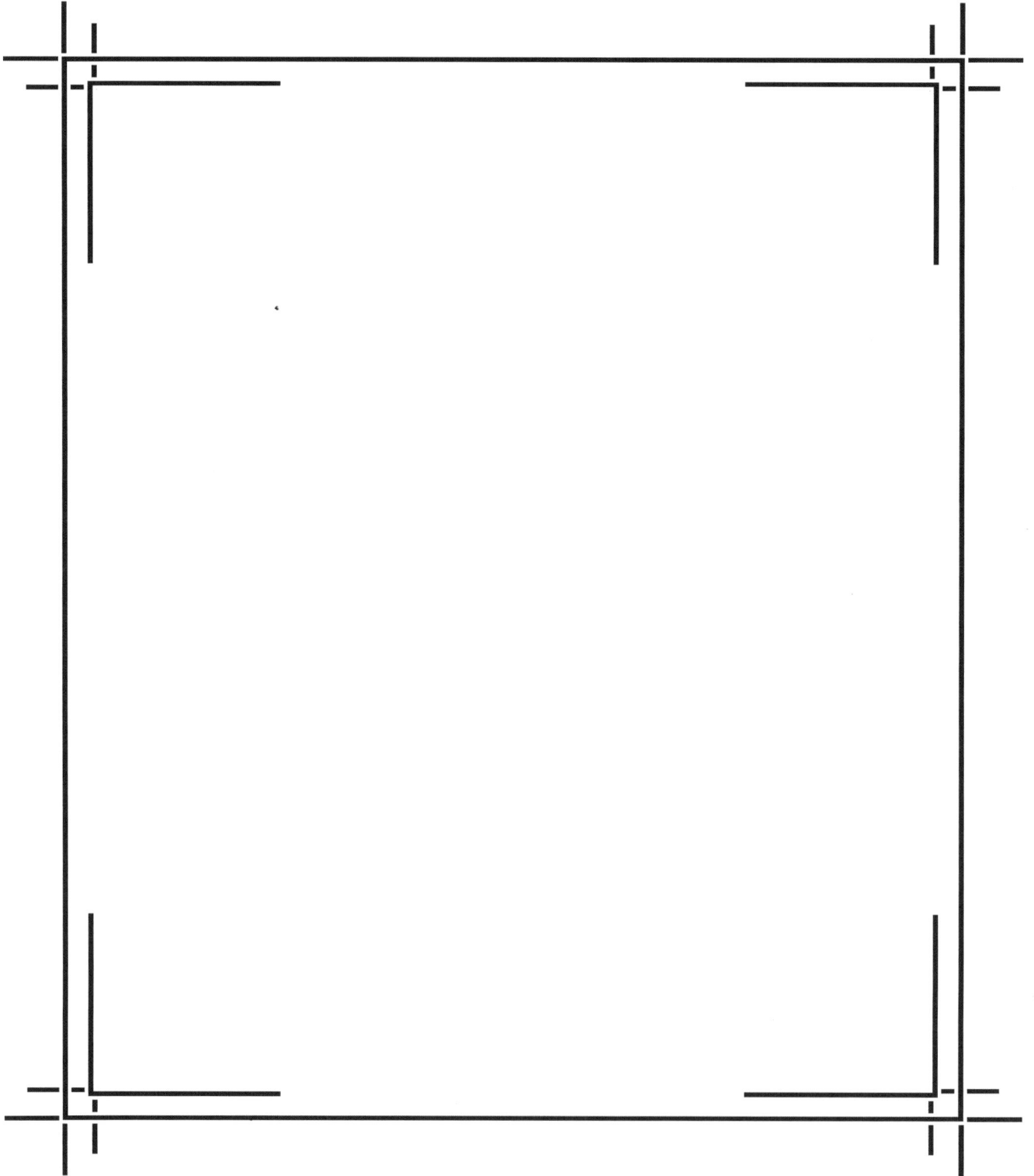

Your canvas...

It is _____ ___, ____
Month   Day   Year

Today, we...
_____
_____
_____
_____
_____
_____

We will always remember...
_____
_____
_____
_____
_____
_____

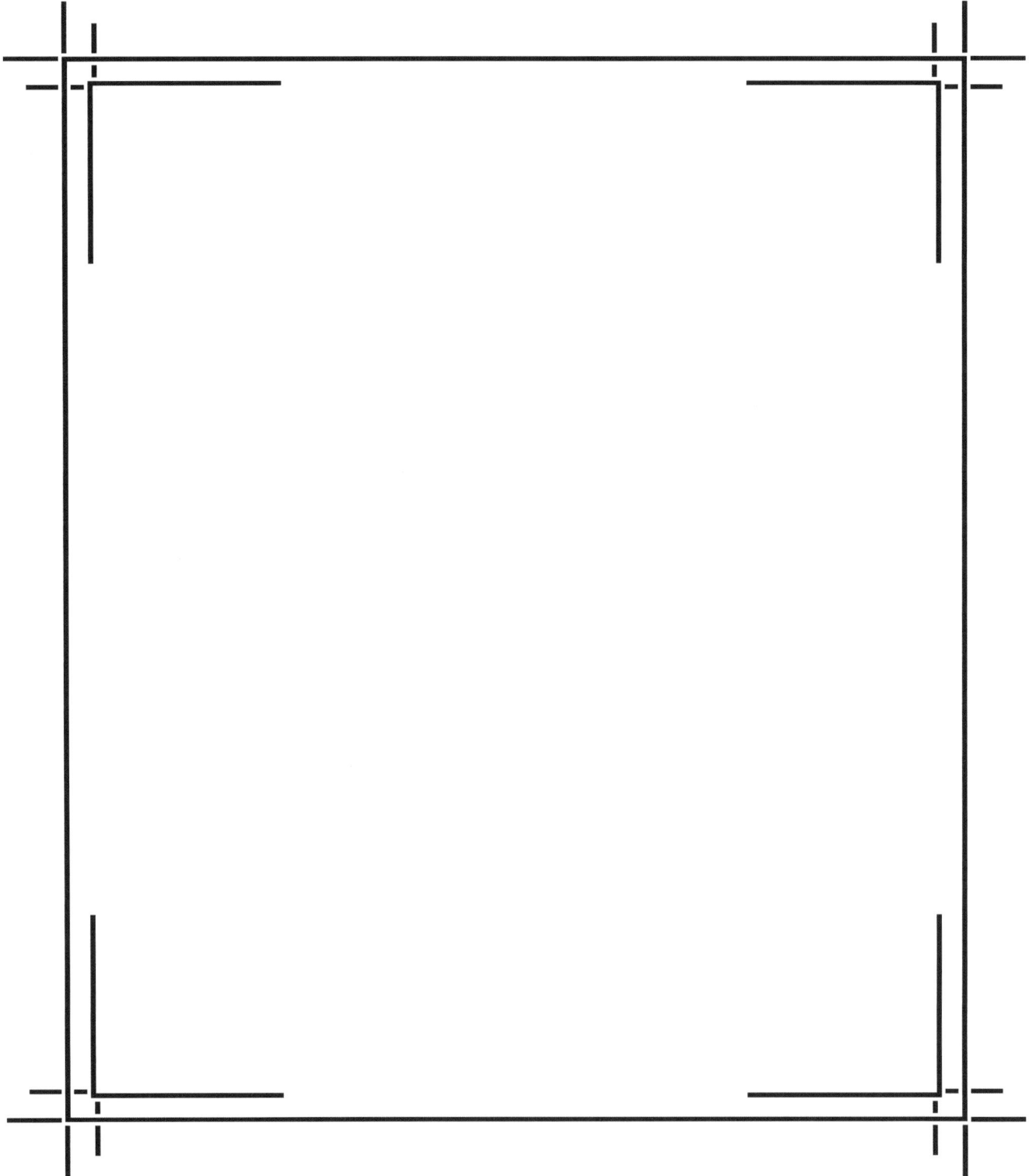

Your canvas...

It is _____ ___ , ___
Month   Day   Year

Today, we...

_____

_____

_____

_____

_____

_____

We will always remember...

_____

_____

_____

_____

_____

_____

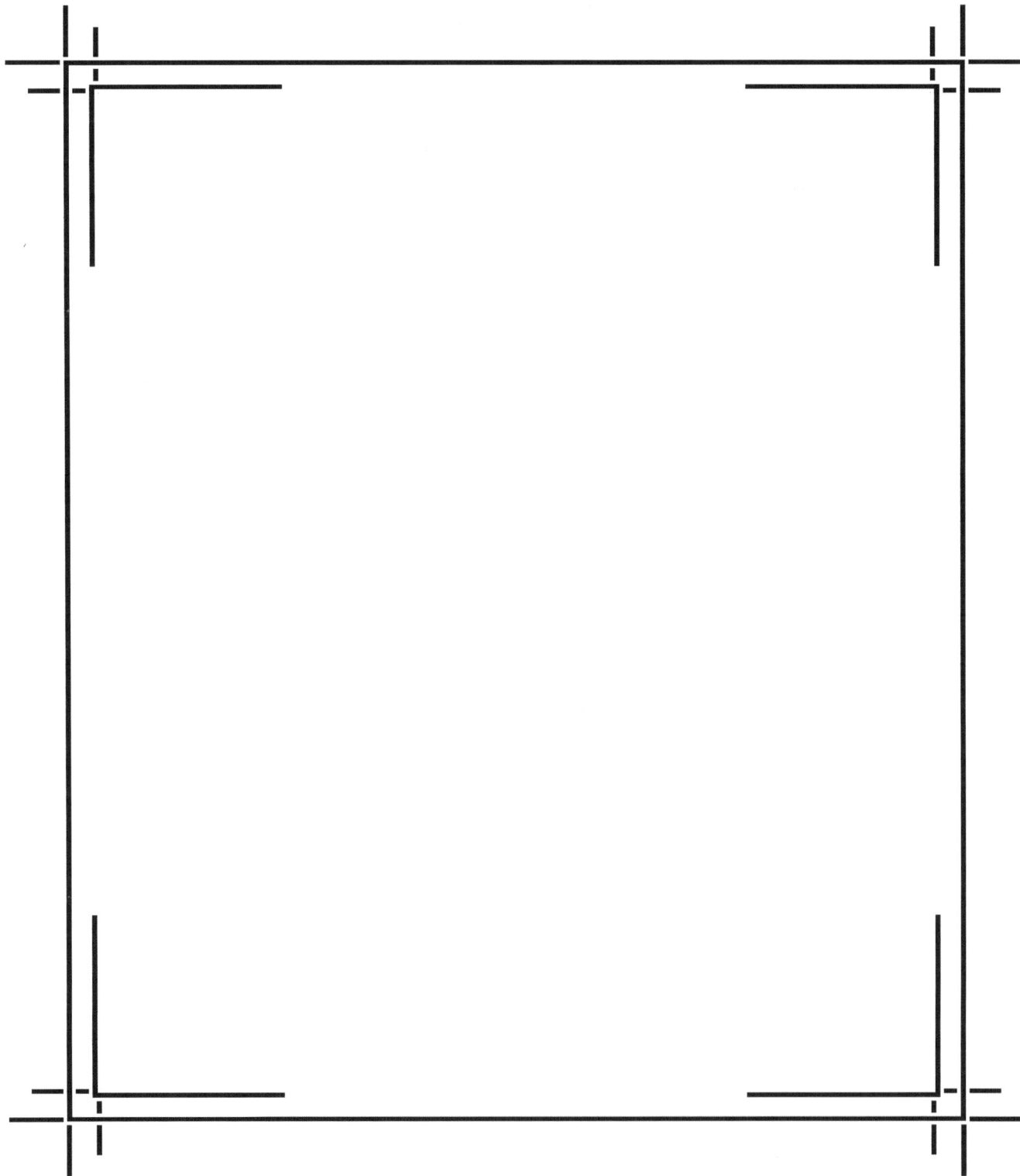

Your canvas...

It is _____ ___ , ___
Month   Day   Year

Today, we...

_____

_____

_____

_____

_____

We will always remember...

_____

_____

_____

_____

_____

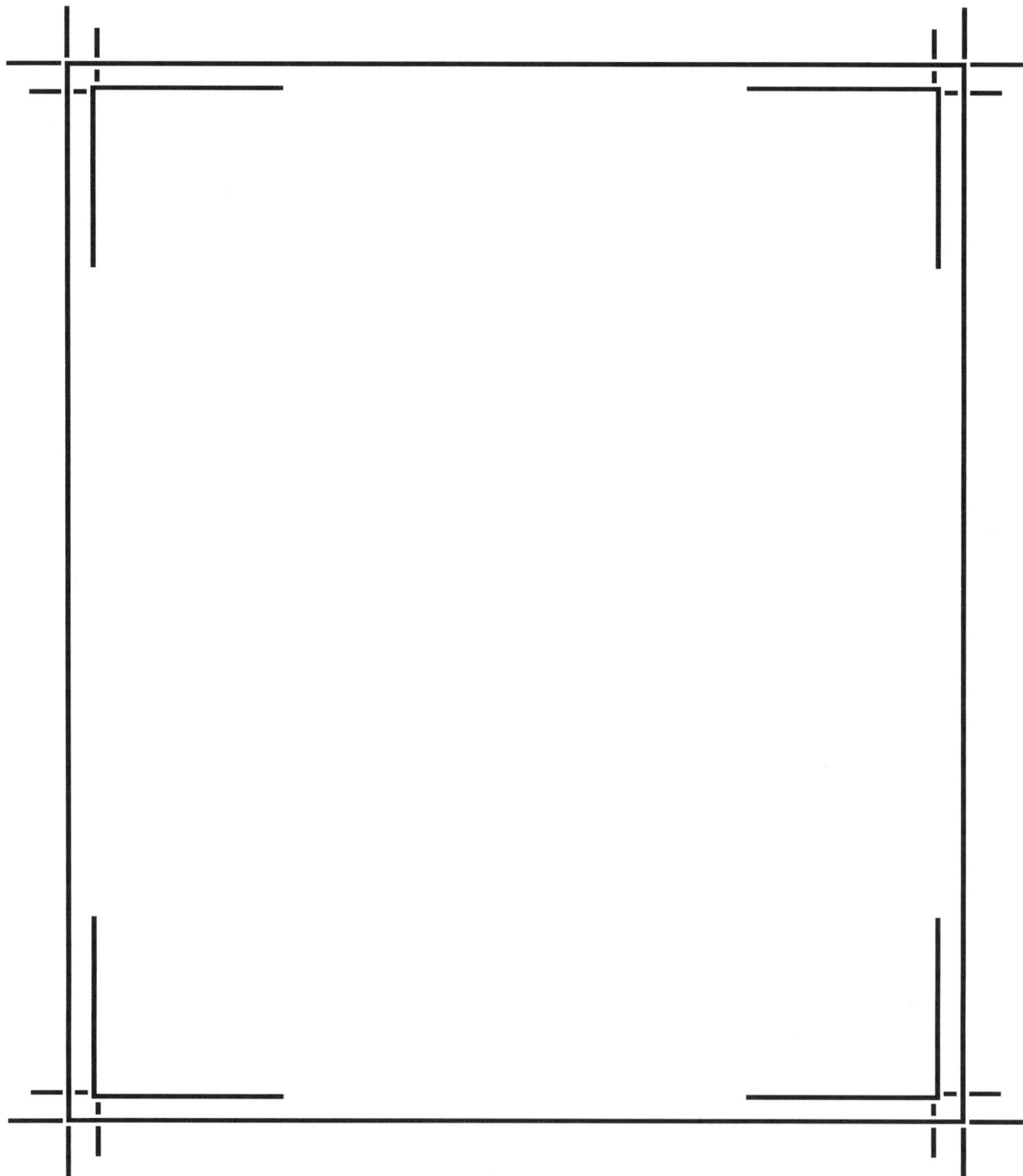

Your canvas...

It is _____ ___, _____
Month   Day   Year

Today, we...
_____
_____
_____
_____
_____
_____

We will always remember...
_____
_____
_____
_____
_____
_____

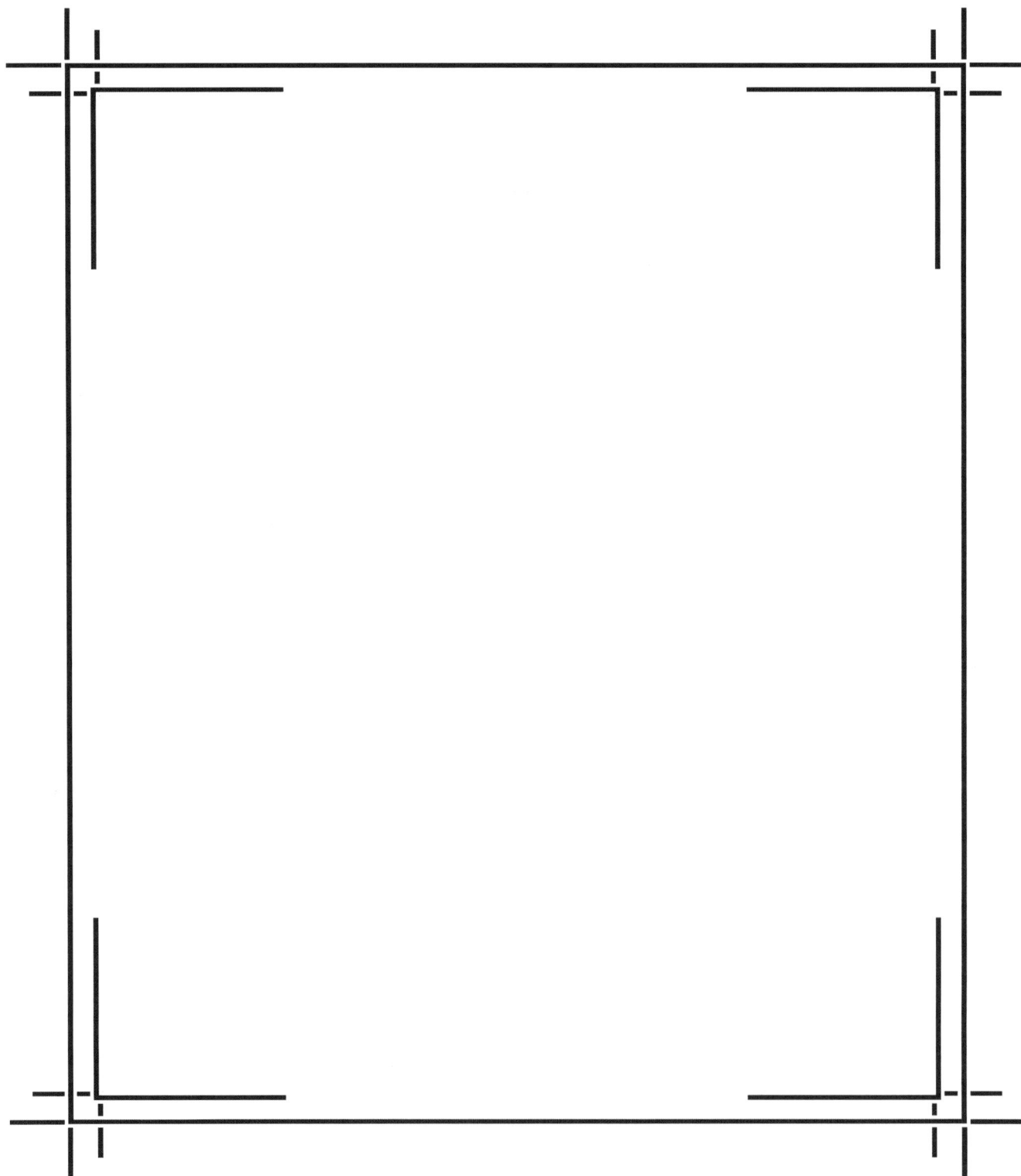

Your canvas...

It is _____ ___, ____
Month   Day Year

Today, we...

_____

_____

_____

_____

_____

We will always remember...

_____

_____

_____

_____

_____

_____

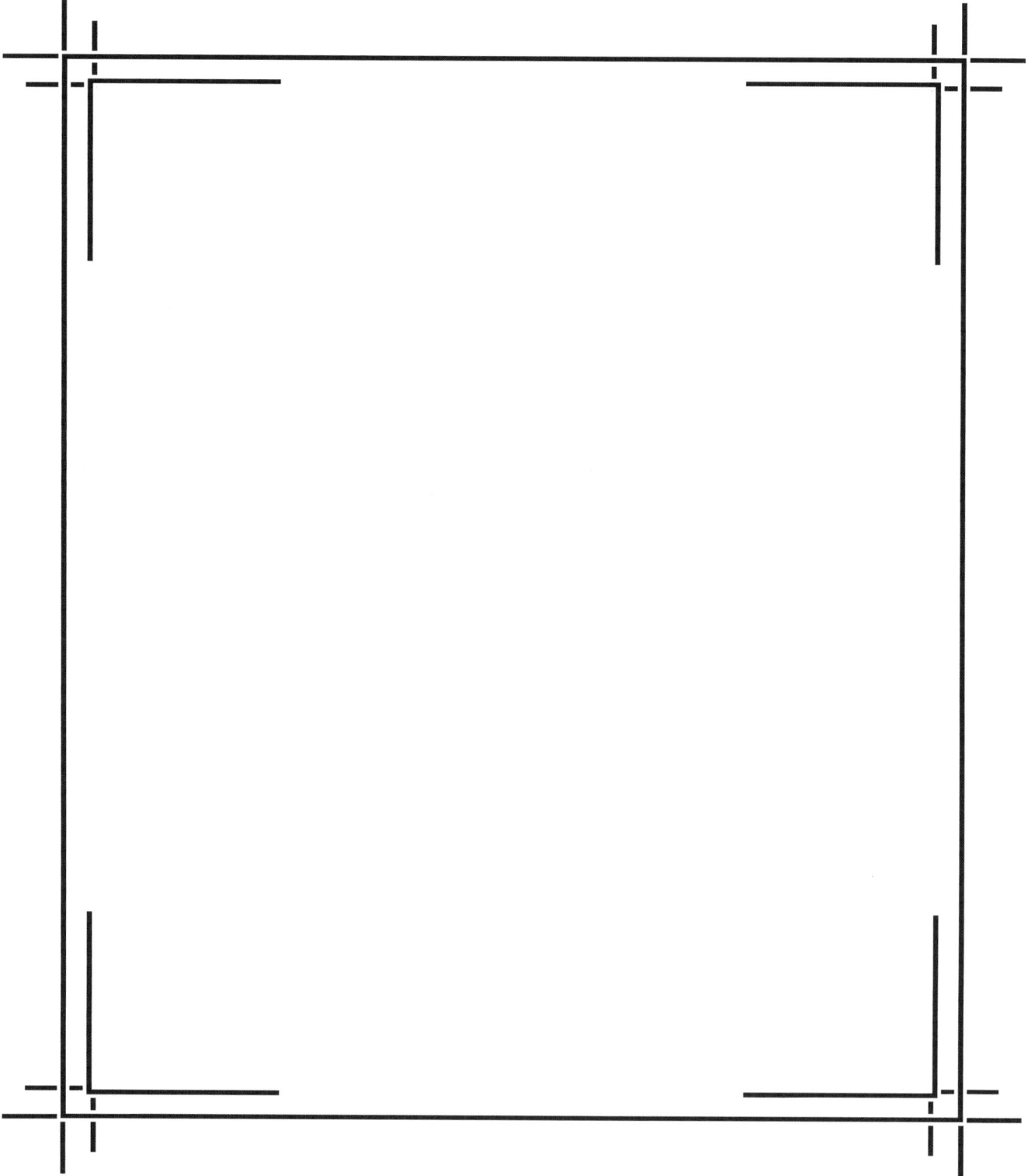

Your canvas...

It is _____ ___, ___
Month   Day   Year

Today, we...

_____

_____

_____

_____

_____

We will always remember...

_____

_____

_____

_____

_____

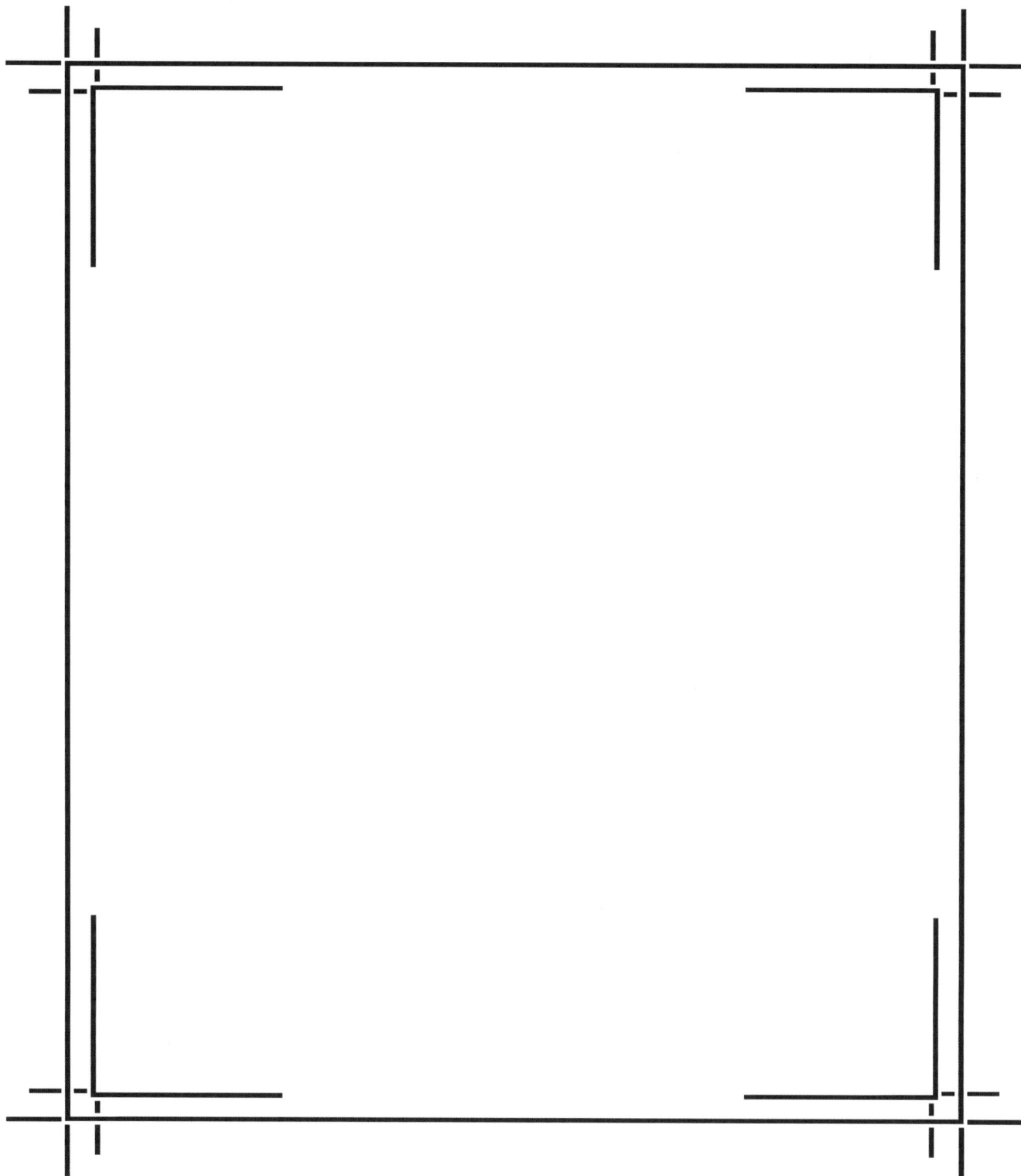

Your canvas...

It is _____ ___, ____
Month Day, Year

Today, we...
_____
_____
_____
_____
_____
_____

We will always remember...
_____
_____
_____
_____
_____
_____

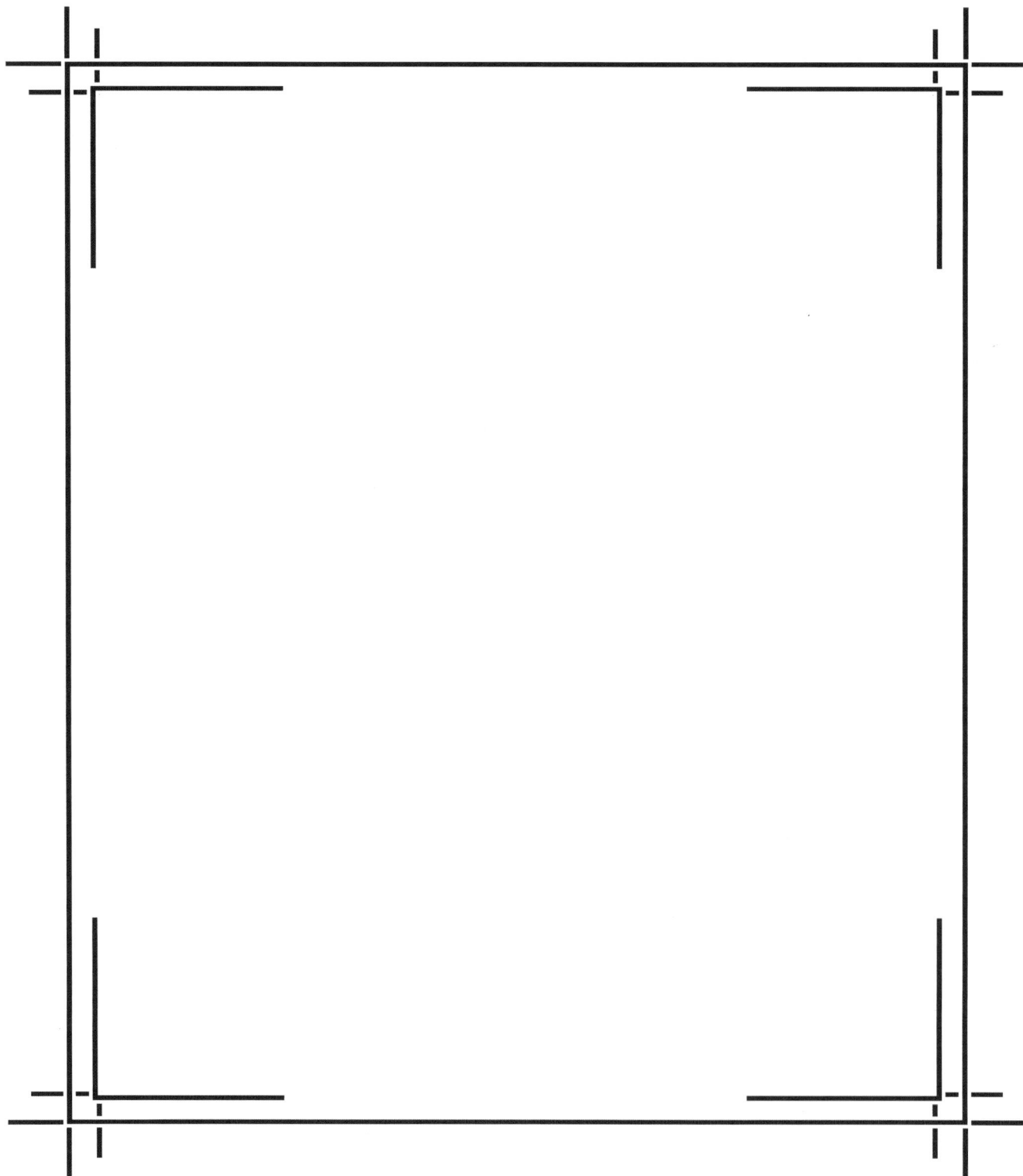

Your canvas...

It is _____ ____, ____
Month   Day   Year

Today, we...

_____
_____
_____
_____
_____
_____

We will always remember...

_____
_____
_____
_____
_____

b396105c-2c71-4a38-b8ce-ea09490f6750R01